Understanding Intercultural Communication

Understanding Intercultural Communication

Larry A. Samovar

San Diego State University

Richard E. Porter

California State University, Long Beach

Nemi C. Jain

Arizona State University

Wadsworth Publishing Company
Belmont, California
A Division of Wadsworth, Inc.

Senior Editor: Rebecca Hayden

Production Editor: Kathie Head

Designers: Detta Penna and Pat Dunbar

Copy Editor: Margo Quinto

Cover: Pat Dunbar

Photo Credits: *Part I*—Andree Abecassis/Represented by Brainen Photography; *Part II*—Burton Berinsky/OPC; *Part III*—Al Kaplan/DPI; *Part IV*—Elizabeth Crews/ICON

Printed in the United States of America

7 8 9 10

ISBN 0-534-00862-3

Library of Congress Cataloging in Publication Data

Samovar, Larry A
  Understanding intercultural communication.

  Includes index.
  1. Intercultural communication. 2. Social perception. 3. Nonverbal
communication. 4. Symbolic interactionism. I. Porter, Richard E., joint author.
II. Jain, Nemi C., joint author. III. Title.
HM258.S254   302.2   80-15425
ISBN 0-534-00862-3

Preface

This book is intended for anyone whose work or lifestyle is likely to involve them in encounters of the intercultural kind. And in this age of world travel, rapid communication, and increased population density, that is likely to be anyone. What was true in the past is even more true today: We must learn to share our perceptions and experiences with others. To do this it is necessary to be prepared and able to accept the perceptions and experiences of others even though they differ vastly from our own. Only through diligent, determined, and effective inter-cultural interactions can we foster the growth of mutual understand-ing, appreciation, and trust.

Intercultural communication is a highly complex dynamic activity in which people participate actively in order to share their inner states and induce one another to attitude and action through symbolic be-havior. Effective intercultural communication requires that people learn how to participate in this form of human interaction. The study of intercultural communication so far has tended to neglect participation and to focus on superficial differences between cultures. Some ap-proaches, for instance, have concentrated on the forms of mass media in various cultures while others appear to be extended versions of *National Geographic* type articles. While these approaches have merit and contribute to an overall knowledge of intercultural communica-tion, they do not stress participation on the individual level.

This book, however, deals primarily with the obstacles to trust and understanding that are usually present when culturally different people with perceptual and experiential backgrounds attempt to communicate. It seeks to enable the reader to recognize and, we hope, learn to overcome some of those obstacles.

A number of people were instrumental in the preparation of this text. The entire manuscript was reviewed by La Ray M. Barna, Kenneth D. Bryson, William S. Howell, Young Y. Kim, and Mary C. Ross. Their criticism and praise was timely, insightful, and extremely useful in the final text preparation. Stephen King of San Diego State University provided invaluable help and is responsible for many of the ideas about interpersonal perception found in Chapter 5. In addition, Jack Mills and Larry Williamson, both also of San Diego State University, aided immensely with their ideas, encouragement, and friendship. Gale Richards and Lara Collins Witt, both of Arizona State University, also contributed significantly to the completion of the text. And to Berta Potter goes special thanks for her preparation of the final manuscript. Finally, as always, the advice and editorial direction of Rebecca Hayden is greatly appreciated. For two of the authors, this is the third project under her guidance, and they have learned to depend on her firmness and charm.

Contents

Contents

III. Interaction:
Verbal and Nonverbal Messages   133

Contents

Understanding
Intercultural
Communication

I

Basic
Elements:
Scope
and
Territory

1

Intercultural Communication: The Inevitable Contacts

The most immutable barrier in nature is between one man's thoughts and another's.

William James

Precision of communication is important, more important than ever, in our era of hair-trigger balances, when a false or misunderstood word may create as much disaster as a sudden thoughtless act.

James Thurber

Intercultural communication, as we might rightly suspect, is not new; as long as people from different cultures have been encountering one another there has been intercultural communication. What is new, however, is the systematic study of exactly what happens when cross-cultural contacts and interaction take place.

The growth of intercultural communication as a field of study is based on a view of history that clearly demonstrates people and cultures have been troubled by a persistent inability to understand and get along with groups and societies removed by space, ideology, appearance, and behavior from their own. What is intriguing about many of civilization's failures is that they appear to be personal as well as global. The story of humankind is punctuated with instances of face-to-face conflicts as well as international misunderstanding—major and minor quarrels that range from simple name-calling to isolationism or even armed conflict.

The Importance of Intercultural Communication

In the past two decades, Americans were forced to focus their attention on a new series of intercultural problems. We began to realize that the ways in which peoples and cultures relate to one another are more complicated than we had previously believed. We can look at some of the specific events, both abroad and at home, that heightened our interest in intercultural relationships.

International Awareness

The late 1960s and the early 1970s might well be characterized as that period when, in a figurative sense, the world began to shrink; the global village prophecy was upon us. We could no longer avoid each other. A combination of increased mobility, modern communication technology, and an awareness of common worldwide problems, seemed to reduce radically the time-space relationships between different cultures. By both chance and design, once remote and isolated cultures were now thrust upon us. A jet airplane could, within hours, place us anywhere in the world. This ease of movement was not uniquely American; businessmen, students, tourists, and diplomats from all nations became increasingly mobile. In 1977, 18.6 million tourists from abroad visited the United States, and the total topped 20 million in 1978. What everyone was discovering, however, was that other cultures seemed unfamiliar, alien, and at times mysterious.

Closer cultural contact was also encouraged by sophisticated and complex communication systems. Communication satellites that allowed governments to teach, persuade, and entertain hundreds of thousands of people at the same time became commonplace during this period. In addition, a well organized international film industry was evolving. We were developing, at a suddenly faster pace, a world communication network.

As earlier travel and communication constraints were removed, the world became cognizant of a compelling need to improve global understanding. A costly, bloody, and protracted confrontation thousands of miles away in Vietnam saw us trying to deal with an enemy whose view of what constituted warfare and victory confused us. During this same period the number of Third World nations grew. These new countries did not follow the traditional and prescribed modes of behavior of the Western world. Revolutionary events in Iran demonstrated vividly our lack of cultural understanding. Why was the modernization that had been pursued by the Shah not valued? Learning to make sense of the behaviors of others, both in and out of the United Nations, became a major concern not only of the government of the United States, but for many social and religious institutions, as well as countless individuals who sought to understand their increasingly complex world.

Shifts in the international business community, coupled with new problems in supply and demand, forced us to re-think our relationships with import and export cultures. In short, some major changes were made in the international business market. OPEC became a household word. Investments, foreign markets, even countries, once controlled by the United States, diversified and would not respond to our wishes or demands. In addition, foreign investors began to influence American markets. "Since 1974 foreign investments in the capitalist bastion of America [grew] by an average 13% annually, and [in 1978 totaled] more than $171 billion, or two-thirds as much as the sum of U.S. investments abroad . . . nearly 1.1 million people work for foreign owned companies in the U.S., and the number is growing daily. . . ."[1] Humorous stories about how the Arabs would soon purchase McDonald's and JC Penney's abounded. Would the Big Mac soon be replaced by *kibbi* and *shrek*?

Domestic companies began to recognize the cultural diversity of their customers. Sears Roebuck, the nation's largest retailer, introduced a bilingual general catalog in some parts of the United States. (Santa Claus could now speak Spanish.) And telephone companies started taking out full-page ads in major news magazines listing international area codes so people could dial direct to most major cities in the world.

The issue of international interdependence was manifested clearly when the Japan Information Center used the American mass media to tell the people of the United States that the Fifth Economic Summit was an important event for the entire world. In one advertisement they noted that the seven countries involved in the summit needed to look at how world trade systems, inflation and monetary instability, energy, and world economic development linked all the issues and all the countries together.

A more serious need for intercultural communication was underscored dramatically as a growing number of countries acquired nuclear capability. Potentially, poor communication or a lack of understanding could mean the end of the world as we know it. Needless to say, these doomsday prophecies seemed to motivate people where simple words could not.

The beginning of the 1970s also brought the realization to many countries that time-space relationships were not the only ways in which the world was shrinking. We were starting to see that the earth's natural resources were not boundless, that they too were diminishing. Shortages in food, oil, copper, and even water, made us aware that we not only shared in the planet's bounty, but we also shared in its limita-

tions. The awesome prospect of major shortages and possible deple-
tions had the effect of making us aware of our common concerns. A yet
unfulfilled need for universal understanding emerged from this new
problem. A residual effect of this need for better international communication is found in President Carter's mandate that changed the
title of the United States Information Agency to the International
Communication Agency.

Domestic Awareness

As these worldwide changes were occurring, a cultural revolution took
place within our own land. From a variety of directions, and with
varying degrees of intensity, we were being made aware of new and
different cultures, subcultures, and groups in conflict with mainstream
America: Blacks, Chicanos, women, the elderly, homosexuals, the
poor, hippies, and countless other groups became highly visible and
vocal.

A number of significant incidents added to the conspicuous nature
of these subcultures and their chief advocates. First, many of these
groups were no longer willing to wait passively for admission into the
dominant culture. They were more aggressive, demanding, and at
times more violent than subcultures of the past. Cries of black, brown,
gray, and red power filled the air. Names such as Mario Savio, Russell
Means, Eldridge Cleaver, Timothy Leary, Cesar Chavez, Huey New-
ton, Betty Friedan, the Chicago Seven, the Weathermen, and the Sim-
bianese Liberation Army appeared on our television screens and in our
newspapers. Phrases such as "burn, baby, burn," "women's liberation," "turn on, drop out," "black is beautiful," and "gay power"
confused and shocked many of us.

Our schools were just one of a host of targets that received a new
and thorough re-examination. One argument maintained that American education gave the impression of being democratic and universal
while in reality "the curriculum remained Waspish in its content and
aristocratic in its expectations."[2] As the schools and the government
responded, these groups became even more conspicuous. As the alle-
gations mounted so did the number of groups seeking recognition.

New legislation and major court decisions in the area of school
busing and open housing placed many of these groups in settings that
made contact between the dominant culture and certain subcultures
impossible to avoid. Many affirmative action rulings had a similar effect. They also forced open doors that the dominant culture had con-
structed out of fear, ignorance, apathy, and prejudice.

When these new and unsolicited contacts took place, they often
were unsuccessful and even counterproductive. Differences in lan-

7

guage, length of hair, treatment of time, dress, and skin color represented only superficial characteristics of the problem. It became obvious that misunderstandings were much deeper and more complex than we had first anticipated. What we were learning in often painful ways was that there were groups of people with different lifestyles, values, and ways of perceiving the universe. The need to comprehend and to interact with these groups became a major stimulus for the study of intercultural communication.

Personal Awareness

It is obvious that this increased contact with other cultures and subcultures makes it imperative for us to make a concerted effort to get along with and to try to understand people whose beliefs and backgrounds may be vastly different from our own. The ability, through increased awareness and understanding, to peacefully coexist with people who do not necessarily share our lifestyles or values could benefit us not only in our own neighborhoods but could be the decisive factor in forestalling nuclear annihilation.

There also are several positive personal rewards that await us as conscientious and effective intercultural communicators. These benefits span psychological pleasure to financial gain. There are four very specific and personal advantages for us that can come from the study of intercultural communication.

First, from personal experience we already know the feelings of enjoyment and satisfaction that accompany the discovery of something new. These same sensations are associated with the discoveries we make about another person's culture. For example, one explanation for the success of Alex Haley's book and television series, *Roots*, was that it offered fresh insights into the black culture. Haley himself noted, "... white people are saying 'I didn't know; I never knew.' "[3] Like a trip to a foreign country, *Roots* afforded us the excitement of learning something new. These same feelings of exhilaration are often expressed by Peace Corps and Vista volunteers. Try to visualize, for example, the fascination of seeing a Buddhist religious ceremony for the first time.

Second, knowledge of intercultural communication can aid us in solving communication problems before they arise. An understanding of some of the reasons why the hard-core poor perceive the schools as they do might well help school counselors in their treatment of young truants. Knowing that Native American Indians and Mexicans employ eye contact in ways that differ from other Americans is also useful information that could avert a misunderstanding. In essence, what we are saying is that many problems can be avoided by understanding the components of intercultural communication.

Third, employment opportunities abound in the area of intercultural communication. As would be assumed, government service is one area where positions are plentiful. Government employment is available not only in the obvious places such as the State Department, United Nations, Department of Agriculture, Export-Import Bank, and the Central Intelligence Agency, but at all levels of government. Most of these agencies need people with an intercultural perspective, for cross-cultural understanding in such positions is not only beneficial, it is crucial.

Educational systems in the United States offer employment opportunities in nearly all communities. Multicultural teacher-training programs are becoming commonplace in most school districts. Originally these programs were begun as bilingual classes. It soon became apparent, however, that teaching a second language only solved part of the problem. Many school boards designed programs that called for full-day classes in history and culture. In 1977 the Department of Health, Education and Welfare sponsored 627 bilingual projects in teacher-training, curriculum development, and schoolroom programs. These programs were estimated to cost over $200 million in federal and state money,[4] and as we indicated, most of them contained an intercultural communication dimension.

The business and industrial community also abounds in employment opportunities for people who can move in and out of different cultures with ease. Over one-hundred and fifty American-based businesses actively recruit people who are interested in intercultural affairs. Such firms as Rockwell International, IBM, Xerox, and General Mills, are some obvious organizations that stress international services and products. Specific needs vary from professional negotiators to salespersons and to people who can prepare dependents for living overseas. New training centers and organizations, such as Applied Intercultural Management Associates and the Center for Research and Education, have evolved in recent years. These companies attempt to train executives in intercultural communication skills.

Of course, the ability to exchange precise, sometimes culture-specific, ideas and meanings with people of other cultures, by itself, is not a sufficient basis for a career in international business. But it greatly enhances the value to employers of people with specific training in such fields as computer technology, business administration, public administration, economics, education, and the like.

Fourth, the study of intercultural communication offers immeasurable opportunities to improve self-perception and understanding. In attempting to grasp another's culture, we can gain a better understanding of ourselves and our own culture. Knowing how Koreans feel about the elderly, for example, can cause us to examine our own beliefs about age. Knowing where, when, and how the Japanese utilize touching as a form of communication can encourage us to explore how we employ this same tactile experience. And understanding how the British view silence can cause us to re-evaluate our personal perception of this concept. Even more serious issues such as our stereotypes and prejudices can be examined rationally by studying intercultural communication.

In these last few pages we have seen the need to learn more about intercultural communication. In the final analysis, of course, how we rank this subject on our scale of priorities is a personal and private matter. However, different cultures and subcultures are exerting an ever-increasing influence on our daily lives. It is an inescapable truism that our world is getting smaller and our lives necessarily must change. "...The conditions of contemporary history are such that we may now be on the threshold of a new kind of person, a person who is socially and psychologically a product of the interweaving of cultures in the twentieth century."[5]

Communication

This book is about what happens when people from different cultures attempt to communicate. To be more specific, it is a book about communication, culture, and the relationship existing between them. These topics (communication, culture, and their link) are of such significance that we will spend the remainder of this chapter and all of the next chapter examining how they form the bases of our investigation of intercultural communication. This chapter defines and describes communication. Chapter 2 will continue our analysis by looking at culture and how communication and culture are inseparable.

To understand intercultural interaction one must first understand human communication. Although the parties involved in intercultural interaction represent diverse backgrounds, they are, nevertheless, subject to the same types of experiences that people of similar backgrounds encounter whenever they attempt to communicate. Understanding human communication means we know something about what happens during an encounter, why it happens, what can happen, the effects of what happens, and finally what we can do to influence and maximize the results of that event.

Defining Communication

Defining and describing communication is a difficult task because of the complexity of the subject. Writers in the field have developed numerous definitions that basically fall into two schools of thought.

One approach describes communication as the process whereby one person deliberately attempts to convey meaning to another. ". . . A communicates B through channel C to D with effect E."[6] Here *A* represents a speaker who communicates a message *B* through a channel *C* which reaches listener *D* and elicits a response *E*. A more general definition of the process approach describes communication as ". . . the process by which an individual transmits stimuli to modify the behavior of other individuals."[7]

These process-oriented definitions state or assume intentionality. They limit communication to those circumstances where one person intentionally sets out to affect the behavior of another through symbolic inducement to attitude or behavior. These definitions, however, do not take into account circumstances in which messages are conveyed unintentionally or unconsciously. Awareness of this possibility is especially important in intercultural communication when we may be transmitting unknown, unwanted, and undesirable messages without realizing it.

In order to avoid the limitations of intentionality, other authors have formulated definitions in which there is no intention to affect another; it just happens. ". . . [As] used in [this] sense the concept of communication would include all those processes by which people influence one another."[8] An even less specific view states, "communication, viewed psychologically, is a process which is concerned with all situations involving meaning."[9]

We now have some idea of how a few writers in the field have attempted to come to grips with this very complex idea. Let us now undertake a more detailed analysis of human communication.

Understanding Communication

We begin with a basic assumption that communication has something to do with human behavior and the satisfaction of a need to interact with other human beings. This last aspect is known as communication hunger. Almost everyone needs social contact with other people, and this need is met through the exchange of messages that serve as bridges to unite otherwise isolated individuals. Messages come into being through human behavior. When we talk, we obviously are behaving; when we wave, smile, frown, walk, shake our heads, or gesture, we also are behaving. Frequently these actions are messages; they are often used to communicate something to someone else.

Before these behaviors can be called messages, they must meet two requirements. First, they must be observed by someone and second they must elicit meaning. Another way to say this is that any behavior to which meaning is attributed is a message.

If we examine this last statement for a moment we can see several implications. First, the word *any* tells us that both verbal and nonverbal behaviors may function as messages. Verbal messages consist of words either spoken or written (speaking or writing is a word-producing behavior) while nonverbal messages consist of the entire remaining repertory of our behaviors to which meaning may be attributed.

Second, behavior may occur either consciously or unconsciously. This means, of course, that we may sometimes behave without being conscious of our actions. This is especially true of nonverbal behavior. Such nervous habits as fingernail biting, toe-tapping, leg-jiggling, head-shaking, staring, smiling, and as many more as we can think of, can and do occur many times without our being aware of them. Even such things as slouching in a chair, chewing gum, or adjusting glasses are frequently unconscious behaviors. And since a message consists of behaviors to which meaning may be attributed, we must acknowledge that it is quite possible to produce messages unconsciously and without awareness. The importance of this implication will be made clearer shortly.

A third implication of behavior-message is that frequently we behave unintentionally. For instance, if we are embarrassed we may blush or speak with vocal disfluencies. We do not intend to blush or stammer, but we may do it anyway. Again, these unintentional behaviors become messages if someone sees them and attributes meaning to them.

Using this concept of conscious-unconscious, intentional-unintentional behavior relationships, we are ready to formulate our own definition of communication. Here, communication is defined as that which happens whenever meaning is attributed to behavior or to the residue of behavior. This definition tells us that when someone observes our behavior or its residue and attributes meaning to it, communication has taken place regardless of whether our behavior has been conscious or unconscious, intentional or unintentional. If we think about it for a moment, we must realize that it is impossible for us not to behave. Just the very act of being is a form of behavior. And if behavior has communication potential, then it is also impossible for us not to communicate; in other words, *we cannot not communicate.*

The notion of behavior residue mentioned in our definition refers to those things that remain as a record of our actions. For instance, the writing of this book involved certain behaviors; the authors had to sit down and write and type, all of which were behaviors. What we hold in our hand is a residue of that behavior; it is a record of earlier behaviors. We may, however, attribute meaning to this book as easily as we could attribute meaning to actual behaviors. Another example of behavior residue might be the odor of cigar smoke lingering in a room after the cigar smoker has departed. Smoking the cigar was the actual behavior; the odor is the residue. The meaning we give to that smell is a reflection of our past experiences and attitudes toward cigars, smoking, and, perhaps, the people who smoke them.

Our approach to communication has focused on the attribution of meaning to behavior. Attribution means that we take meaning which we already have and assign or attach it to behavior we observe in our environment. We might imagine that stored somewhere in our brain is a meaning reservoir in which we have stored all of the meanings we possess. These various meanings have developed throughout our lifetime as a result of our culture acting upon us as well as the result of our individual experiences within that culture. Meaning is relative to each of us in that we are all unique human beings with unique backgrounds and experiences.

When we encounter a behavior in our environment we dip into our unique meaning reservoir and select from it the meaning we believe has the highest probability of being the most appropriate for the behavior we encounter and the social context in which the behavior occurred. Sometimes this works quite well, but at other times it lets us down and we misinterpret a message; we attribute the wrong meaning to the behavior we have observed.

Thus far, our definition of communication has been kept general in order to accommodate the many circumstances under which communication may occur and the cases of unconscious and unintentional communication. What we are going to do now is propose a modified definition that assumes a conscious intention to communicate but still realizes that unconscious and unintentional behavior may be present to complicate communication situations. Further, our definition will specify the ingredients of communication and specify some of the dynamics present.

The Ingredients of Communication

Before we can examine the ingredients of communication, we must have a definition that specifies these ingredients and their relationships. As we have already seen, communication may be intentional or unintentional, and it may be conscious or unconscious. Since our purpose in studying intercultural communication is to develop skills we will apply with conscious intention, our working definition of communication will specify intentional communication.

Communication is defined as *a two-way, on-going, behavior-affecting process in which one person (a source) intentionally encodes and transmits a message through a channel to an intended audience (receivers) in order to induce a particular attitude or behavior*. Communication is complete only when the intended receiver perceives the message, attributes meaning to it (decodes it), and is affected by it. In this process must be included all conscious or unconscious, intentional or unintentional verbal, non-verbal, or contextual stimuli that act as cues to both the source and receiver about the quality and credibility of the message. We also must realize that although we are concerned primarily with intentional communication situations, behavior that may be perceived as messages may be generated without intention and intended messages may be received by unintended receivers.

This definition allows us to identify eight specific ingredients of communication within the context of intentional communication. First is the *source*. A source is a person who has a need to communicate. This need may range from a social desire for recognition as an individual to the desire to share information with others or to influence the attitudes and behaviors of one or more others. The need to communicate can be seen as a desire to share an internal state of being, whether it be emotional or informational, with another human being. Communication, then, is really concerned with the sharing of internal states of being with varying degrees of intention to influence the attitudes and behaviors of others.

Internal states of being, however, cannot be shared directly. We lack the means of directly inducing a state of being in another person; we must rely on symbolic representations of our internal states. This brings us to the second ingredient, *encoding*. Encoding is an internal activity in which a source creates a message through the selection of verbal and nonverbal symbols that are put together according to the rules of grammar and syntax applicable to the language being used.

The result of encoding is a *message*, which is the third ingredient of communication. A message is a set of verbal and/or nonverbal symbols that represent a source's particular state of being at a particular moment in time and space. Although encoding is an internal act that produces a message, a message is external to the source; the message is what must pass between a source and a receiver if the source is to influence the receiver.

Messages, however, must have a means by which they move from source to receiver. The fourth communication ingredient is the *channel*, which provides the connection between source and receiver. A channel is the physical means by which the message is transmitted. For instance, in this book, the words printed on the page constitute the message and the channel is light. Light reflects from the pages of the book and carries reflections of the words to the retina of our eyes where we begin to convert these reflections into our own internal states of being. If we are listening to someone speak, the channel is the air. Physical differences in air pressure carry a speaker's voice to the listener who receives the message at the ear in the form of varying air pressures impinging on the ear drum.

14

Another way to think of the connection between source and receiver is in terms of the means of conveying a message. The term *media* is most frequently used to distinguish channels in the physical sense from means of conveyance. In this case we think of various ways of linking people together: face-to-face oral communication, letters, magazines, books, newspapers, billboards, radio, television, tape recorders, records, sky writers, and telephones. All these are media by which messages may be conveyed from one person to another. This consideration of channels or media is important in intercultural communication because the preference of channel or media to be used for various types of communication varies from one culture to another. For example, the preferred channels of white Anglo school administrators in East Los Angeles for conveying messages to parents about their children differ considerably from the channels preferred by the Mexican-American parents.[10]

Fifth among our ingredients of communication is the *receiver*. The term receiver represents the person or persons who intercept the message and as a consequence become linked to the message source. Receivers may be those intended by the source or they may be others who, by whatever circumstance, come in contact with the message once it has entered the channel.

Receivers have a problem with messages that is not unlike the problem sources have with internal states of being. Messages impinge on receivers in the form of raw energy. For the most part this energy is in the form of light waves and sound waves. But it also may be in forms that stimulate any of our senses, such as pressure applied to our skin as we shake hands, chemicals that bombard our olfactory senses as we smell things, or chemicals that stimulate our taste receptors as we eat or drink things. Whatever the form of sensory stimulation, receivers must convert these raw energies into meaningful experiences.

Converting external energies to meaningful experience is the sixth ingredient, called *decoding*. It is akin to the source's act of encoding, as it also is an internal activity of the receiver. This internal function, which also is sometimes called information processing, constitutes the decoding of a message and the attribution of meaning to the source's behaviors which constitute symbols representing the source's internal state of being.

The seventh ingredient we need to consider is *receiver response*. This is most easily thought of as what a receiver decides to do about the message. Response may vary along a minimum-maximum dimension. Minimum response can be described as the receiver's decision to ignore or do nothing about the message. Maximum response, on the other hand, is characterized as an immediate overt physical act of possibly violent proportion. If communication has gone somewhat successfully, the response of the receiver will to some degree resemble that desired by the source who created the response-eliciting message.

The final ingredient we will consider is *feedback*. This is information available to a source that allows the source to make qualitative judgments about the effectiveness of the communication situation in order to adjust and adapt to the on-going situation. Although feedback and response are not the same thing, they are clearly related. Response is what the receiver decides to do about the message while feedback is information about communication effectiveness. The two concepts are related because response or a lack of response is the normal source of feedback.

The eight ingredients just discussed are but a partial listing of the factors that function during a communication event. These eight, however, were selected because there cannot be communication without all of them. In addition to these elements, when we approach communication as a process there are several other characteristics that, when understood, help clarify how communication actually operates.

First, communication is *dynamic*. This means it is an on-going, ever-changing activity. As participants in communication we constantly are affected by other people's messages and, as a consequence, we undergo continual change. This does not mean radical change, although radical change can occur. The transformation of Patty Hearst into Tanya in a period of about three months is an example of radical change. But each of us in our daily lives meets and interacts with people and these people exert some influence over us. Each time we are influenced we are changed in some way, which means that as we go through life we do so as a continually changing individual—a dynamic person.

A second characteristic of communication is its *interactive nature*. Communication must take place between a source and a receiver. Usually this implies two or more people. It is possible, however, for one person to fulfill simultaneously the roles of both source and receiver. We call this *intra*personal communication as it refers to those situations where we become aware of ourselves and attribute meaning to our behaviors. This includes thinking, talking to ourselves, or evaluating our appearance as we gaze in a mirror. When the source and receiver are different people, we call the form of communication *inter*personal. In this situation communication is characterized by the fact that both parties bring to a communication event their own unique backgrounds and experiences, which serve as a backdrop for communicative interaction. Interaction also implies a reciprocal situation in which each party attempts to influence the other. That is, each party simultaneously functions as both source and receiver, creating messages designed to elicit specific responses from the other.

Third, communication is *irreversible*. Once we have said something and someone else has received and decoded the message, we cannot retrieve the message. This circumstance is sometimes called "putting-your-foot-in-your-mouth." The point to be made here is that because of the process nature of communication, once a receiver has been affected by a message that result cannot be recalled. We may send other messages in attempts to modify the effect, but we cannot eliminate it. This is one of the big problems that occur when we unconsciously or unintentionally send a message to someone. We may affect them adversely and not even be aware of it. Then during future interaction we may not be able to understand why someone is reacting to us in an unusual way.

Fourth, communication takes place in both a *physical and social context*. When we interact with someone it is not in isolation but within a specific physical surrounding and under a set of specific social dynamics. The physical surrounding includes specific physical objects such as furniture, window coverings, floor coverings, lighting, noise levels, acoustics, vegetation, presence or absence of physical clutter, as well as competing messages. Many, many aspects of the physical environment can and do affect communication. The comfort or discomfort of a chair, the color of walls, or total atmosphere of a room are but a few. There is also the symbolic meaning of the physical surroundings that falls into the arena of nonverbal communication. This will be discussed later in Chapter 6, which deals with the nonverbal aspects of intercultural communication. By way of illustration, however, we briefly recall the Paris Peace Talks in which much time was spent in deciding on a table shape acceptable to all parties. While this may seem trivial to us, to the negotiators it was very important because a table with equal sides symbolically represented an equality of all parties at the table. And the South Vietnamese did not want to give this recognition to the Viet Cong any more than North Vietnam wished to give this recognition to the United States.

Social context defines the type of social relationships that exist between source and receiver. In our American culture we tend to be somewhat cavalier toward social hierarchies and we pay much less attention to them than people do in other cultures. Nevertheless, such differences as teacher-student, employer-employee, parent-child, admiral-seaman, senator-citizen, friend-enemy, physician-patient, and judge-attorney affect the communication process. And, quite frequently, the physical surroundings help define the social context. The employer may sit behind a desk while the employee stands before the desk to receive an admonition. Or, in the courtroom, the judge sits elevated facing the courtroom, jurors, and attorneys, indicating the social superiority of the office of judge relative to the other officers of the court. The attorneys sit side-by-side indicating a social equality between accuser and accused until such time as the jury of peers renders a verdict.

No matter what the social context, there will be some effect on communication. The form of language used, the respect or lack of respect shown one another, time of day, personal moods, who speaks to whom and in what order, and the degree of nervousness or confidence people may express are but a few of the ways in which the social context can affect communication.

At this point, we should see clearly that human communication does not take place in a social vacuum. Rather, communication is an intricate matrix of interacting social acts that occur in a complex social environment. This social environment reflects the way people live, how they come to interact with and get along in their world. In short, this social environment is culture, and if we truly are to understand communication, we must also understand culture.

Studying Intercultural Communication

We have spent some time discovering that human communication is complex, multidimensional, and subject to a countless number of variations. When the component of culture is added to human communication the complexities and the problems facing any systematic study of the two is compounded greatly. The study of culture is as elusive as the study of human communication.

Because culture lacks a distinct crystalline structure, it is riddled with contradictions and extremes. Culture is learned on both the cognitive and affective levels. We are told some of what our culture is, but most of it we simply absorb without being aware of it. Culture is vague and it is specific; it is all of an individual, and it is but part of an individual. Lacking consistencies and any clearcut distinction between what is an individual trait or what is a cultural characteristic, we sometimes tend to oversimplify and overgeneralize. Both of these actions are wrong. Cultural generalizations must be viewed as approximations, not absolutes. As our own experiences have taught us, there are occasions when people do not act out the prescribed and accepted modes of cultural behavior. Even though not all human transactions follow a prepared script, the study of culture does help explain much of what takes place between people. The important consideration at this point is that we be mindful of oversimplification and remember there are many exceptions.

Another problem in studying intercultural communication is that culture cannot be manipulated. Unlike scientific experiments where a researcher controls and manipulates the variables, culture cannot be controlled or made to cease evolving. What we know about intercultural communication, therefore, is not only somewhat tentative, it comes from a variety of sources—some reliable and some highly speculative, some from personal observations and some from specific studies. Hence, once again a reminder that intercultural generalizations must allow for exceptions, and they are most useful when viewed as guidelines rather than absolutes.

Our final problem is an impossible one to overcome completely, for in this instance we are the problem. In studying other cultures, and in making cultural comparisons, we do so from the perspective of our own culture. Our observations and our conclusions are colored by the specific orientation of our culture. It is difficult to see and to give meaning to words and movements we are not familiar with. How, for example, do we make sense of someone's silence if we come from a very verbal culture. There also is a danger that we might allow our judgments to take on evaluative interpretations. Phrases such as "if our males do not kiss each other in greeting, why should they do something so silly," tend to creep into the perception process. This inclination to believe that our own group is superior to and the only basis for judging other groups (or cultures) is called ethnocentrism. Although we shall return to this idea later, we should be mindful of our propensity toward ethnocentrism during the introductory stages of our study.

Preview of the Book: What Lies Ahead?

This book is divided into four interrelated parts. Part I, which has two chapters, serves as an introduction to intercultural communication. Chapter 1 has four objectives: to talk about the importance of intercultural communication, to discuss human communication, to discuss the study of intercultural communication, and to preview the major chapters or themes of the book. Chapter 2 will examine the theoretical concepts that help explain and define the field of intercultural communication. Elements such as culture, society, ethnic and racial differences, and group traits will be explored. In addition, the major components of intercultural communication will be presented. Understanding is the touchstone of improvement, and our progress is aided by our understanding of the theory as well as the practice of intercultural communication.

Part II moves us from the theoretical to the practical. There are three chapters in this section, and each attempts to examine the people involved in intercultural transactions. Chapter 3 is predicated on the notion that we must understand our own behavior before we can understand the behavior of others. We shall look, therefore, at the dominant factors in American culture that influence the way we communicate. In Chapter 4 we examine some of the dominant patterns in other cultures that affect how people communicate. A culture's history, social organizations, values, and lifestyles offer us insights into the communication patterns of that culture. Chapter 5 looks at issues related to perception, stereotypes, and prejudices. These three constituents often impede intercultural understanding and must be surveyed before we move to our analysis of actual communication encounters.

In Part III the elements of interaction are discussed. Chapters 6 and 7 focus on the verbal and nonverbal systems used in communication. Looking at the messages that are exchanged will help us appreciate the responses those messages often produce.

Part IV, the final section, is concerned with improvement of intercultural communication skills. In a sense, our entire study focuses on the issue of improvement, but in Chapter 8 we find specific advice and recommendations. We hope these guidelines will make our intercultural meetings more productive, rewarding, and successful.

Notes

1. *Time* Magazine, May 29, 1978, p. 68.

2. Alfred C. Aarons, Barbara Y. Gordon, and William A. Stewart, "Linguistic-Cultural Differences and American Education," *Florida FL Reporter,* Spring/Summer 1969, p. 1.

3. *Time* Magazine, February 7, 1977, p. 96.

4. *Newsweek* Magazine, February 7, 1977, p. 64.

5. Peter S. Adler, "Beyond Cultural Identity: Reflections on Culture and Multicultural Man" in *Topics in Cultural Learning,* ed. Richard W. Brislin, vol. 2 (Honolulu: East-West Center, 1974), p. 23.

6. Wilbur Schramm, ed., *Communication in Modern Society: Fifteen Studies of the Mass Media Prepared for the University of Illinois Institute of Communication Research* (Urbana: The University of Illinois Press, 1948), p. 24.

7. Carl Hovland, "Social Communication," *Proceedings of the American Philosophical Society,* 92 (1948): 371.

8. Jurgen Reusch, "Values, Communication, and Culture" in *Communication: The Social Matrix of Psychiatry,* eds. Jurgen Ruesch and Gregory Bateson (New York: W. W. Norton, 1951), pp. 5–6.

9. Henry C. Lindgren, *The Art of Human Relations* (New York: Hermitage House, 1953), p. 135.

10. Howard P. Holiday, "Communication of Mexican Americans with Public School Personnel: A Study of Channel, Code, Receiver, and Source Preferences," (doctoral dissertation, University of Southern California, 1972).

11. Dean C. Barnlund, *Private and Public Self in Japan and the United States* (Tokyo: Simul Press, 1975).

Additional Readings

Burgoon, M. and M. Ruffner. *Human Communication.* New York: Holt, Rinehart & Winston, 1978, Chapter 1.

Devito, J. A. *Communicology: An Introduction to the Study of Communication.* New York: Harper & Row, 1978, Units 1–3.

McCroskey, J. and L. R. Wheeles. *Introduction to Human Communication.* Boston: Allyn & Bacon, 1976, Chapters 1 and 2.

Prosser, M. H. *The Cultural Dialogue: An Introduction to Intercultural Communication.* Boston: Houghton Mifflin, 1978.

Rich, A. L. *Interracial Communication.* New York: Harper & Row, 1974.

Sitaram, K. S. and R. T. Cogdell. *Foundations of Intercultural Communication.* Columbus, Ohio: Charles E. Merrill, 1976.

Concepts and Questions

1. Can you think of some intercultural conflicts that seemed to start over a simple misunderstanding?

2. What are the newest subcultures that are asking to be heard?

3. Is foreign investment in the United States harmful to the country? Why?

4. Why is the study of human communication an essential part of the study of intercultural communication?

5. What is meant by a meaning approach to communication?

6. Are there ethical considerations inherent in the idea that communication is irreversible?

7. What are some problems in studying intercultural communication? How can they be overcome?

Exercises

1. Ask your career counseling service about job opportunities in foreign countries. If possible, interview some people who have

worked abroad recently. Select a job opportunity that interests you and investigate the types of intercultural contacts or communication situations involved. Discuss briefly the importance of intercultural communication for effective performance of this job.

2. Locate some agencies or organizations that work with minority groups in your area. Interview some officials of these agencies to identify the racial and ethnic composition of the groups they work with and discuss the major problems encountered. Discuss the importance of intercultural communication in improving the work of these agencies.

3. Interview the foreign students adviser on your campus to find out: (a) the nature and size of foreign student population on your campus, (b) the major communication problems encountered by the foreign student advising office in working with foreign students, and (c) the types of communication problems most frequently reported by foreign students. Discuss briefly the importance of intercultural communication in improving the work of the foreign student adviser and in dealing with the problems encountered by foreign students.

4. Attend an intercultural event (e.g., foreign students' reception on your campus, international students' picnic, international night, and international students' dinner) involving persons from several countries. Try to meet some persons from foreign countries and find out the purpose of their visit, their intercultural adjustment experiences, and their future plans. Keep track of your communication experience and problems with each person. In what ways are these experiences and problems different from communication with persons of your own culture?

2

Culture and Communication: The Crucial Link

Culture is man's medium; there is not one aspect of human life that is not touched and altered by culture. This means personality, how people express themselves (including shows of emotion), the way they think, how they move, how problems are solved, how their cities are planned and laid out, how transportation systems function and are organized, as well as how economic and government systems are put together and function. However . . . it is frequently the most obvious and taken-for-granted and therefore the least studied aspects of culture that influence behavior in the deepest and most subtle ways.

Edward T. Hall

Communication is far more complex and much more important to us than we may thus far suspect. With rare exception, our daily lives almost constantly are acts of communication. As was brought out in Chapter 1, we cannot not communicate, and "the way people communicate is the way they live."[1]

When we begin to talk about the way people live we are thrust immediately into the arena of culture because culture is the form or pattern for living. People learn to think, feel, believe, and strive for what their culture considers proper. Language habits, friendships, eating habits, communication practices, social acts, economic and political activities, and technology all follow the patterns of culture. If people speak Tagalog, avoid members of another race, eat snakes, avoid wine, live in communal housing, bury their dead, talk on the telephone, or rocket to the moon, it is because they have been born into or at least reared in a culture that contains these elements. What people do, how they act, and how they live and communicate is both a response to and a function of their culture.

Culture and communication are inseparable because culture not only dictates who talks with whom, about what, and how the communication proceeds, it also helps to determine how people encode messages, the meanings they have for messages, and the conditions and circumstances under which various messages may or may not be sent, noticed, or interpreted. In fact, our entire repertory of communicative behaviors is dependent largely on the culture in which we have been raised. Culture, consequently, is the foundation of communication. And, when cultures vary, communication practices also vary.

Culture and communication are so inextricably bound to one another that some cultural anthropologists have argued persuasively that the terms culture and communication are essentially synonymous.[2] This inseparable relationship between culture and communication is the key factor in our fully understanding communication. Our ability to fathom the complexities of intercultural communication must begin with a sound grasp of cultural influences on the way people communicate. Cultural variance in how people encode and decode messages is the foremost problem in intercultural communication. To help us develop an appropriate perspective for the study of intercultural communication, we are going to survey the notion of culture, describe and define intercultural communication, and then consider in detail some socio-cultural elements that affect intercultural communication most directly.

Culture

Culture is an intriguing concept. Although we can easily read a definition of it, when we begin to consider that definition and what it implies, culture becomes a prodigious and commanding notion. Formally defined, culture is the deposit of knowledge, experiences, beliefs, values, attitudes, meanings, hierarchies, religion, timing, roles, spatial relations, concepts of the universe, and material objects and possessions acquired by a large group of people in the course of generations through individual and group striving. Culture manifests itself in patterns of language and in forms of activity and behavior that act as models for both the common adaptive acts and the styles of communication that enable us to live in a society within a given geographic environment at a given state of technical development at a particular moment in time. It also specifies and is defined by the nature of material things that play an essential role in common life. Such things as houses, instruments and machines used in industry and agriculture, forms of transportation, and instruments of war provide a material foundation for social life. Although this definition is considerable and covers a wide range of human endeavor, we can easily see that culture is persistent, enduring, and omnipresent, and that it includes all of the behavioral reinforcements that we receive during the course of our lifetime. Culture also helps dictate the form and structure of our physical realm, and it encompasses and specifies the social environment permeating our lives.

The effect of culture on our lives is largely unrealized. Over the period of time we have been raised in our culture, many of the influences culture has had on us have become buried in the primitive portions of our brains beneath the neocortex, where they largely are below our levels of awareness. Whether any cultural knowledge is transmitted by heredity is unknown, but even this possibility cannot as yet be ruled out. Perhaps another way to understand cultural influence is by way of analogy with electronic computers: As we program computers to do what they do, our culture to a great extent programs us to do what we do and to be what we are. Our culture affects us in a deterministic manner from conception to death—and even after death in terms of funeral rites.

The effect of this cultural influence is found in our everyday modes of behavior and in our communication practices. Culture includes all of the behavioral reinforcements we receive during our lifetime, and it is through rewarding reinforcements that we learn how to act and how to communicate in a manner that is both effective and acceptable within our cultural context. Of course, culture is not the sole determinant of behavior and communication. There are also many social, physical, and psychological factors that motivate our behavior. But, these various motivating forces occur within specific cultural contexts. In a sense, the influence of culture on communication can be summed up by the idea that what we talk about and how we talk about it is for the most part determined by the culture in which we have lived. More will be said later about the relationship between culture and communication when we examine the socio-cultural elements most relevant to intercultural communication.

Culture Is a Model for Life

Culture conditions us unconsciously toward particular modes of behavior and communication. Such conditioning might seem repugnant to those of us who think of ourselves as self-motivated individuals, free thinkers who decide what we are going to do and what our fate will be. We may feel uncomfortable with the thought that we are programmed by our culture. But cultural influences in our development as individuals are vital because it is culture that gives us the skills, knowledge, customs, traditions, material objects, and social organization that make living in groups possible. It teaches us how to live in our particular social environment. Without culture we would be helpless floundering animals in an unfathomable realm. We might even go so far as to say that "our primary mode of biological adaptation is culture, not anatomy."[3]

Culture is the basis of the structure, stability, and security that both individuals and a society must possess if they are to maintain themselves. Culture provides this foundation because it is dynamic and develops along the lines of self and societal survival. In essence, culture is the medium through which a society survives and perpetuates itself by the survival, reproduction, and training of the individuals who comprise the society. An example of how culture works to perpetuate society can be found by looking at a cultural custom in Africa and seeing how it operates to benefit a part of African tribal society.

Lobola is a traditional marriage custom practiced by the Zulu and Sotho tribal people of South Africa. A lobola is a payment made by the family of a man to the family of a woman when the couple marry. In rural South Africa, a lobola usually is in the form of ten cows each with a value of about $11. This makes the total value of the lobola approximately $110. Urban Zulus and Sothos also practice lobola, but since cows are not practical in cities, the payment is made in money. This change in the form of lobola payment maintains the custom and its social benefit, and demonstrates to us the dynamic quality of culture by showing how it persists and adapts to on-going changes in the social environment.

How lobola helps to perpetuate a social order can be seen by noting that a lobola is refundable if a marriage is not successful or if the woman is unable to bear children. In order to help ensure successful marriages and lobola retention, parents often seek out compatible marriage partners for their children. Among Zulus and Sothos arranged marriages are quite common. And, as we can imagine, a great deal of family social pressure is imposed on couples to remain married.

Lobola and its accompanying social pressures produce strong socio-cultural forces toward maintaining a high degree of stability in immediate as well as in extended family groups. As this stability persists, it becomes felt throughout the entire fabric of the society. This stability also is accomplished because lobola functions as a form of financial security. Just as the Social Security System in the United States provides a base of financial security for senior citizens, South African children provide security for their parents through the payment of the lobola. Daughters, of course, become financial assets that are redeemed when they marry.

Another glimpse of how culture functions to maintain social stability can be found in India. Among the Hindus of India, women generally are accorded an inferior social position. Men are the acknowledged superiors. Family and social order is maintained because the Hindu culture teaches its women their appropriate sex roles. This cultural conditioning prepares the Indian woman for her position in society, which through its acceptance helps to eliminate sex role conflict and marital discord, which in turn promotes social stability.

We so far have seen examples of how cultures develop customs and traditions to foster, protect, and perpetuate a society as well as to provide for the survival and well-being of the people in that society. Lobola and subservient roles for women in India are but two ways in which cultures provide mechanisms for maintaining society.

So far we have been given an overview of culture that has shown how it functions to maintain structure, stability, and security in a society. While this discussion has been brief, it is sufficient for us to proceed to the specifics of intercultural communication.

Intercultural Communication

In all respects, everything so far said about communication applies to intercultural communication. The functions and relationships between the components of communication outlined in Chapter 1 obviously apply. But, what especially characterizes intercultural communication is that sources and receivers come from different cultures. This alone is sufficient to identify a unique form of communicative interaction that must take into account the role and function of culture in the communication process. In this section, intercultural communication will first be defined and discussed through the perspective of a model and then its various forms will be shown.

Intercultural Communication Model

Intercultural communication occurs whenever a message producer is a member of one culture and a message receiver is a member of another. In this circumstance, we are faced immediately with the problems inherent in a situation where a message encoded in one culture must be decoded in another. As we have already seen, culture shapes the individual communicator. It is largely responsible for the entire repertory of communicative behaviors and meanings we possess. Consequently, those repertories possessed by two people from different cultures will be very different, which can lead to all sorts of difficulties. But, through the study and understanding of intercultural communication, we can reduce or nearly eliminate these difficulties.

The influence of culture on the individual and the problems of encoding and decoding messages across cultures are illustrated in Figure 2-1. Three cultures are represented in this model by three distinct geometric shapes. Cultures A and B are relatively similar to one another and are represented by a square and an irregular octagon which is nearly square. Culture C is quite different from cultures A and B. This greater difference is represented both by the circular shape of culture C and its physical distance from cultures A and B.

Within each culture is another shape similar to the shape of the culture. This represents an individual who has been shaped by the culture. The shape of the individual is slightly different from that of the influencing culture. This is to suggest two things. First, there are other affecting influences besides culture that help shape the individual. And, second, although culture is the dominant shaping force on an individual, people vary to some extent from each other within any culture.

Message encoding and decoding across cultures is illustrated by a series of arrows connecting them. These arrows indicate the transmission of messages between cultures. When a message leaves the culture in which it was encoded, it contains the meaning intended by the encoder. This is represented by the arrows leaving a culture containing the same pattern as that within the individual encoder. When a message reaches the culture where it is to be decoded, it undergoes a transformation in which the influence of the decoding culture becomes a part of the message meaning. The meaning content of the original messages becomes modified during the decoding phase of intercultural communication because the culturally different repertory of communicative behaviors and meanings possessed by the decoder does not contain the same cultural meanings possessed by the encoder.

The degree of influence culture has on intercultural communication situations is a function of the dissimilarity between the cultures. This is indicated in the model by the degree of pattern change shown in the message arrows. The change between cultures A and B is much less than the change between cultures A and C and between cultures B and C. This is due to the greater similarity of cultures A and B. Hence, the repertory of communicative behaviors and meanings is similar and the decoding effort produces results more nearly like those intended in the original message encoding. But, since culture C is represented as being vastly different from cultures A and B, the decoding is also vastly different and more nearly represents the pattern of culture C.

The model suggests that there can be wide variation in cultural differences during intercultural communication. This is due in part to circumstances or forms. Intercultural communication takes place

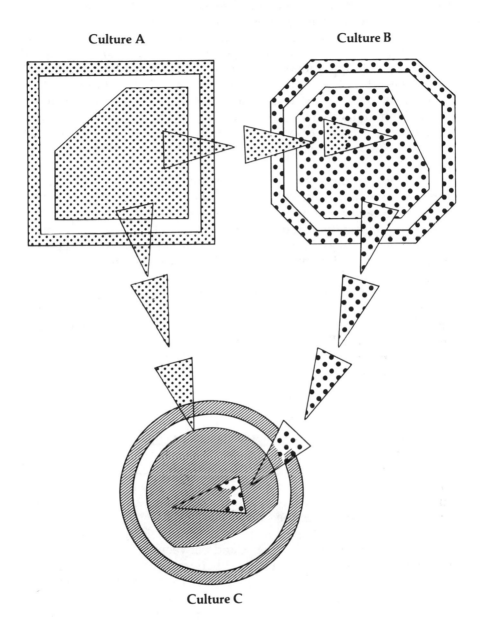

Figure 2-1

Model of Intercultural Communication

among a wide variety of situations that range from interactions between people for whom cultural differences are extreme to interactions between people who are members of the same dominant culture and whose differences are reflected in subcultures or subgroups. If we think of differences varying along a minimum-maximum dimension (see Figure 2-2), the amount of difference between two cultural groups can be seen to depend on the relative social uniqueness of the two groups. Although this scale is crude, it permits us to examine an intercultural communication act and to gain insight into the effect of cultural differences. In order to see how using this dimension helps, we can look at some of the examples of cultural differences positioned along the scale.

The first example represents a maximum difference—differences between Asian and Western cultures. This can be typified as a conversation between two farmers, one from a communal farm on the outskirts of Beijing in China and the other who operates a large mechanized wheat and corn farm in Iowa. In this example, we find the greatest number of cultural factors subject to variation. Physical appearance, religion, philosophy, social attitudes, language, heritage, basic conceptualizations of self and the universe, and degree of technological development are among the cultural factors that differ sharply. We must recognize, however, that these two farmers also have the commonality of farming and a rural lifestyle. In some aspects of cultural patterns they may be more closely related than they are to members of their own cultures who live in a large urban metropolis. In other words, across some cultural dimensions, the Iowa farmer may share more in common with the Chinese farmer than with a New York City stock broker.

An example nearer the center of the scale is the difference between American culture and German culture. Less variation is found; physical characteristics are similar, and the English language is derived in part from German and its ancestor languages. The roots of both German and American philosophy lie in ancient Greece, and most Americans and Germans share the Christian religion.

Examples near the minimal end of the dimension are characterized in two ways. First are variations found between members of separate but similar cultures—for instance, between U.S. Americans and English-Canadians. The difference is less than that found between American and German cultures, between American and Greek cultures or even between American and British cultures but greater than that generally found within a single culture. Second, minimal differences may be seen in the variance between subcultures or subgroups of the same dominant culture. Socio-cultural differences can be found between members of the Catholic church and the Baptist church, between members of the Sierra Club and advocates of off-shore oil drill-

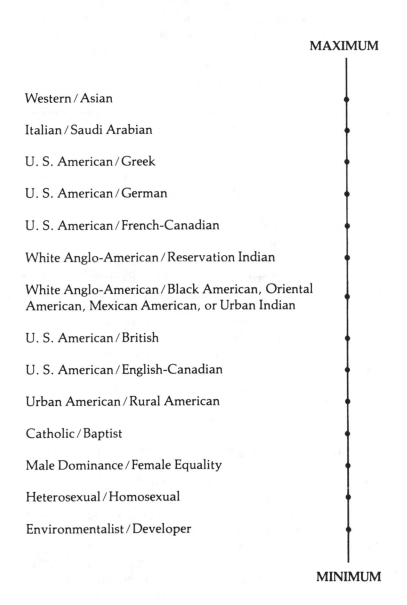

MAXIMUM

Western / Asian

Italian / Saudi Arabian

U. S. American / Greek

U. S. American / German

U. S. American / French-Canadian

White Anglo-American / Reservation Indian

White Anglo-American / Black American, Oriental
American, Mexican American, or Urban Indian

U. S. American / British

U. S. American / English-Canadian

Urban American / Rural American

Catholic / Baptist

Male Dominance / Female Equality

Heterosexual / Homosexual

Environmentalist / Developer

MINIMUM

Figure 2-2

**Arrangement of Compared Cultures, Subcultures, and Subgroups
along a Scale of Minimum to Maximum Socio-cultural Differences**

ing, between middle-class Americans and the urban poor, between mainstream Americans and the homosexual community, or between male dominance advocates and female equality advocates.

In both of these categorizations, members of each cultural group share much more in common than in the examples at the maximum end of the scale. They probably speak the same language, share the same general religion, attend the same schools, and inhabit the same geographical area. Yet, these groups are somewhat culturally different; they do not share the same experiences nor do they share the same perceptions. They see their worlds differently. Their lifestyles may be vastly different, and their beliefs, values, and attitudes are far from being the same. Because of their cultural similarity, they differ primarily in limited aspects of their social perception.

Social perception is the process by which we attach meaning to the social objects and events we encounter in our environments and is an extremely important aspect of communication. Culture conditions and structures our perceptual processes in such a way that we develop cuturally determined perceptual sets. These perceptual sets not only influence which stimuli reach our awareness, but more important, they have a great influence on the judgmental aspect of perception—the attachment of meaning to these stimuli. It is our contention that intercultural communication can best be understood as cultural variance in the perception of social objects and events. The barriers to communication caused by this perceptual variance can best be lowered by a knowledge and understanding of cultural factors that are subject to variance, coupled with an honest and sincere desire to communicate successfully across cultural boundaries.

A sincere desire for effective communication is critical because a successful exchange may be hampered not only by cultural variations but also by unfriendly or hostile attitudes. There exist problems of ethnic and racial prejudice that inhibit communication between cultures and races. If these problems are present, no amount of cultural knowledge or communication skill will make the encounter a pleasant one. A discussion of stereotypes and prejudices is presented in Chapter 5 with the hope that a recognition of our prejudicial and stereotypic behavior will cause reflection on our behavior with an ultimate reduction of prejudice and stereotyping. Our major concern, however, will be with those situations where there are cultural differences in the encoding and decoding of verbal and nonverbal messages during intercultural interaction and the problems inherent in the varying situations.

We now will focus on the composition of various cultural groups and on the forms and types of intercultural communication associated with them. We will be dealing primarily with subcultures, subgroups, and races because most of our intercultural contacts will be with members of subcultures, subgroups, or other races, rather than with members of other cultures.

Subcultures and Subgroups

A subculture is a racial, ethnic, regional, economic, or social community exhibiting characteristic patterns of behavior sufficient to distinguish it from others within an embracing culture or society. Subcultures in the United States include, for example, Oriental Americans, Polish Americans, Jews, hard-core urban poor, Hari Krishnas, and the Mafia.

A second important societal element that does not meet the necessary criteria to be called a subculture, but nevertheless poses similar problems, is the subgroup. Included among United States subgroups are gays, pimps and prostitutes, the drug community, youth gangs, religious cults, and revolutionary organizations. Subgroups are products of the dominant culture; their group existence has not persisted long enough nor developed a sufficiently wide enough pattern of deviant behaviors to qualify as a culture or subculture. The main distinguishing feature of subgroups is that their values, attitudes, and behavior or elements of their behavior are at odds with the majority community. Subgroups exist within a community that is displeased with them, generally disagrees with them, and has difficulty understanding and communicating with them. In this book, these subgroups are treated as if they are subcultures.

Because of our culture's relative youth, the way in which our country was settled, and some tendency toward tolerance for those that differ from ourselves, the United States is in many ways a culture of subcultures. If we use the definition of subculture given above, we can divide our population into many subunits that qualify as subcultures. Looking around, we can find immediately subcultures defined by racial, ethnic, economic, religious, and geographical characteristics. In most instances these identifying qualities overlap one another. For instance, there may be a black living in Alabama who is a Baptist and whose income is $15,000 a year. This set of characteristics would give our friend membership in subcultures based on race and location. Since $15,000 is the economic middle class, and the Baptist religion is mainstream Protestant, economic and religious consideration would be among the dominant cultural characteristics rather than subcultural characteristics.

In the United States we find subcultures based on race that transcend ethnic identities. For instance, Orientals are a racial subculture that transcend such ethnic identifications as Japanese, Chinese, Korean, Thai, or Cambodian. On the other hand, we also find ethnic or religious subcultures that transcend race. Sammy Davis, Jr., for example, is both a black and a Jew. When we consider economic influences, we find economic subcultures that transcend religion, race, ethnicity, and geographic location. The ultrawealthy, although tending to be white, may also be Afro-, Latin, Oriental, Arabic, or Native American. The wealthy also may be Catholic, Protestant, Jew, Taoist, Buddhist, or Moslem. They may live in Beverly Hills, New Mexico, Florida, Ohio, New Jersey, Kansas, Hawaii, Maine, or Manhattan. The same can be said for the urban poor who as a group are found in all major urban locales and also represent all racial, ethnic, and religious groupings although containing a disproportionally large share of nonwhite and non-European ethnic representations.

Each subculture or subgroup is a social entity that, although a part of the dominant main culture, is unique and provides its members with a set of experiences, backgrounds, social values, and expectations that may not be found elsewhere in the dominant culture. Hence, communication between people who appear similar may not be easy because in reality they are members of very different subcultures or subgroups and their experiential backgrounds are so different they may be unable to relate meaningfully.

As an example of the problems of members of different subcultures and subgroups relating, let us imagine a highly skilled, competent, and successful black neurosurgeon earning upwards of $200,000 annually. This doctor, who was born and raised in the British cultural environment of Trinidad and emigrated to the United States at the age of nineteen, came from a well-to-do family and never knew or experienced ghetto life or poverty. It would be extremely difficult for this person to relate to or even begin to understand the psychological environment of another black who was born and reared in the Detroit ghetto; whose father deserted the family when the child was an infant; whose mother barely subsisted on welfare and occasional odd jobs; whose preteen and teen years were spent on the streets among prostitutes, pimps, drug pushers and users, and a white police authority that constantly harassed any black youth who happened to be on the street. Yet, in our naive approach to intercultural communication we sometimes expect that because people are black, brown, red, yellow, or white, they ought to be able to relate to and to understand one another. We base such expectations on perhaps the only commonly shared characteristic: similarity of skin pigmentation.

Forms of Intercultural Communication

There are a number of terms that describe various aspects and levels of communication between people of varying backgrounds. *Intercultural communication* is the overall encompassing term that refers to communication between people from different cultural backgrounds. Frequently the terms *cross-cultural communication* and *transcultural communication* are also used. These terms are synonymous with intercultural communication and designate the same form of interaction.

Interracial Communication. This form of communication occurs when source and receiver are from different races. It is characterized by the fact that there are racially identifiable physical differences between source and receiver. Interracial communication may or may not be intercultural. For instance, a third generation Japanese-American whose family has become firmly enculturated in North American culture, talking with a white Anglo-American would be a case of interracial communication but hardly intercultural. On the other hand, a recently arrived Panamanian talking with the same Japanese-American illustrates a case of both interracial and intercultural communication.

The major difficulty encountered in interracial communication is an attitudinal problem associated with racial prejudice. A person who holds stereotypes about other races often expects certain behaviors or responses that actually might not occur. Another characteristic of interracial communication is that the ruling or governing race controls the degree to which other races may intrude into the mainstream of society.[4] In the United States the white race is both the governing and the predominant race, and it is the whites who determine the degree and the extent members of other races may interact within the United States society. In the South African nation of the Republic of South Africa, a minority white race holds the reins of power and has been responsible for determining the degree to which the majority black race may mingle or interact in the minority white society.

Interethnic Communication. Interethnic communication refers generally to situations where source and receiver are of the same race but of different ethnic origins or backgrounds. Interethnic communication is characterized by such situations as German-Americans talking with Greek-Americans. Both are members of different ethnic backgrounds, but at the same time they are also members of the same pervading predominant North American culture and probably of the same race. Interethnic communication also describes the current situation in Canada between English-Canadians and French-Canadians. Both are citizens of Canada and members of the same race, yet they maintain quite different backgrounds, perspectives, viewpoints, goals, and languages.

International Communication. Finally, there is international communication, which refers primarily to communication between nations and governments. It is the communication of diplomacy and propaganda, and it frequently involves both intercultural and interracial situations. In the case of international communication, however, interaction is influenced by the policies, aims, needs, and economics of nations. This form of communication is highly ritualized, taking place in neutral countries, the United Nations, or by diplomatic third parties. International communication also is regulated by international law, military strength, treaties, secret agreements, and world opinion. Its analysis is a field unto its own and will receive no further formal attention here.

Intercultural communication has been portrayed as a multidimensional form of interaction between members of national, ethnic, racial, and cultural groups. It also has been shown to include communication between members of the dominant culture and members of subgroups or subcultures within a cosmopolitan society. Intercultural communication is unique in that it involves sources and receivers from different cultures who are affected by their differing cultural backgrounds and experiences. The effect of culture on an individual's behavior and communication habits has been discussed in general terms. Now our attention will focus directly on the relationship between culture and communication, and we will examine a number of specific sociocultural elements that have the greatest degree of influence on intercultural communication.

Culture and Communication

The link between culture and communication is crucial to understanding intercultural communication because it is through the influence of culture that people learn to communicate. A Korean, Egyptian, or American learns to communicate like other Koreans, Egyptians, or Americans. Their behavior can convey meaning because it is learned and shared; it is cultural. People view their world through categories, concepts, and labels that are products of their culture.

Cultural similarity in perception makes the sharing of meaning possible. The ways in which we communicate, the circumstances of our communication, the language and language style we use, and our nonverbal behaviors are all primarily a response to and a function of our culture. Communication is cultural. And, as cultures differ from one another the communication practices and behaviors of the individuals reared in those cultures also will vary.

Culture, as the concept has been presented, is an all encompassing form or pattern for living. It is complex, abstract, and pervasive. Numerous aspects of culture help to determine communicative be-

36

havior. These influences on communication, called *socio-cultural elements,* are diverse and cover a wide range of human social activity. For the sake of simplicity and to put some limitation on our discussion, we will examine a few of the socio-cultural elements associated with *perception, verbal processes,* and *nonverbal processes.* Our discussion here will be brief and introductory; in following chapters, each of these categories will be the subject of a separate and detailed discussion.

These socio-cultural elements are the constituent parts of intercultural communication. When we combine them, as we do when we communicate, they are like the components of a stereo system—each one related to and needing the other. In our discussion, the elements will be separated in order to identify them and to discuss them. In actuality, however, they do not exist in isolation nor do they function alone. They all are at work together in a complex matrix of interacting elements that operate together to form the complex phenomena we call intercultural communication.

Perception

In its simplest sense, perception is "the process by which an individual selects, evaluates and organizes stimuli from the external world."[5] In other words, perception is an internal process whereby we convert the physical energies of our environment into meaningful experience. A number of corollary issues arise out of this definition that help to explain the relationship between perception and culture. For example, many students of intercultural communication maintain that people behave as they do because of the ways in which they perceive the world, and that these behaviors are learned as a part of their cultural experience. Whether it be a judgment of beauty or a description of snow, we respond to stimuli as we do primarily because our culture has taught us to do so. We tend to notice, reflect on, and respond to those elements in our environment that are important to us. In the United States we might respond to something because of its size and cost, while in Japan, color might be the important criterion. As we can see, our culture tends to determine which are the important criteria of perception.

There are many researchers who believe that intercultural communication can best be understood as cultural variance in the perception of social objects and events. A central tenet of this position is that minor problems in communication often are exaggerated by these perceptual differences. To understand others' words and actions, we must try to understand their perceptual frames of reference. We must learn to understand how they perceive the world.

In the ideal intercultural encounter we would hope for many over-lapping experiences and a commonality of perceptions. The nature of culture, however, tends to introduce us to dissimilar experiences, and hence, to varied perceptions of the external world. A few cross-cultural examples will help us visualize this point.

The manner in which a culture responds to and treats females demonstrates clearly the connection existing between culture and per-ception. We earlier looked at India and South Africa in this regard, but further examples will clarify this relationship even more. In Saudi Arabia, due to strict Islamic laws, women are raised in a style that is bound to influence how people in that culture will perceive one's sex. One grows up in Saudi Arabia knowing that women have few legal rights and in most instances are not allowed to drive a car nor even to obtain a passport without the written consent of a male family member. Arranged marriages are still the rule and many men, when asked how many children they have, automatically state the number of sons. As we can see, women's liberation has not yet arrived in Saudi Arabia. A vivid cultural comparison emerges when we think about the notion of growing up female in the United States. Although the women's movement in the United States is still evolving, it is a safe assumption to conclude that Saudis perceive women differently than do people in the United States.

Each subculture and culture even has a specialized way of teaching its members what constitutes status—and hence what will be per-ceived as status. In the United States, the dominant culture has taught us that status is achieved by wealth and material possessions. Certain subcultures, however, teach their members that status is measured by yet another set of standards. The hard-core urban poor often perceive status in light of physical strength and street wisdom. In prisons, status is also based on strength and even on the type of crime one has committed on the outside.

When we look to foreign cultures we can see other examples of perceptual differences in status. In Thailand the number of friends one has is often a sign of status, while in Ethiopia one inherits status.

Three major socio-cultural elements have a direct and major influ-ence on the meanings we develop for our percepts. These are our *belief, value, attitude systems,* our *world view,* and our *social organization.*

When these three elements influence our perceptions and the meanings we develop for them, they are affecting primarily our indi-vidual, subjective aspects of meaning. We all may see the same social object or event and agree upon what it is in objective terms, but what the object or event means to us individually may differ considerably. Both a Saudi and an American would agree in the objective sense that a particular person is a woman. But, they most likely would disagree completely on what a woman is in a social sense. Each of these three elements will be considered individually to show how they affect our perception.

Belief, Value, Attitude Systems.   Beliefs, in a general sense, can be viewed as uniquely held subjective probabilities that some object or event is related to some other object or event or to some value, concept, or attribute. In short, an object or event possesses certain characteristics. For instance, we may believe that we are intelligent, witty, and charming. Or, we may believe that rain will cause the grass to grow (a causal relationship) or that our next door neighbor is unfriendly. Any belief, therefore, involves a link between the belief object and the characteristics that distinguish it. The degree to which we believe that an event or object possesses certain characteristics reflects the level of our subjective probability and, consequently, the depth or intensity of our belief. The more certain we are in a belief, the greater is the intensity of that belief.

Three types of beliefs may be distinguished: experiential, informational, and inferential. The type of belief depends on the manner in which the belief was formed or how it was learned.

Experiential beliefs come through direct experience. Through direct sensory contact, we learn and thus believe that a particular object or event has certain characteristics. By touching a hot stove, for instance, we learn to believe it has the capacity to burn our fingers. Experiential beliefs usually are held with the highest degree of probability because of our direct sensory experience in their acquisition. There is minimal cultural influence on experiential beliefs beyond the limits culture places on our experience. We normally would not expect Eskimos to form experiential beliefs about camels. Informational and inferential belief formations, on the other hand, are strongly influenced by culture.

Many times we form or come to hold beliefs that are not the result of direct experience. Many of these beliefs come from outside sources such as other people, books, magazines, news media, and text books. We may, for instance, now believe that the United States has normalized diplomatic relations with the People's Republic of China. We probably do not believe this through direct experience unless we actually participated in the event. We probably believe this because we heard President Carter's announcement of normalization or read about it in our newspaper. This type of belief is called an *informational* belief, and it is formed from information provided by an outside source we choose to believe.

Informational beliefs are subject to wide cultural variation. In many respects the formation of an informational belief is dependent upon a higher level belief known as an authority belief. This basically is a culturally influenced individual belief about who or what institution is an authority on various topics or concerns. Our informational beliefs are beliefs derived from authority, which we hold because someone or some institution we believe to be an authority has given us the information. In other words, if we believe that the *New York Times* is a good place to find unbiased news reporting (an authority belief) we may therefore believe what we read in the *New York Times* (a belief derived from authority). Or, we may believe that the Bible is an infallible source of knowledge about the ministry of Christ (an authority belief) and thus believe the miracles of Christ (beliefs derived from authority).

Culture plays an important role in informational belief formation because it largely specifies our authority beliefs. Whether we accept the *New York Times*, the Bible, the entrails of a goat, tea leaves, the visions induced by peyote, or the changes specified in the Taoist I Ching as sources of knowledge and beliefs depends upon our cultural backgrounds and experiences. And, in matters of intercultural communication, there are no rights and wrongs as far as a particular interaction is concerned. If someone believes that the voices in the wind can guide their behavior along the proper path, we cannot throw up our hands and declare the belief is wrong; we must be able to recognize and to deal with that belief if we wish to obtain satisfactory and successful communication.

Quite clearly, though, we form many, if not most, of our beliefs by going beyond direct observation and information. Beliefs formed in this manner are called *inferential* beliefs, and they involve the use of internal logic systems in their formation. This type of belief is typified by the observation of a behavior and the inference that the behavior is generated or caused by a particular emotion; if we observe people shouting obscenities, we may assume or believe them to be angry.

Although internal logic systems differ from one individual to another within a culture, they differ more from one culture to another. The most dramatic difference in cultural variance in thinking lies between Western and Eastern cultures. The Western world has a logic system built upon Aristotelian principles, and it has evolved ways of thinking that embody these principles. The use of syllogistic or deductive reasoning has been a basis of Western thought for almost twenty-five centuries. Eastern cultures, however, developed before and without the benefit of Athens or Aristotle. As a consequence, their logic systems are sometimes called non-Aristotelian, and they can often lead to quite different sets of beliefs. Even within Western cultures, an examination of thought processes will show that there can be considerable differences in the ways in which internal logic systems operate. These systems differ primarily according to the emphasis they place on intuition, rationalism, and empiricism as means of gaining knowledge.

Values are the evaluative aspects of our belief, value, attitude systems. Evaluative dimensions include qualities such as usefulness, goodness, aesthetics, need satisfaction ability, and pleasure production. Although each of us has a unique set of values, there also are values that tend to permeate a culture. These are called *cultural values,* and it is these that are of significance to us here.

Cultural values usually are derived from the larger philosophical issues that are part of a culture's milieu. These values generally are normative in that they inform a member of a culture what is good and bad, right and wrong, true and false, positive and negative, and the like. Cultural values define what is worthwhile to die for, what is worth protecting, what frightens people and their social systems, what are considered proper subjects for study and for ridicule, and what types of events lead individuals to group solidarity. Cultural values also specify what behaviors are of importance and which should be avoided within a culture. Values "represent a learned organization of rules for making choices and for resolving conflicts."[6]

As already indicated, values are learned; they are not universal, and they tend to differ from culture to culture. A society's outlook toward age is one of the values that differs among cultures. In Korea, for example, age is highly revered. Older people are sought out and asked to take part in family decisions. In fact, in Korea, at age sixty one is considered to be reborn and entering into the second and more important cycle of life. This positive value placed on age is in sharp contrast to the "Pepsi generation" outlook in the United States.

The value placed on privacy is another instance of how cultures differ. In Japan and China, privacy is valued highly and openness is not encouraged. Openness, in fact, often is considered to be a sign of weakness in these cultures. We can see an opposite disposition toward privacy, however, when we look at Israel or Italy. In these cultures solitude is shunned.

The values held by participants in intercultural communication are important because values develop standards and guidelines that establish appropriate and inappropriate behaviors in a society. Values, in other words, help determine how people ought to behave with the result that people will exhibit and expect behaviors according to their value systems. To the extent that cultural value systems differ, we may expect that intercultural communication participants will tend to exhibit and to expect different behaviors under similar circumstances.

A key ingredient in intercultural communication is value clarification. This consists of each person discovering the crucial value structures of the other in order to eliminate confusion and conflict. People may differ significantly along many value dimensions and unless these differences are understood, communication can fall victim to confusion and conflict.

Cultural values may be identified as primary, secondary, or tertiary, depending on the location of particular values in a culture's hierarchy of values.[7] Americans, for instance, value democracy as a primary value; indeed, many believe it is worth fighting and dying for. To many Asians and Africans, however, democracy is not so important; it even may be a tertiary value having little significance. Secondary values are those that people believe necessary, but not to the degree of significant sacrifice. Modern technology is a secondary value for most Americans. They believe it necessary, but few would deem it worth going to war in order to force Singapore to modernize its agriculture by switching from water buffalo to tractors. Table 2-1 summarizes some significant cultural values according to their importance in a number of cultures.

Values also may be classified according to whether they are positive, negative, or neutral. Supporting primary values is positive. Thus, maintaining capitalism is a positive value for most Americans and a negative value for most communists. Values that do not seem to make sense are neutral; they cannot be classified as either positive or negative.

Values express themselves within a culture by prescribing behaviors that members of the culture are expected to perform. These are called *normative* values. Thus, Catholics are supposed to attend Mass, motorists are supposed to stop at stop signs, and workers in our culture are supposed to arrive at work at the designated time. Most people follow normative behaviors, a few do not. Failure to do so may be met with sanctions either informal or codified. Thus the Mass avoider may receive a visit from the priest, the stop sign violator may receive a traffic ticket and fine, and the tardy employee may be fired. Normative behavior also extends itself into everyday manners and becomes a guide to individual and group behavior that minimizes or prevents harm to individual sensitivities within cultural groups.

In traditional cultures there are strong norms for behaving according to cultural expectations. In the traditional Greek culture, norms are strong and rigidly followed. Traditional Greeks use the word *philotimos* to describe a person who behaves according to the norms of the culture, which is a positive primary value. To be known as a philotimos by one's associates is the highest of compliments.

Difficulty may arise when a member of one culture is accustomed to weak norms and the person from another culture is a philotimos or strong adherer to group norms. In this situation, weak normative behavior may be perceived as inexcusable by the philotimos because it does not follow prescribed patterns, and the other person may think the philotimos is too formal.

A value dimension of major concern to intercultural communicators is the individual-group orientation. In most cultures, the group, be it family, work, or social, is superior to the individual. This orientation is expressed frequently as collective responsibility. In this situation

Table 2-1

Value Classification System

Value	Primary	Secondary	Tertiary	Negligible
Individuality	W	B	E	M
Motherhood	BE	MW	—	—
Hierarchy	WEMA	B	—	—
Masculinity	BMEWA	—	—	—
Gratefulness	EA	MB	W	—
Peace	E	B	WA	M
Money	WAB	M	E	—
Modesty	E	BAM	—	W
Punctuality	W	B	ME	A
Saviorism	W	M	—	EBA
Karma	E	—	—	MWBA
Firstness	W	B	—	EAM
Aggressiveness	WB	M	AE	—
Collective Responsibility	EAM	B	—	W
Respect for Elders	EAM	B	—	W
Respect for Youth	W	MABE	—	—
Hospitality to Guests	EA	B	MW	—
Inherited Property	E	—	MWAB	—
Preservation of Environment	E	BA	W	M
Color of Skin	EWB	M	—	A
Sacredness of Farm Land	E	A	—	BMW
Equality of Women	W	EB	A	M
Human Dignity	WB	EAM	—	—
Efficiency	W	B	EM	—
Patriotism	BMAE	W	—	—
Religion	WBMAE	—	—	—
Authoritarianism	EMA	WB	—	—
Education	WB	EAM	—	—
Frankness	W	BEMA	—	—

SOURCE: K.S. Sitaram and Roy T. Cogdell, *Foundations of Intercultural Communication* (Columbus, Ohio: Charles E. Merrill, 1976), p. 191. Used by permission.

Legend: W = Western cultures   E = Eastern cultures
         B = Black cultures   A = African cultures
         M = Muslim cultures

individuals owe primary allegiance to the groups to which they belong. This allegiance may require the sacrifice of individuality to the benefit and welfare of the group. Giving up of individual rights might mean living with an incompatible spouse for the benefit of the family. Because of this orientation, divorce is valued negatively in Oriental cultures because it destroys the family unit and reflects a failure to perform one's duty. Sacrifice of individuality also may require forsaking self interest, desire, and pleasure in order to dutifully carry out roles prescribed for the positions one holds in a group. Thus, to be a parent might require giving up individual pleasures for the benefit of the children.

In Western cultures, the individual is supreme and individualism is a primary positive value. This value probably is most dominant in the United States. Americans are taught from birth to compete and to excel in their endeavors. Such accomplishment may be at the expense of others, even family and friends. Americans have the right to make money at the expense of society. People who exploit what they own are viewed as smart and successful. Even admiration and respect may be accorded. In non-Western cultures, the society comes first. People who exploit their property for profit are seen as menaces to society.

Age is a dominant value in most cultures, for the elders of society are the repositories of knowledge as well as the locus of power and authority. Only in highly technological urbanized areas is the value of age being transferred to youth. This is especially true in the United States where most of us do everything possible to maintain our youth and to refrain from growing old or at least looking old. We keep secret our ages, dress in "mod" attire, twinge at the sight of a wrinkle or a gray hair, and spend literally millions of dollars avoiding the stigma of old age.

In cultures where age is revered, this respect for age is manifest in numerous ways. It may be through special forms of address reserved for any old person regardless of social rank or position. Japanese elders are always addressed by their last name no matter how familiar they may be. This is in contrast to the American penchant for getting on a first name basis.

Age also reflects itself culturally in terms of specifying who is too old or too young to marry, rule, or fight. Marriage between a sixty-year-old man and a twelve-year-old girl is normal in some cultures, but in the United States it would cause an outcry and probably be deemed illegal by the courts. In recent years, there have been numerous news accounts about armed conflict in Southeast Asia where the armed conscripts were young teenagers barely past puberty. In Western cultures, childhood is viewed as more or less sacrosanct and induction of very young teenagers would violate our sense of morality.

In all but a very few places in the world, sexual equality is of low priority and is viewed negatively. Male supremacy is a particularly dominant value in Islamic cultures. Only in some parts of the Western world is sexual equality valued positively to any degree. But even so, where sexual equality is claimed as a value, it exists more as a myth or goal than as a fact. Even in the United States, it still is not possible to pass an Equal Rights Amendment.

Formality is a value dimension bound by extremely ritualized behavior at one extreme and by totally unstructured behavior at the other. Formal relations require the use of titles, honorifics, and polite forms of speech. To those of us who value informality, these behaviors seem unnecessary and perhaps disruptive to communication. In cultures where formality is valued, its practice permits predictable relationships that avoid awkward and embarrassing moments.

Closely akin to formality is modesty, whose opposite extreme is boastfulness. There are degrees of modesty and pompousness among people in any culture, but generally, Eastern cultures hold modesty to be much more of a virtue than does Western culture. "Easterners say that a fragrant flower does not have to announce its existence to the world."[8] Westerners, on the other hand, say "if you've got it, flaunt it."

Beliefs and values contribute to the development and content of our *attitude systems*. Formally we may define an attitude as a learned tendency to respond in a consistent manner with respect to a given object of orientation.

Any attitude is composed of at least three components: a *cognitive or belief component*, an *affective or evaluative component*, and an *intensity or expectancy component*. Attitudes are founded on learned beliefs and values. The intensity of our attitudes is based on the degree of conviction that our beliefs and evaluations are correct. These three elements interact to create a psychological state of readiness to react to objects and events in our environment. Thus, if we believe, for instance, that physically abusing another person is wrong or fear being hurt when hit, and further believe boxing has a high probability of producing physical abuse, we may have an internalized negative predisposition toward boxing (an attitude) which manifests itself in avoidance behavior that prohibits our attending or participating in boxing matches.

Attitudes are learned within a cultural context. Whatever cultural environment surrounds us helps to shape and form our attitudes, our readiness to respond, and ultimately our behavior. The cultural bias of belief, value, attitude systems can be seen in the example of bullfighting. A vast number of North Americans believe that cruelty to animals is wrong and that the systematic wearing down and killing of a bull is an example of that cruelty. Consequently, many North Americans view bullfighting within a negative attitude frame and actively will avoid attending bullfights or even viewing them on television. For most Latin Americans, however, bullfighting is believed to be a contest of courage between man and beast. It is evaluated positively, and witnessing the triumph of the matador is not witnessing cruelty to animals but the exercise of courage, skill, and physical agility. In this cultural context, to witness a bullfight is to witness one of life's finer moments when man again demonstrates his dominance over the beast. This mastery of the bull even has metaphorical overtones of good triumphing over evil.

In this discussion of beliefs, values, and attitudes, we have seen how they can vary from one culture to another. Intercultural communicators are concerned, chiefly, with the difficulties that can occur when cultural beliefs, values, and attitudes come in conflict and clash with one another. Violations of expectations based upon deeply structured value systems can produce hurt, insult, and lead to misunderstandings and, ultimately, violence.

World View. This cultural element, though abstract in concept and description, is one of the most important elements found in the perceptual aspects of intercultural communication. Because world view is so complex, it is often difficult to isolate during an intercultural encounter. In our examination, we seek to understand its substance and its elusiveness.

World view deals with a culture's orientation toward such things as God, man, nature, the universe, and the other philosophical issues that are concerned with the concept of being. In short, our world view helps us locate our place and rank in the universe.

As we can see, these issues are timeless and represent the most fundamental basis of a culture. A Catholic will surely have a different world view than will a Moslem, Hindu, Jew, Taoist, or atheist. The way in which Native American Indians view the individual's place in nature differs sharply from the middle-class Euro-American's view. Native Americans have a world view that places them at one with nature. They perceive a balanced relationship between man and the environment, a partnership of equality and respect. On the other hand, middle-class Euro-Americans have a human-centered picture of the world. Because of their profound belief that humans are supreme and are apart from nature, they treat the universe as theirs—a place to carry out their desires and wishes through the power of science and technology.

World view influences a culture at a very deep and profound level. Its effects often are quite subtle and do not reveal themselves in obvious and often superficial ways as do dress, gestures, and vocabulary. It might be helpful for us to think of a culture's world view as being analogous to a pebble being tossed into a pond. Just as the pebble causes ripples that spread and reverberate over the entire surface of the pond, world view spreads itself over a culture and permeates every facet of it. World view influences beliefs, values, attitudes, uses of time, and many other aspects of culture. In many subtle and often not obvious ways it is a powerful influence in intercultural communication because as members of a culture, our world view is so deeply imbedded in our psyches that we take it completely for granted and assume automatically that everyone else views the world as we do.

Social Organization. The manner in which a culture organizes itself and its institutions also affects how members of the culture perceive the world and how they communicate. There are two forms of societal composition that relate to intercultural communication. The first consists of geographic cultures. These are the nations, tribes, castes, religious sects, and the like defined by geographic boundaries. The second form is called role cultures, and it relates to membership in clearly defined social positions that are more specific and offer us specialized communicative behaviors. These role societies transcend geographic societies and range from professional groups to organizations that stress specific ideologies. Because role cultures teach appropriate modes of behavior for the social positions we occupy, we must recognize the influence they can have on intercultural communication. For example, a member of a university faculty in China has learned a repertory of communicative behaviors that are quite different from those possessed by a prostitute in San Francisco. In this case, two social role cultures have given their members defined patterns of behavior and elaborate communication networks. While members of differing geographic cultures may find difficulty in intercultural communication due to very different experiential backgrounds that give them vastly different perceptual frames of reference, members of a role culture may be able to communicate quite well within the confines of their roles even though coming from different geographic cultures.

It might be helpful if we look briefly at a few of the dominant social units found in a culture (granting, of course, that there are countless others that we shall pass by at this time). The family, though it is the smallest social organization in a culture, is one of the most influential. Families set the stage for a child's development during the formative periods of its life. The family presents the child with a wide range of cultural influences that affect almost everything from a child's first attitudes to its selection of toys. The family also guides children's acquisition of language. Skills from vocabulary building to dialects are the purview of the family. Even the amount of emphasis placed on language falls to the family. The family also offers and withholds approval, support, rewards, and punishments, which has a marked effect upon the values children develop and the goals they pursue. If, for example, children by observation and communication learn that silence is paramount in their culture, as it is in Japan, they will reflect that aspect of culture in their behavior and bring it to intercultural settings.

The school is another social organization that is important for a number of reasons. First, by definition and history, schools are endowed with a major portion of the responsibility for passing on and maintaining a culture. They are a community's basic link with its past as well as its taskmaster for the future. Schools maintain a culture by relating to new members what has happened, what was important, and what one as a member of the culture must know. Schools may teach geography or wood carving, mathematics or nature lore; they may stress revolution based on peace or one predicated on violence. Or they may relate a particular culturally accepted version of history. But, whatever is taught in a school is determined by the culture in which that school exists. Recognition of this fact has motivated some black communities in the United States to open storefront alternative schools that stress black power and that "black is beautiful." These concerns are strictly a part of the black cultural experience and are not found as integrated components of the dominant culture's school functions.

Second, schools transmit more than facts; they inculcate cultural beliefs, values, and attitudes as well as prescribe modes of behavior acceptable within the larger culture. In many traditional cultures students seldom communicate orally with their teachers, and always address them respectfully with such phrases as "yes, sir," and "no, sir." In many urban areas of the United States today it is not uncommon for students to address their teachers rudely with expressions such as "ya," "I don't want to," or "you can't make me."

As we can see from our brief look at social institutions as an aspect of culture, these institutions are largely responsible for the transmission of culture from generation to generation and for its maintenance within generations. We all are members of a vast array of social institutions, some for short spans of our lives such as school, and others, such as our families, in which we have life membership. All of these institutions have some degree of influence in shaping and molding us to our culture. But, families, schools, and churches are by far the strongest and most influential institutions within any culture.

We have looked at some of the socio-cultural elements that affect our perceptual processes. Among these we found belief systems, world view, and social organization. Although these are major contributors to how we learn to perceive our world, they are not exhaustive. Two points should be clear, however. First, what is perceived as important tends to vary from culture to culture. Second, what and how a person communicates are reflections of what his culture perceives. Hence, a crucial precept of intercultural communication is that the world we perceive and communicate about may not be the same world being experienced and expressed by someone from another culture.

Having established the importance of perceptual systems to an understanding of culture and intercultural communication, we shall now turn our attention to verbal processes.

Verbal Processes

Verbal processes include not only how we talk to each other, but also the internal activities of thinking and of meaning development for the words we use. These processes, language and patterns of thought, are vitally related to perception, and the attachment of and expression of meaning.

Verbal Language. Any discussion of language in intercultural settings must include an investigation of language issues in general before specific problems dealing with foreign language, language translation, and questions regarding the argot and vernacular of subcultures and subgroups can be understood. Most of this discussion will be left until Chapter 6, which is concerned entirely with language as it affects intercultural communication. Here, in our introduction to the various dimensions of culture, we will look at verbal language as it relates to our understanding of culture.

In the most basic sense, language is an organized, generally agreed upon, learned symbol-system used to represent the experiences within a geographic or cultural community. Each culture places its own personal and individualistic imprint on a word symbol. Objects, events, experiences, and feelings have a particular label or name solely because a community of people have arbitrarily decided to so name it. Thus, because language is an inexact system of symbolically representing reality, the meanings for words are subject to a wide variety of interpretations. In fact, it often is stated that meanings are in people rather than in words.

Language is the primary means by which a culture transmits its beliefs, values, and norms. It gives people a means of interacting with other members of the culture and a means of thinking. Through their studies of American Indian languages, Edward Sapir and Benjamin Whorf concluded that language not only serves as a mechanism for communication, but as a guide to social reality. Their studies resulted in what today is called the Sapir-Whorf hypothesis, which maintains that language influences perceptions and transmits thoughts, as well as helping pattern them.[9]

If we extend the notion that our culture teaches us an internalized response to a word, then various cultures will have specialized responses to the same words. In the United States, for example, the word *dog* in most instances conjures up an image of a furry, domesticated family pet. In some areas of the world, such as Hong Kong, however, dogs are considered to be a culinary amenity and often are eaten. In many parts of Southeast Asia, the word *dog*, therefore, elicits a quite different meaning because of different cultural experiences. Even the same word when used by two different cultures that share a common language can call forth vastly dissimilar meanings. In England, for example, a *joint* is a roast (meat), a *wing* is a car fender, and *braces* are suspenders. In the United States these same words refer usually to quite different aspects of the environment.

Language problems based on varied experiences represent but one of many issues we face as intercultural communicators. Another major concern about foreign language communication centers on translation. The matter of equivalencies is a case in point. Translation might be a simple matter when we speak in Spanish of *gato* for cat. But there are countless instances where there are not direct equivalencies. In many cases, words simply do not exist in one language for ideas or concepts found in another culture. The Pueblo Indian languages of North America, for instance, do not possess words for late or waiting. Some Arabic languages have no equivalency for the words *rape* or *trespass*, and the Eskimo language has no word for *rice*. If we add the problems of syntax, idioms, and grammar to foreign language translation, we begin to see how complex a problem we are dealing with.

Even when people live within the same geographic boundaries, there are problems in the use of language. We must keep in mind the notion that word usage and meanings are learned, and that each culture, subculture, or subgroup has different experiences that help shape usage and meaning. A few examples demonstrate this idea. Within prison communities, to *tip* is to leave prison and *doing a pound* is an eight-year sentence. Among many hard-core urban poor, a *headknocker* is a policeman. Prostitutes use such common words as *steak, roast*, and *hamburger* to describe prices for their services in an effort to hamper charges of solicitation. And, a lesbian may call someone who steals her lover a *black widow*. We are all aware of the rich argot contained in the black culture. To *mack*, to *jive*, and to *shine on* are but a few examples. Usually, rather elaborate vocabularies surround subcultures and subgroups.

Discussion of language is important and must occupy a large part of any analysis of intercultural communication. In Chapter 6, we will expand our examination of language.

Patterns of Thought.   The mental processes, forms of reasoning, and approaches to problem solution prevalent in a community is another major component of culture. Unless we have had experiences with people from other cultures who follow different patterns of thought, it is quite common to assume everyone thinks in the same way. But we should be aware that there are cultural differences in aspects of thinking. These differences can be clarified and related to intercultural communication by making a general comparison between Western and Eastern patterns of thought. In most Western thought there is an assumption of a direct relationship between mental concepts and the concrete world of reality. This orientation places great stock in logical considerations and rationality. There is a belief that truth is out there where it can be discovered by following the correct logical sequences. We need only turn over the right rock and there it will be. The Eastern view, best illustrated by Taoist thought, holds that problems are solved quite differently. To begin with, people are not granted instant rationality. Truth is not found by active searching and the application of Aristotelian modes of reasoning. On the contrary, one had best wait, and if truth is to be known it will make itself apparent. The major difference in these two views is in the area of activity. To the Western mind, human activity is paramount and will lead ultimately to the discovery of truth. In the Taoist tradition, truth is the active agent, and if it is to be known it will be through the activity of truth making itself apparent.

A culture's thought patterns affect the way individuals in that culture communicate which in turn will affect the way we respond to individuals from another culture.

> Mutual understanding and peaceful relations among the peoples of the earth have been impeded not only by multiplicity of languages but to an even greater degree by differences in patterns of thought—that is, by differences in the methods adopted for defining the sources of knowledge, and for organizing coherent thinking. [10]

We cannot expect everyone to employ the same patterns of thinking, but understanding that many patterns exist and learning to accommodate them will facilitate our intercultural communication.

Nonverbal Processes

Verbal processes are the primary means for the exchange of thoughts and ideas, but there are also closely related nonverbal processes that often can overshadow them. Although there is not complete agreement as to what constitutes the province and domain of nonverbal processes, most authorities agree that the following topics must be included: gestures, facial expressions, eye contact and gaze, posture and movement, touching, dress, objects and artifacts, silence, space, time, and paralanguage. As our investigation turns to nonverbal processes relevant to an understanding of culture, we will consider three aspects: nonverbal behavior that functions as a silent form of language, conceptualizations of time, and the use and organization of space.

Nonverbal Behavior. It would be folly for us to try to examine all of the elements that constitute nonverbal behavior at this time for our goal here is a general introduction to the major socio-cultural elements of intercultural communication. An example or two should enable us to visualize how nonverbal issues fit into the overall scheme of intercultural understanding. Instances of touch as a form of communication demonstrate how nonverbal communication is a product of culture. In Germany women as well as men shake hands at the outset of every social encounter; in the United States, women seldom shake hands. In Thailand people do not touch in public, and to touch someone on the head is a major social transgression. You can imagine the problems that could arise if one did not understand some of the variances.

Another illustrative example is eye contact. In the United States, we are encouraged to maintain good eye contact when we communicate. In Japan eye contact often is not as important. And in some American Indian tribes young children are taught that eye contact with an elder is a sign of disrespect. A white school teacher working on an Indian reservation was not aware of this and thought her students were not interested in school because they never looked at her.

As a component of culture, nonverbal expression has much in common with language. Both are coding systems of communication that are learned and passed on as part of our cultural experience, Just as we learn that the word *stop* can mean to halt or to cease, we also have learned that an arm up in the air, with the palm facing another person, frequently means the same thing. Because most nonverbal communication is culturally based, what it symbolizes is often a case of what a culture has transmitted to its members. The nonverbal symbol for suicide, for example, varies among cultures. In the United States it is a finger pointed at the temple, in Japan it is a hand thrust into the stomach, and in New Guinea, it is symbolized by a hand on the neck.

Also, both verbal and nonverbal coding systems use a symbol to represent something else. In verbal systems, the word *love* stands for or represents a feeling or a sensation, which in reality is an internal state. The same is the case for words that represent things or objects. Try as you will, you cannot spread the word *butter* on your bread. Nonverbal systems operate in the same way. A smile, wave, wink, or touch are often used to convey feelings.

As has already been indicated, both nonverbal symbols and the responses they generate are part of our cultural experience—part of what is imparted from generation to generation. In the United States our culture has taught us that the thumb extended from the fist usually is employed by the hitchhiker as a form of asking for a ride. This same gesture in some other country might well secure the symbol-maker physical harm. Every symbol takes on significance because of our past experience with it. Our culture influences and directs those experiences, and is, therefore, a major contributor to how we send, receive, and respond to these nonverbal symbols.

Concept of Time.   A culture's concept of time is its philosophy toward the past, present, and future, and the importance, or lack of importance, it places on time. Most Western cultures think of time in lineal-spatial terms. We are timebound and well aware of the past, present, and future. Countries such as Germany and Switzerland are even more aware of time. Trains, planes, and meals must always be on time. In contrast, the Hopi Indians pay very little attention to time as we know it. They believe that each thing, whether a person, plant, or animal, has its own time system.

Even within a dominant culture we find groups that have learned to perceive time in ways that may appear strange to many outsiders. Mexican-Americans frequently speak of Chicano time when their timing varies from the predominant Anglo concept. And blacks often use what is referred to as BPT (black people's time), or hang-loose time. This outlook maintains that priority belongs to what is happening at that instant.

Time, like other components of culture, serves to underscore a basic theme of this book—vast differences exist between diverse cultures, and those differences affect communication.

Use of Space.   The way in which people use space as a part of interpersonal communication is called *proxemics*. It involves not only the distance between people engaged in conversation but also their physical orientation. We all most likely have some familiarity with the fact that Arabs and Latins tend to interact closer together than do North Americans. What is important is for us to realize that people of different cultures do have different ways in which they relate to one another spatially and that when talking to someone from another culture we must expect what in our culture would be violations of our personal space and be prepared to continue our interaction without reacting adversely. We may experience feelings that are difficult to handle; we may believe that the other person is overbearing, boorish, or even making unacceptable sexual advances when indeed these are not the case but instead only are manifestations of another's cultural learning about how to use space.

Physical orientation is also culturally influenced, and it helps to define social relationships. North Americans prefer to sit where they are face-to-face or at right angles to one another. We seldom seek out side-by-side arrangements. Chinese, on the other hand, often prefer and feel more comfortable in a side-by-side arrangement and may feel uncomfortable when placed in our preferred face-to-face situation.

We also tend to define social hierarchies through our nonverbal use of space. Sitting behind a desk while speaking with someone who is standing is usually a sign of a superior-subordinate relationship, with the socially superior person being seated. This same behavior, however, can also be used to convey disapproval, disrespect, or insult if one violates cultural norms. It is easy to have misunderstandings in intercultural settings when two people, acting according to the dictates of their cultures, violate each other's expectations. If we were to remain seated while expected to rise, we could easily violate a cultural norm and insult our host or guest inadvertently.

How we organize space also is a function of our culture. The following scenes illustrate how courtroom arrangements show cultural values and organization in nonverbal displays:

> The judge's commanding seat catches first attention, but the eye soon wanders to the other furniture. In a British or American courtroom, the jury box stands out to the right of the enclosure behind the "bar." Between it and the judge's bench on a raised platform somewhat lower than that of the judge stands the chair waiting for the witness, facing outward into the room so that all can hear, including the press for whom a gallery or at least a bench is often reserved to give meaning to the concept of "publicity" characteristic of the common law concept of "due process."
>
> Compare the Assize court in the canton of Geneva, and you will find the jury, but in a different place. It is in no box separated from the judge, but arranged on two rows of chairs to the judge's left behind the great semi-circular bench that extends the width of the room. One scarcely needs to be told that the judge retires with the jury in this Swiss canton, and that he shares with the jurymen the decision on guilt and punishment. At the eastern end of Europe there is no jury box at all, for the Soviet legal procedure relies on two lay assessors in every type of case, both criminal and civil, to share with the judge the decisions on matters both of fact and law. This is so in all of the Eastern European states that have adopted the Soviet legal system, and has been accepted even in Communist China.
>
> Witness stands in continental Europe traditionally face in toward the judge rather than out toward the courtroom. The assembled public sees only the back of the witness's head when he testifies and hears little of what he says unless he raises his voice.[11]

Our homes also reflect and help preserve nonverbally our cultural beliefs and values.[12] South American house designs are extremely private with only a door opening directly onto the street and everything else being behind walls. North Americans are used to large unwalled front yards with windows looking into the house where we can get an idea of what goes on inside a particular house. In South America, we are liable to feel excluded and wonder about what goes on behind all those closed doors.

Again, we have not even begun to discuss nonverbal communication in detail. Our attempt has been only to show how nonverbal processes are related to culture and how they can vary from one culture to another. This subject will be given greater consideration in Chapter 7.

Summary

In many respects the relationship between culture and communication is reciprocal. They affect and influence each other. What we talk about, how we talk about it, what we see, attend to, ignore, how we think, and what we think about are all influenced by our culture. In turn, what we talk about, how we talk about it, and what we see help shape, define, and perpetuate our culture. One cannot exist without the other. One cannot change without causing change in the other.

This chapter has stressed the role of culture in providing structure, stability, and security to a society. We applied our knowledge of communication to the special circumstances of intercultural communication and saw many of the difficulties inherent in a situation where a message that is encoded in one culture must be decoded in another. We examined the differences between culture, subcultures, and subgroups as well as between such forms of intercultural communication as interracial, interethnic, and international communication. Finally, we presented several important socio-cultural elements that affect the perception of people within a culture and saw how these elements may confound intercultural communication. With this fundamental grasp of the nature of intercultural communication and its constituent elements, we now are ready to move to the next part of this book where we will consider the participants in intercultural communication.

Notes

1. Alfred G. Smith, ed., *Communication and Culture: Readings in the Codes of Human Interaction* (New York: Holt, Rinehart & Winston, 1966), p. 1.

2. See Edward T. Hall, *The Silent Language* (Greenwich, Conn.: Fawcett, 1959); *The Hidden Dimension* (Garden City, New York: Doubleday, 1966); *Beyond Culture* (Garden City, N.Y.: Anchor, 1977); and Smith, pp. 1–10.

3. Marvin Harris, *Cows, Pigs, Wars, and Witches: The Riddles of Culture* (New York: Random House, 1974), p. 84.

4. For a good overview of the degree to which interracial interaction is permitted in a society see Andrea L. Rich and Dennis M. Ogawa, "Intercultural and Interracial Communication: An Analytic Approach," in Larry A. Samovar and Richard E. Porter, eds., *Intercultural Communication: A Reader*, 2d ed. (Belmont, Calif.: Wadsworth, 1976), pp. 24–32.

5. Marshall Singer, "Culture: A Perceptual Approach," *The Bridge*, Occasional Paper No. 11 (October 1971), p. 1.

6. Milton Rokeach, *Beliefs, Values, and Attitudes* (San Francisco: Jossey-Bass, 1968), p. 161.

7. K.S. Sitaram and Roy T. Cogdell, *Foundations of Intercultural Communication* (Columbus, Ohio: Charles E. Merrill, 1976), p. 164.

8. Sitaram and Cogdell, p. 183.

9. Harry Hoijer, "The Sapir-Whorf Hypothesis" in Larry A. Samovar and Richard E. Porter, eds., *Intercultural Communication: A Reader*, 2d ed. (Belmont, Calif.: Wadsworth, 1976), pp. 150–58.

10. Karl Pribram, *Conflicting Patterns of Thought* (Washington, D.C.: Public Affairs Press, 1949), p. 1.

11. John N. Hazard, "Furniture Arrangements as a Symbol of Judicial Roles," *ETC: A Journal of General Semantics* 19 (1962): 181–88. Used by permission.

12. Hall, *The Silent Language*.

Additional Readings

Freilich, Morris, ed. *The Meaning of Culture.* Lexington, Mass.: Xerox College Publishing, 1972.

Hall, Edward T. *Beyond Culture.* Garden City, N.Y.: Anchor Books, 1977.

Harms, L.S. *Intercultural Communication.* New York: Harper & Row, 1973.

Harris, Marvin. *Cows, Pigs, Wars, and Witches: The Riddles of Culture.* New York: Random House, 1974.

Newmark, Eileen and Molefi K. Asante. *Intercultural Communication.* Urbana, Ill.: ERIC Clearinghouse on Reading and Communication Skills, 1976.

Rich, Andrea L. *Interracial Communication.* New York: Harper & Row, 1974.

Sitaram, K.S. and Roy T. Cogdell. *Foundations of Intercultural Communication.* Columbus, Ohio: Charles E. Merrill, 1976.

Smith, Alfred G., ed. *Communication and Culture.* New York: Holt, Rinehart & Winston, 1966.

Concepts and Questions

1. Why are culture and communication considered to be inseparable?

2. What is culture? How does it affect our daily lives?

3. How does culture affect us throughout the course of our lives?

4. What are the unique distinguishing characteristics of intercultural

communication? How does intercultural communication differ from everyday forms of communication?

5. What are the differences between subcultures and subgroups? How can we determine whether a particular group of people are members of a subgroup or a subculture?

6. What are the differences between intercultural, interracial, and interethnic forms of communication?

7. What is perception, and how is it related to intercultural communication?

8. What are some value dimensions that vary culturally? How might cultural variation in values affect intercultural communication?

9. How can the way in which a society is organized differ across cultures? How might these differences affect intercultural communication?

Exercises

1. Identify both material and nonmaterial cultural elements used by you during a week. To what extent do you share these cultural elements with your family members? How are these cultural elements interrelated?

2. Participate in a small group discussion aimed at determining the five most important elements of culture that affect communication. For every element selected, provide an intercultural example showing the effect of the cultural element on communication.

3. Drawing upon your own experiences and those of some other students in your class, prepare a list of intercultural contacts. Classify these contacts in terms of the cultural difference continuum presented in this chapter. What difficulties did you experience in classifying these contacts along the continuum?

4. Analyze the news stories published in a major newspaper during a week to determine: (1) international news items, (2) interracial news items, (3) interethnic news items, (4) minority news items, and (5) intracultural news items. What difficulties did you experience in classifying news items into the above categories?

5. Which of the socio-cultural elements discussed in Chapter 2 have you personally experienced in your intercultural encounters? Which of these elements have you experienced in your interracial encounters? Which of these have you experienced in your intracultural encounters?

II

The
Participants:
Ourselves
and
Others

3

Understanding Ourselves: American Cultural Patterns

The obstacles to cross-cultural understanding may be conceptualized as differences in cultural assumptions and values. From the American's point of view, his own values and assumptions prevent him from objectively perceiving and understanding the underpinnings of the behavior of his counterpart. His performance overseas would be enhanced if he understood both his own culture and that of his counterpart.

Edward C. Stewart

Our effectiveness as intercultural communicators depends largely upon the cultural similarities and differences between ourselves and others. Cultural similarities usually facilitate communication while cultural differences tend to inhibit it. There are three types of cultural dimensions that affect communication. First is an awareness of the cultural patterns that influence our own perception, thinking, encoding, and other communication behaviors. This is referred to as cultural self-awareness. Second is an awareness of the cultural patterns influencing the communication behavior of people from other cultures. Third is identification of cultural differences and their effect on communication.

In this chapter we will look at the first of these three cultural dimensions, cultural self-awareness. We first will discuss the importance of cultural self-awareness. Then we will examine several dominant cultural patterns prevalent in the United States, hereafter called American cultural patterns. We will focus primarily on those aspects of our culture that seem to have the most direct influence on communication in intercultural settings.

Becoming Aware of American Culture

Importance of Cultural Self-Awareness

Why should we understand our own cultural patterns? How does cultural self-awareness help us in intercultural communication? Although most people recognize the importance of understanding the culture of the other person involved in the communication, very few of us see the need to understand our own cultural conditioning and its influence on our communicative behavior. For instance, various area training programs, which are designed to prepare us for overseas assignments requiring intercultural communication with host nationals, focus primarily on the foreign culture and its unique characteristics. Many large universities have area studies programs that deal with certain aspects of foreign cultures. When we receive training about various aspects of a given culture with a view toward improving our effectiveness in working with people from that culture, it is called culture-specific training. On the other hand, when the training we receive is aimed at cultural self-awareness and other concepts that prepare us to communicate effectively in *any* culture (rather than a specific culture), it is called culture-general training. Culture-specific approaches with their emphasis on learning about the other culture are much more common than are culture-general approaches. Most people that conduct intercultural training programs agree, however, that culture-general training is often necessary because some of us (in the military, industry, academia, etc.) are not assigned to specific country until the last minute, or because some programs have participants about to depart for a variety of countries. Persons going to a specific country need both culture-general and culture-specific training. Proponents of culture-general training programs recognize the need for us to understand our own cultural patterns and have suggested several benefits of cultural self-awareness for intercultural communicators.

Probably the most common mistake we make during interpersonal encounters is that we assume the other person's cognitions are similar to what our own would be if we were in the other's place. This assumption, known as *projected cognitive similarity*, [1] can hamper our effectiveness, depending largely on the degree to which our experiences are similar. Quite often our assumptions of projected cognitive similarity are made unconsciously. People whose experience has been limited to the norms of their own culture often misinterpret a communication based on a different set of norms. They also may not be able to understand why a "self-evident" remark from them cannot be comprehended by others. The problem of unwarranted, culturally conditioned assumptions of projected cognitive similarity can be considerably resolved if we become aware of our own cultural conditioning and if we recognize that our cultural patterns may have influenced our behavior. In other words, cultural self-awareness should make it easier for us to diagnose difficulties in intercultural communication. It enables us to examine such difficulties from the point of view of discovering what cultural aspects of our own thinking may have caused the difficulty. Ordinarily we react to not being able to communicate what seems to be a self-evident idea by speculating on what shortcomings of the other person might explain the difficulty. As we increase our cultural self-awareness we should be able to suspend judgment when confronted in an intercultural encounter by behavior that appears odd. We should be more ready to suspect that the appearance of oddness may be caused by cultural influences in our own thinking and behavior. This suspension of our judgment and subsequent diagnosis are very useful in continuing intercultural relationships, because the next encounter with the same person offers us an opportunity to try to correct previous misunderstandings.

An awareness of our own culture induces understanding of ourselves as cultural beings. It prepares us for the hardships of culture shock and frustrations common to overseas missions and to dealing with foreign nationals in this country. Cultural self-awareness promotes objectivity in appraising ourselves as well as in evaluating our counterparts. In particular, it prepares us to separate cultural factors from idiosyncratic ones in ourselves and in others.

Another benefit we gain from increased cultural self-awareness is a greater awareness of our ignorance of other cultures and a corresponding increase in motivation to learn more about them. As long as we assume that a particular communication behavior is universal, we have no reason to look for a cultural variation. When we recognize its cultural aspects we should see that the communication behavior may not be shared to the same extent in the other culture and be curious as to its nature and variation there.

> Take, for example, the way Americans with occupations tend to think of themselves and of other persons. It manifests itself in a question such as "What kind of work do you do?" that one American might ask another just after they have been introduced at a social gathering. That question is a manifestation of the idea that people are primarily known by their work and their achievements—an idea not equally common in other cultures.
>
> Having discovered in training how their way of thinking and talking about themselves is culturally influenced, Americans abroad would be more likely to pay close attention to the way host nationals think and talk about themselves. They might listen carefully to an exchange between host nationals who have just met for the first time. What might otherwise have been thought of as an insignificant event

is now recognized as an opportunity to learn. Thus, apart from its contribution to effectiveness in communication, the ability to recognize cultural aspects of one's own cognitions can serve as a stimulus and as a conceptual tool for learning the host culture.[2]

Often the concepts or categories of cultural patterns we use in understanding our own culture can serve as bridges to other cultures and help us in understanding them. Some cultural patterns are unique to a given culture and cannot be literally translated into other cultures. But all cultures are characterized by certain universal patterns including cultural values, beliefs, attitudes, and norms. An understanding of our own cultural patterns, their strong and weak points, and their variants, may induce in us an attitude called cultural relevance. This attitude, which predisposes us to recognize that many social customs and patterns of behavior have relevance only in the context of the culture in which they occur, is essential if we are to be effective intercultural communicators.

We can gain, from cultural self-awareness, a perspective or a frame of reference for identifying cultural similarities and cultural differences between ourselves and the others involved in an intercultural encounter. If we understand our own cultural patterns, we are more likely to compare and contrast them with the other culture. We can then begin to identify those specific cultural patterns that usually facilitate our work with the foreign counterpart, and those that usually inhibit it. For instance, several American cultural patterns have been identified as serious problems for us when conducting business abroad: pragmatic thinking, straight talk, separating work and life, and a sense of inevitability. There are other American cultural patterns that seem to facilitate our work abroad: problem-solving perspective, skill training, and success-failure split.[3]

Low Level of Cultural Self-Awareness

Most of us do not know much about our own culture and its influence on our behavior because culture so permeates our lives that a great deal of its effect on us is below our levels of consciousness. Since our cultural patterns are shared to some extent by most people with whom we ordinarily communicate, there is nothing in the behavior of others to draw our attention to them. For instance, when we talk with a neighbor and use the English language, which is a shared cultural characteristic, we are not likely to realize that the English language is facilitating our conversation. We just take it for granted. On the other hand, if we were talking to someone who does not know English or does not know it well, we are more likely to think about the influence of language on our communication.

We learn culture in very indirect and subtle ways, through our parents, schools, mass media, peers, and personal observations. Much of our learning is implicit rather than explicit. We rarely have any need or opportunity to learn to recognize cultural influences, while our learning to recognize other social influences (such as age, sex, occupation, and social status) is part of our socialization. Cultural influences manifest themselves only in combination with other influences, such as education, age, occupation, role, group membership, or situational constraints. Consequently, when we try to understand or explain a given behavior, we are very likely to see it as a function of one of these more apparent characteristics rather than as a function of our cultural conditioning. It is a function of the cultural bondage we all share that we forget our own culture.

Origins of North American Culture

Location and history are important factors in cultural evolution. As a prelude to our examination of dominant American cultural patterns, we will look briefly at the origins of our culture.

During the fifteenth, sixteenth, and seventeenth centuries, European nations explored the world and established numerous colonies. These colonies usually were exploited by the European aristocracy who extracted their wealth in order to support the expensive aristocratic way of life. This happened in Central and South America, the East and West Indies, the Indian subcontinent, and Africa.

North American colonization was an exception. The original settlers were not the established aristocracy with strong ties to the homeland. Instead, most original colonizers as well as many later arrivals were the unwanted, the outcasts, the nonconformists who, if they had remained in their native lands, would have been persecuted, jailed, or worse. Early North American folklore tells us how the Pilgrims and other groups fled their European homelands to avoid persecution—to start afresh in America where they could be free.

The important issue for us here is that the settlers of North America did not have strong ties to their homelands. The extended family was broken and the nuclear family developed in its place. In a very real sense, our forebears had to create their own culture. Their old cultures were no longer acceptable or satisfactory; ties to the past had been severed. The only way they could look was forward to an uncertain future. Consequently, a culture was formed that centered on change and the development of a bigger and better future. This cultural development tells us in part why North America has developed the highest, most advanced and sophisticated technological society in the world while South America, which was colonized simultaneously, has not developed a comparable technology. North America's greatest exports have been its technologies, and Latin America's exports have been primarily raw materials and labor.

Another important aspect of North American culture is its emphasis on the individual. Since the beginning, when North American culture was developing in a survival environment, emphasis has been placed on individual accomplishment and independence. The more people were able to accomplish on their own, independent of others, the more able they were to survive in the unsettled land.

Individualism is a virtue that came to be admired highly in the North American culture. Today we continue to express it in such terms as rugged individualism. New Englanders are appreciated and admired for their individualism and independence. We have developed a pride in individualism which has become fixed in our folk history. Daniel Boone's father, for instance, knew it was time to move whenever he could see smoke from his neighbor's fireplace. People actively avoided having to rely on other people, or at least on people outside the immediate family. Charity became an unsavory word for some. It implied failure, the inability to succeed in a world of individualism and independence. The founding of our North American culture reflected the dissolution of the extended family and severance of the ties of responsibility and obligation to those outside the immediate family. Others became responsible for themselves. Self-reliance was paramount. Today these values are prominently displayed for us through such television programs as "Little House on the Prairie," "Bonanza," and "The Waltons." The Ingalls, the Cartwrights, and the Waltons display close ties in the nuclear sense, but they tend not to rely on outsiders for help. They can do it themselves; they are individual, independent, and self-reliant; they view outside help as interference and refuse it stubbornly.

The culture we have developed in North America is unique. Most of the rest of the world perceives North Americans as "Yankees" even if they are Afro-American, Mexican-American, Native American, or Canadian. Our unique culture manifests itself in our daily life. Without ties to the past where social status was tied to ancestry and who you were, we often speak about status in terms of our employment and wealth. When we inquire of another's social status, we often ask, "what do you do?" and the reply often is in the form "I'm a physician," "I'm a banker," "I'm an auto assembler," or "I own a cabinet shop."

American culture also is unique because of its freedom, tolerance, and, hence, diversity. Cultures that offer freedom and toleration can accommodate great diversity of individuals and institutions, which in turn leads to diversity of lifestyles, creativity, and expression.

Having considered the importance of cultural self-awareness, our low level of cultural awareness, and the origin of our culture, we now are ready to examine the major cultural patterns that influence communication behavior in intercultural settings.

Dominant American Cultural Patterns

Like any other culture, the American culture is complex and consists of interrelated cultural patterns including cultural beliefs, values, attitudes, norms, and material aspects. In our society the range of cultural patterns is so great that we can make precise and detailed characterizations only for carefully delimited segments of our society. Any attempt to delineate a national culture or typical American cultural patterns is extremely hazardous, not only because of serious gaps in the requisite data but also because of the heterogeneity of the American society. A common core of cultural patterns that could be said to hold for our whole population would have to be kept very general. Therefore, let us limit our discussion to *dominant* American cultural patterns. In our society, white American middle-class cultural patterns are considered dominant. Clearly, these dominant cultural patterns do not encompass all the significant cultural characteristics shared by a large number of Americans. Cultural patterns shared by members of a distinct racial and/or ethnic group (such as American Indians, blacks, Mexican-Americans, and Japanese-Americans) constitute subcultural variations of American cultural patterns.

In Chapter 2 we saw that a culture includes both material and nonmaterial aspects. We believe that nonmaterial aspects of a culture, such as cultural values, beliefs, attitudes, and norms, tend to affect communication behavior more than the material aspects, such as houses, machines, and instruments of war. Accordingly our discussion of dominant cultural patterns is limited to various nonmaterial cultural characteristics. Material cultural aspects do play a significant role in nonverbal communication, and they will be discussed in the chapter on nonverbal factors.

The components we use to analyze a given culture are arbitrary and depend to a large extent upon our purpose. We have identified a variety of cultural components or patterns that are shared by a majority of Americans, especially white middle-class Americans, and which are highly pervasive in terms of their influence on communicative behavior. For convenience, various cultural patterns are grouped into six categories: (1) world view, (2) activity orientation, (3) time orientation, (4) human nature, (5) perception of the self, and (6) social organization.

Each of these categories includes several specific cultural patterns, and each cultural pattern affects the others, and in turn, is limited by them. Contradictions among cultural patterns are probably universal throughout societies. Each cultural pattern represents a continuum, and within the same culture variations of the pattern normally occur. Despite internal variations and contradictions, there is an overall integration to the pattern of white middle-class American culture. It is possible for us to simplify its description by isolating various cultural patterns and considering them one at a time.

World View

The world view concept is a complex set of interrelated beliefs, values, and attitudes concerning the nature of the universe, the relationship between human beings and nature, and other philosophical issues or orientations regarding the cosmos. The three most significant cultural patterns concerning our world view are: (1) the individual and nature relationships, (2) science and technology, and (3) materialism.

The Individual and Nature Relationship. Every culture has a set of beliefs concerning the relationship between individual human beings and nature. Americans view humans separately from nature and all other forms of life. Nature and the physical world are viewed as living but are conceived of as material and mechanistic. The dominant individual and nature belief in the United States is that nature and the physical world should be controlled in the service of humanity. This twofold category in American culture separates humanity from nature and is an important contributive factor in the exploitative attitude toward nature that has contributed to the material richness of American society.

In addition to the mastery-over-nature orientation that is most widely shared among Americans, there are two other prominent subcultural individual and nature relationships in the United States. The Mexican-American culture in the Southwest is characterized by a very definite subjugation-to-nature orientation. Under this belief system, humanity is at the mercy of nature; there is very little or nothing that people can do to change things in the world. The second subcultural human-nature relationship belief is that of harmony where there is no real separation of humanity, nature, and supernature. One is simply an extension of the other, and a conception of wholeness derives from their unity. This orientation is widely distributed among the Native American Indian cultures.

Our belief about the relationship between human beings and nature gives us a perspective from which we shape and form our values and attitudes. These beliefs, values, and attitudes provide us with a frame of reference that influences our perception, thinking, encoding, and other communicative behaviors. When we communicate with a person from another culture whose perspective on individual and nature relationships is very different from ours, we are bound to experience differences in perception that may affect our communication with each other.

Science and Technology. The American belief of mastery-over-nature has influenced their values and attitudes toward science and technology. Americans place a high value on science and technology. They believe science and its related technologies are the major tools for understanding and controlling nature. Science is based upon the assumption that reality is or can be rationally ordered by humans and that such an ordering implies predictability through the empirical testing of phenomena by methods designed to secure objectivity and control. Another major metaphysical assumption of science is the belief that events are atomistic and repeatable. They are atomistic in the sense that causes can be isolated from effects and that the most appropriate cause is the one immediate to the effect. Science is rooted in the belief that events can be isolated, analyzed, and recorded, and that reliable inferences can be derived from such observations. The prime quality of science is not in its applications but in its basic method of approaching problems—a way of thought and a set of procedures for interpreting experience.

Very broadly, American emphasis upon science reflects the values of the rationalistic-individualistic tradition. Science is disciplined, rational, functional, active; it requires systematic diligence and objectivity; it is congruent with pragmatism and efficiency and the tendency to minimize absolutes and ultimates. These science-oriented values, beliefs, and attitudes play a significant role in communication. Americans tend to value objectivity, empirical evidence, rationality, and concreteness in their communication, and they often experience considerable difficulty in understanding persons who do not reflect these values.

Materialism. Americans consider it almost a right to be materially well off and physically comfortable. They expect swift and convenient transportation—preferably controlled by themselves—a variety of clean and healthful foods and comfortable homes equipped with labor-saving devices. Associated with the values of physical comfort and health is the acceptance of cleanliness as being nearly identical with health, if not with Godliness. Materialism is a major force behind the American genius for devising and employing machines to provide efficiency and convenience in daily life. Americans are famous for taking all kinds of gadgets and machines with them on their trips abroad. They exhibit a strong tendency to perceive their tasks as requiring the use of machines, tools, and equipments. Although Americans are usually correct in recognizing that machines can facilitate the tasks at hand, they frequently overlook the fact that American machines and techniques of operation and maintenance are both integral parts of American technology. One cannot be exported without the other because the successful use of machinery requires a broad base of values and a social organization of roles to operate, maintain, and repair the machines.

The high value placed on materialism is sometimes reflected in ethnocentric attitudes toward individuals, groups, and societies that do not have high standards of living as measured by American standards of material welfare. The achievement level or success of an individual is often judged in terms of concrete, material possessions. Americans tend to view racial and ethnic groups and societies that do not have a high materialistic standard of living as "underdeveloped" or poor. These attitudes often create problems in intercultural communication.

Activity Orientation

The activity orientation describes the form of human activity or the self expression of human beings in activity. Three common modes of activity expression are: (1) Being, (2) Being-in-Becoming, and (3) Doing. The Being orientation refers to the kind of activity that is a spontaneous expression of the human personality. It is a nondevelopmental conception of human activity. Being-in-Becoming stresses the idea of development or growth. It emphasizes the kind of activity that contributes to the development of all aspects of the self as an integral whole. The Doing orientation describes the kind of activity that results in accomplishments measurable by standards external to the acting individual. Of these three modes of human expression, the Doing orientation is most common in the American culture and Doing is the dominant activity for Americans. Doing is reflected in the primary questions used in the appraisal of persons: What does the individual do? What can or will he accomplish? "Getting things done" and "let's do something about it" are stock American phrases. The foreign visitor in the United States quickly gains an impression of life lived at a fast pace and of people incessantly active.

The Doing orientation impinges upon several other beliefs and values of the American culture. We will examine three interrelated cultural patterns: (1) activity and work, (2) efficiency and practicality, and (3) progress and change.

Activity and Work.   Americans seek to dominate the world of nature, to subdue and to exploit the physical world around them through activity and work. This country is an almost perfect example of a culture that stresses activity. This pattern may be explained historically as developing out of our religious tradition, frontier experience, ceaseless change, vast opportunity, and fluid social structure.

Directed and disciplined activity in a regular occupation, referred to as work, is valued highly in the American society. Work often involves a desired and desirable expenditure of energy, a means of controlling and expressing strong affective states, an avenue for gaining recognition—not to mention its instrumental rewards in money or power. Work represents a cluster of moral and affective conditions of great attractiveness for Americans; involuntary idleness often constitutes a severely threatening and damaging social condition.

One of the most important distinctions in the forms of activity in American life is the separation of work from play. Work is pursued for living. It is what a person must do and a person is not necessarily supposed to enjoy it. Play, on the other hand, is relief from the drudgery and regularity of work and is enjoyable in its own right. This emphasis on play can be seen in the rush many Americans make each weekend to "get away" in their recreation vehicles. The United States has developed a large and complex recreation industry to satisfy American desires for play.

Efficiency and Practicality.   American emphasis upon efficiency has consistently impressed outside observers. *Efficient* is a word of high praise in this society that has long emphasized adaptability, technological innovation, economic expansion, mass production, standardization, up-to-datedness, practicality, expediency, and "getting things done." The mere listing of these words and phrases reveals how the multiple extensions of efficiency are used as a standard against which activity is judged. This standard is premised largely upon the active orientation to the world of the immediate present so characteristic of the American culture's concern with the here and now. American concern for efficiency at once sets this society apart from others that place greater emphasis upon aesthetic, contemplative, ritualistic, mystical, or other-worldly concerns.

American concern for efficiency is obviously related to the high place accorded science and technology and to the overweening importance attributed to practicality. Practical orientation is basically short-range adjustment to immediate situations. The practical person concentrates upon goals attainable in a given situation and solves immediate problems as they arise, leaving to others the more abstract and long-range problems. Practicality or pragmatism as a positive value involves important presuppositions as to other beliefs and values. For instance, it typically assumes the worth of the basic social order within which action occurs. It characteristically rests on a whole set of implicit premises, among which are the stress on activity, rationality, and efficiency. The theme of practicality points us again to the activistic, rational, and secular emphases of our culture. At the same time, it hints of possible tendencies toward the dissipation of the content of ultimate values in favor of adaptability to immediate interests and satisfactions. American emphasis on efficiency and practicality indicates an implicit value framework within which practical action acquires meaning and rationale.

Our concern for efficiency and practicality influences communication quite often. We tend to apply an "efficiency-practicality" frame of reference in perceiving, interpreting, and evaluating communication experiences. "How effective and efficient is this type of communication?", "What factors affect the efficiency of this communication style?", and "What approach is most practical?" are questions commonly used in our perception and thinking process. When persons from other cultures do not show similar concern for efficiency or practicality we become very frustrated. Such frustrations often lead to negative stereotypes and attitudes toward the persons from other cultures or subcultures.

Progress and Change.   Americans place a high value on progress and change. From the society's earliest formation as a distinct national entity there has been a diffuse constellation of beliefs and attitudes that may be called the cult of progress. This broad theme has no unitary value but is rather a certain "set" toward life that has permeated a wide range of behavior patterns. Various aspects of this complex include optimism, receptivity to change, an emphasis upon the future rather than the past or present, faith in our ability to control the environment, and faith in the perfectibility of the common person. Belief in progress involves acceptance of changes, the idea that changes are tending in a definite direction, and the belief that the direction is good. To generations of Americans all three components seemed verified; things were changing, they were moving in a central direction, they were getting better.

Although progress in American society finds many expressions, it is perhaps most frequently associated with the technological control of the environment. Most Americans tend to believe that the basic problems of the world are technological and their solution will bring about economic welfare. Materialism is the final arbiter of the good and desirable. Progress, then, quite often means the achievement of material possessions, physical comfort, and a high standard of living. Many cultures do not share our beliefs and values concerning materialism, and therefore define progress in very different terms. Likewise, many cultures do not value change as much as Americans do. The differences in values, beliefs, and attitudes toward progress and change often create communication problems in intercultural settings.

71

Time Orientation

Cultures vary widely and importantly in their conceptions of time. The possible cultural interpretations of the temporal focus of human life break easily into the three-point range of past, present, and future. Obviously, every society must deal with all three time problems; all have their conceptions of the past, the present, and the future. Where they differ is in the preferential ordering of the three alternatives (rank-order emphasis). A great deal can be told about a particular society or part of a society and much can be predicted about the direction of change within it if one knows the rank-order emphasis.

Americans, more strongly than most peoples of the world, place an emphasis upon the future—a future that is anticipated to be bigger and better. This does not mean they have no regard for the past or no thought of the present. But it certainly is true that no current generation of Americans ever wants to be called old-fashioned. The ways of the past are not considered good just because they are past, and middle-class Americans are seldom content with the present. This view results in a high evaluation of change, providing the change does not threaten the American way of life.

For Americans, the orientation toward the future and the high value placed on work yield the principle that one can improve upon the present through hard work. Most Americans have an attribute called effort-optimism, which leads them to believe that action and hard work will bring about what the individual wants. No goal is too remote for the individual who has the will and the determination and who expends the effort. The converse also holds—failure means the individual did not try hard enough, is lazy, or is worthless. These harsh evaluations may be moderated, since one can have bad luck. Nevertheless, they remain as vital American values that often create frustrations for Americans trying to initiate action and attain achievements with people who are oriented to the past or present, who assume a fatalistic outlook toward the future, and who are upset by American drive and energy.

There is another important aspect of time orientation. Americans believe that time is a flow in one direction, proceeding from the past, barely slowing for the present, and rushing to the future. "Time moves fast." It is important for Americans to cope with this flow, for "you've got to keep up with the times." This concept of time is eminently suited to a rational view of the world. It is easy to distinguish various moments in time, note their relationship, and signal the relation by seeing the preceding moment as a cause and the next one an effect. Although over-simplified, this description identifies the American predilection for seeing the world in rather simple terms and, ideally, evoking a simple cause and effect sequence to explain events. On this firm foundation one can see the evolution of the dominant American belief in one's ability to master his environment.

Another dimension of time orientation is the high value placed upon time in this society. Americans view time as a precious commodity; it has to be carefully used, properly budgeted, and should not be wasted. "Time is money," "let us not waste time," "I don't have time," and "how much time do you have?" are common expressions in American culture that reflect our concern and high value for time. Chapter 7 will discuss in more detail the effects of time on communication in intercultural settings.

Human Nature Orientation

What is the character of human nature? This question has concerned great thinkers for centuries. Every judgment about human behavior involves one's beliefs about human nature. Of all the cultural patterns discussed in this chapter, the human nature orientation is perhaps the most complex. The mere cataloging of questions that those holding differing concepts of human nature will answer differently suggests the complexity of this particular cultural pattern:

> Ought man to regulate his life with reference to the achievement of certain temporal conditions or with reference to his individual eternal salvation? What are the relative effects of "grace," "will," genetic heredity, geographical conditions, social institutions, and historical accident on the behavior of an individual? Would the "natural" man tend toward love and altruism in his treatment of others, or would he be dominated by greed and brutality? Is reason capable of dominating the behavior of man or merely a tool which he uses to mediate between the demands of an insatiable *id* and an uncompromising *super-ego*? Does human nature ever change, or is it..."human nature to change itself?" Can virtue be taught? What are the limits of educability?[4]

The above passage identifies three major dimensions of human nature orientation that influence communication behavior in intercultural settings: (1) goodness of human nature, (2) rationality of human nature, and (3) mutability of human nature. Let us examine briefly dominant American beliefs concerning these.

Goodness of Human Nature. To the question of what is the innate goodness or badness of human nature, there are three logical divisions: Evil, Good-and-Evil, and Good. Although it may be argued that the category of Good-and-Evil is not one but two categories, the three categories are adequate for the analysis of dominant American beliefs about the goodness of human nature.

Few disagree that the orientation inherited from Puritan ancestors and still strong among many Americans is that of a basically Evil but perfectible human nature. According to this view constant control and discipline of the self are required if any real goodness is to be achieved, and the danger of regression is always present. But some in the United States today, perhaps a growing number, incline to the view that human nature is a mixture of Good-and-Evil. These would say that although control and effort are certainly needed, lapses can be understood and need not always be condemned.

Rationality of Human Nature. Cutting across the arguments concerning the virtue or evil of human nature has been the question of the essential rationality of human nature. Tension between the mystic and the intellectual has been present throughout history. There have been those who "felt" their way to truth as well as those for whom rational analysis was considered essential to understanding. The early arguments between the rationally oriented Puritans and those who would exploit religious "enthusiasm" was but one of many conflicts on this issue. So, too, was the nineteenth-century frontier struggle between those churches that insisted upon a learned ministry and those that stressed the simple faith of the relatively unlettered.

With the growing acceptance of science and technology in this society, Americans seem to assume that people are basically rational and thus, while they may make mistakes, they can generally be trusted to make decisions for themselves. This premise underlies the democratic ideal, trial by a jury of one's peers, and free enterprise, which allows the consumer to choose for himself the goods he will buy from a selection offered in the open competition of a free marketplace.

Mutability of Human Nature. This refers to the possibility of change in human nature. Americans believe that human nature is highly plastic and subject to being molded by social and cultural environments. Human behavior is believed to be the result of biological inheritance interacting with numerous environmental factors. Thus, the use of intelligence in the control and manipulation of various environmental factors can improve human behavior. This conviction in the mutability of human nature provided a major argument in the American campaign for universal education, which would expand the use of intelligence in social affairs. As social institutions were reformed in light of new knowledge, the mind and character of people would be raised to new heights. These people would then be capable of further institutional reform and more effective utilization of natural forces and resources. Progress would be dynamic and continual.

Americans believe that human tendencies are so easily shaped by experience that social institutions largely determine whether a specific individual will be noble or mean. This view has been shocking and frightening to many Americans, particularly when they perceive that the communist world has used scientific psychological knowledge to undermine such values as religion, democracy, and free enterprise that Americans had thought to inhere in the soul and conscience of human beings.

Perception of the Self

The self is a very important concept underlying the American culture. We carry with us a sense of who we are, what we should be, and what we want to be. Our behavior to a large extent is determined by our perception of the self. In the American culture, the word *self* occupies an important place. We speak of self-concept, self-image, self-esteem, self-reliance, self-help, self-awareness, self-actualization, self-determination, and so on.

> A searching look at any aspect of American culture readily brings the self to the surface as a unifying concept. The self provides a perspective in thinking, a direction for activity, a source of motivation, a locus in decision-making and a limit to group involvement. Although personality is fragmented to accommodate to the demands of the culture, the identity of the individual is held together by the self. Providing continuity for the individual, the self furnishes the quantum of the culture. All messages, transactions and activities in life which yield an impact upon Americans must be translated into the language of the self. . . . This concept of the self as the quantum of the culture draws together various strands of activity and belief in American culture and deeply affects its values and assumptions.[5]

Psychologists have long recognized a person's perception of the self as an important aspect of human personality. Since culture and personality are integrally related through the socialization process, persons from different cultures tend to have differing perceptions of the self. In the American cultural context, the perception of the self involves a set of beliefs, values, and attitudes concerning the role and responsibilities of the individual in the society. We will discuss two cultural patterns concerning the perception of self: (1) individualism, (2) self-motivation.

Individualism. Americans believe that each person has his own separate identity, which should be recognized and stressed. The individual self is viewed as a distinct entity apart from other people and apart from the world. Broadly speaking, the concept of individualism refers to a doctrine that the interests of the individual are or ought to be paramount and that all values, rights, and duties originate in individuals. It emphasizes individual initiative, independence, action, and interests. Americans believe that to be a person is to be independent, responsible, and self-respecting, and thereby to be worthy of concern and respect in one's own right. To be a person, in this sense, is to be an autonomous and responsible agent, not merely a reflection of external pressures, and to have an internal center of gravity, a set of standards, and a conviction of personal worth.

The American value of individualism begins at a very early age when the child is encouraged to be autonomous. The self-centeredness of the child is seldom questioned. Children are encouraged to make their own decisions, develop their own opinions, solve their own problems, have their own things, and in general, learn to view the world from the point of view of the self. People are not expected to bow unquestioningly to authority or tradition. The pressures on the individual are usually informal since one is assumed to be a free agent.

In American culture, individualism emphasizes the individual while accepting affiliations within a group. A consequence of American individualism is that a person's self-concept usually does not merge with a group. People maintain a separate sense of individuality. To them, any group ranging from a small one to the nation is a collection of individuals. People require that their individuality be recognized by being given opportunities to express their opinions and take part in group decisions, since as a member of a group they presumably are pursuing their own self-interest. An American does not like to get lost in or to become deeply identified with large groups or collectivities.

The value of individualism in American culture represents a complex cluster of more specific desirable states or conditions such as self-reliance, autonomy of choice, privacy, freedom of expression, respect for other persons, equality, and democratic processes. These dimensions of individualism influence communication behavior and thus affect the outcome of intercultural communication.

Self-motivation.   The American value of individualism is strongly reflected in the patterns of motivation in the American culture. Americans believe in self-motivation. Individuals should set their own goals and then make up their own minds on how to pursue them. Motivation, in the sense of long-range goals and plans, as well as motivation for a specific and immediate task, should originate with the person.

The idea of self-motivation is related to the American use of persuasion:

Americans tend to dislike motives originating in others which are then applied to them. They strongly reject motivation in the form of orders, injunctions and threats emanating from authority. Probably it is this dislike which makes Americans anti-militaristic rather than a rejection of fighting or violence. . . . The American concept of the self and self-motivation causes stress both in American institutions and in the general lifestyle prevalent in the United States. If coercion is disapproved and authority rejected, how do Americans manage to coordinate their lives and activities? The answer is through persuasion. The desire to act according to the wishes of others is instilled in the individual by means of examples, incentives and subtle hints of failure.[6]

American emphasis on self-motivation is also related to the high value of personal achievement and success in the American culture. It is marked by a central stress upon personal achievement, especially secular occupational achievement. The "success story" and the respect accorded to the self-made person are distinctly American. Ascribed status (in the form of fixed, hereditary social stratification) has been minimized, and achieved status through self-motivation and hard work has been maximized.

Social Organization

Social organization refers to cultural patterns concerning social relationships among the members of a society. Every society has a wide variety of social relationships which are crystallized in the form of social groups, large or small, permanent or temporary, formally organized or unorganized. Of the various ways of classifying the groups that represent the crystallization of social relationships, there is one that is of particular interest to us here. It is based on the concept of the primary group and includes the obverse concept of the secondary group. The primary group is a group in which contact is personal, intimate, and usually face-to-face, and which involves the entire personality, not just a segmentalized part of it. The family, the child's play group, and social cliques are all examples of a primary group. In direct contrast, the secondary group is a group in which contacts tend to be impersonal, formal, or casual, nonintimate, and segmentalized; in some cases they are face-to-face, in others not. Examples of secondary groups involve various interest groups, associations, and organizations. Obviously, there are groups that are hard to classify because they seem to have both primary and secondary aspects. Using the concepts of primary and secondary groups, we can think of *primary relationships* with other persons, which are personal, intimate, emotionally affective, and which bring into play the whole personality, as contrasted with *secondary relationships*, which are impersonal, formal, and segmentalized, and tend not to come very close to the core of personality. Both types of social relationships tend to have a pattern of some repetition and can to some degree be predicted, and are based, at least to some extent, on a set of shared expectations. Since these social relationships occur within the cultural framework of a society, they are influenced by a set of cultural beliefs, values, attitudes, and norms that transcend various types of relationships. In other words, there are certain cultural patterns—called social organization cultural patterns—that influence all types of social relationships within a society. We will discuss two major social organization cultural patterns in the American culture: (1) equality, and (2) conformity.

Equality. Compared to many other cultures, American culture emphasizes equality in social relationships. As discussed earlier, Americans believe that each person is a unique individual worthy of respect and capable of making autonomous choices. Consistent with this high value on individualism and human dignity, our interpersonal relations are usually egalitarian and horizontal, conducted between presumed equals. When there is a social interaction between two persons of different hierarchical levels, there is an implicit tendency to establish an atmosphere of equality.

> Thus even within the definitive authoritarian structure of the military, a commanding officer may ask a subordinate a personal question, or offer a cup of coffee, before beginning a conversation. Furthermore, the officer is not expected to call attention to his rank and authority or exercise his personal power over a subordinate. One mark of a good officer from the enlisted man's point of view is that he does not "pull rank" or "use his authority as a crutch." In short, the good officer promotes a feeling of equality, the preferred social mode among Americans.[7]

The value of equality is prevalent in both primary and secondary social relationships in the American society. For instance, most of the primary social relationships within a family tend to emphasize equality rather than authoritarian or hierarchial orientation. Friendships, co-worker relationships, and other kinds of secondary relationships are characterized by equality.

The value of equality in the American culture sometimes conflicts with the value of individualism and freedom. Americans believe in individualism in the sense that individuals are free to pursue their self-determined goals for personal achievement, success, and reward with minimum interference from the government or other social institutions. Americans prefer to have the freedom to decide who to relate with, what groups to join, and how to conduct social relationships. Sometimes, these "inalienable" rights and freedoms create problems of inequality and discrimination in social relationships with persons of different racial and ethnic groups. Equality of opportunity receives emphasis in American culture; equality does not extend to achievements, success, or reward.

Like many other cultural patterns, the value of equality in social relationships creates communication problems in intercultural settings. Americans like to treat others as equals and prefer to be treated as equals in intercultural settings. Persons from cultures that have rigid, hierarchical social structures find it very frustrating to work with Americans, who negate the value of such hierarchical structures by such behaviors as calling social superiors by their given names.

Conformity. People universally seek the approval of some of their fellows and therefore try to succeed according to shared standards of achievement or conformity. This characteristic is the outcome of universal requirements of social life and of the basic nature of the socialization process. Otherwise stated, conformity and the desire for social approval are part of the very definition of society. In this sense, conformity is not a distinct cultural value or cultural pattern at all but simply an end product of other cultural patterns and the necessary adjustments entailed by life in social groups. In other words, all cultures have some degree of conformity in social relationships.

Cultures tend to differ in the content or type of conformity. Some cultures emphasize conformity to traditional or past-oriented social norms while others emphasize conformity to modern or future-oriented norms. Americans tend to be highly future-oriented and value progress and change. This future-orientation and high value of change are reflected in the future-oriented conformity found in America. Americans prefer to conform to standards that momentarily are current and up-to-date rather than old-fashioned. For instance, "keeping up with the Joneses" in car purchases, in household furnishings, in the schooling of children, and keeping one's ideas in line with those of others are matters of far greater concern than an adherence to traditional standards in the American society.

One argument suggests that Americans emphasize external conformity, which is to be expected when upward social mobility and competition are highly valued. The competitive striving of an upwardly mobile group in a society organized around economic enterprise requires stringent discipline over the expression of sexual and aggressive impulses, over patterns of consumption, over the uses of time and resources. Furthermore, an emphasis on external conformity easily develops out of the American premise of basic human equality: if all are equal, then all have an equal right to judge their fellows and to regulate their conduct according to commonly accepted standards.[8]

In terms of social relationships, external conformity would require that the individuals involved in a social relationship conform to some basic "externals" in the social interaction—elements that are external from the point of view of the individuals involved but are necessary for developing and maintaining the social relationship. Some examples are: a common language, conformity to some agreed upon rules of social interaction, and disagreement on individual beliefs, values, and attitudes. Without these external conformities, it is difficult to develop and maintain any social relationships.

> . . .The very heterogeneity of American culture tends to produce a stress upon external conformity. Given the varied cultural backgrounds of the population and the desire that the various groups should continue to live together in the same society, conformity in externals becomes a sort of "social currency" making it possible to continue the society in spite of many clashes of interests and values. If it is gradually learned that the exhibition of cultural differences— whether they be of dress, or language, or religious faith, or political philosophy—seems to lead to friction in interpersonal relationships or even to public disturbances, a whole series of complex adjustments are set in motion.[9]

The American values of future-oriented and external conformity sometimes create serious problems in intercultural situations involving persons who value past-oriented and internal conformity.

Summary

In this chapter we have examined six categories of dominant American cultural patterns: (1) world view, (2) activity orientation, (3) time orientation, (4) human nature orientation, (5) perception of the self, and (6) social organization. The cultural patterns discussed here are commonly associated with white middle-class Americans. As stated earlier, there are important subcultural variations of these dominant cultural patterns. In Chapter 2, we explained various types of subcultural variations in American society including racial differences, ethnic differences, and social class differences. We should also remember that the cultural patterns discussed here are not static; they change over time. If we view each cultural pattern representing a continuum, we can begin to understand the relative position of various subcultures on these cultural patterns. Also, we can see cultural changes in terms of minor or major shifts on a given continuum. An understanding of these American cultural patterns can facilitate our understanding of other cultures, which is the major focus of the next chapter.

Notes

1. See Alfred J. Kraemer, *Development of a Cultural Self-Awareness Approach to Instruction in Intercultural Communication* (Alexandria, Va.: Human Resources Organization, 1973).

2. Kraemer, p. 6. Used by permission.

3. Jean Marie Ackermann, "Skill Training for Foreign Assignment: The Reluctant U.S. Case," in Larry A. Samovar and Richard E. Porter, eds., *Intercultural Communication: A Reader,* 2d ed. (Belmont, Calif.: Wadsworth, 1976), pp. 298–306.

4. Merle L. Borrowman, "Traditional Values and the Shaping of American Education," in John H. Chilcott, Norman C. Greenberg, and Herbert B. Wilson, eds., *Readings in the Socio-Cultural Foundations of Education* (Belmont, Calif.: Wadsworth, 1968), p. 175.

5. Edward C. Stewart, *American Cultural Patterns: A Cross-Cultural Perspective* (Pittsburgh: Intercultural Communications Network, 1972), p. 74. Used by permission.

6. Stewart, p. 71. Used by permission.

7. Stewart, p. 46.

8. Robin M. Williams, Jr., *American Society,* 3d ed. (New York: Alfred A. Knopf, 1970), p. 486.

9. Williams, p. 486.

Additional Readings

Chilcott, John H., Norman C. Greenberg, and Herbert B. Wilson, eds. *Readings in the Socio-Cultural Foundations of Education.* Belmont, Calif.: Wadsworth, 1968, pp. 162–222.

Condon, John C. and Fathi Yousef. *An Introduction to Intercultural Communication.* Indianapolis: Bobbs-Merrill, 1975, pp. 47–121.

Kluckhohn, Florence R. and Fred L. Strodtbeck. *Variations in Value Orientations.* Evanston, Ill.: Row, Peterson, 1961, pp. 1–48.

Kraemer, Alfred J. *Development of a Cultural Self-Awareness Approach to Instruction in Intercultural Communication.* Alexandria, Va.: Human Resources Research Organization, 1973.

Rhinesmith, Stephen H. *Cultural-Organizational Analysis: The Interrelationship of Value Orientations and Managerial Behavior.* Cambridge, Mass.: McBer, undated.

Stewart, Edward C. *American Cultural Patterns: A Cross-Cultural Perspective.* Pittsburgh: Intercultural Communications Network, 1972.

Williams, Robin M., Jr. *American Society*. New York: Alfred A. Knopf, 1970, pp. 483–504.

Concepts and Questions

1. Why is it necessary to learn about one's own culture for effective intercultural communication?

2. How does learning about one's own culture help in understanding other cultures? How do we learn our own culture? How do we learn about other cultures? In what ways are these two types of culture learning similar? In what ways are they different?

3. What are the main reasons for our low level of cultural self-awareness? Is the low level of cultural self-awareness a common problem across all cultures or is it only true in America? Why? What could be done to increase the level of cultural self-awareness among Americans?

4. What are the main types of subcultural variations found in the American society? How do these variations influence communication?

5. What are some other ways of classifying dominant American cultural patterns? In what ways are these better than the ones used in this chapter?

6. Are there some dominant American cultural patterns missing from the discussion presented in this chapter? What are they?

7. Why do cultural patterns change over time? What cultural patterns are relatively stable? Do cultural patterns change faster in America than in some traditional societies? Why?

8. What American cultural patterns operate on or influence our communication behavior in a conscious and deliberate manner in the form of values, beliefs, attitudes, or opinions? What cultural patterns inadvertently or unconsciously affect our behavior? How can we achieve congruence between these conscious and unconscious cultural influences on our behavior?

Exercises

1. Ask your friends and family members to list ten of the most important characteristics of the American culture. Compile these lists to

identify the most commonly mentioned American cultural patterns. Compare this list with the cultural patterns discussed in this chapter. Discuss briefly why these two lists are different and what problems you encountered in doing this exercise.

2. Observe your own communication behavior for a week. Try to determine the main reasons for your participation in each communication encounter. Also, try to determine the main reasons for participation by the other persons in the encounter. Now correlate these reasons for communication with the American cultural patterns discussed in this chapter. What American cultural patterns affected your communication behavior most? Were you aware of these cultural influences before doing this exercise?

3. Discuss some topic of mutual interest with two or three foreign students. Observe and analyze your discussions to identify similarities and differences in communication behaviors between you and the foreign students. Which of these communication differences were influenced by cultural factors? Which were influenced by personality factors? Which were influenced by situational factors? How do you know?

4. Interview some faculty members at your campus who have worked abroad. Ask them what American characteristics facilitated their work abroad and what American characteristics hindered their work abroad. Collect some specific examples of successful and unsuccessful intercultural communication experiences and try to analyze these experiences in terms of the American cultural patterns discussed in this chapter.

5. Write a dialogue between an American and a non-American. Incorporate appropriate American cultural characteristics in the statements and responses made by the American. Incorporate appropriate contrasting cultural characteristics in the statements and responses made by the non-American. List briefly (on a separate sheet) American cultural characteristics used in the dialogue. If possible, role play this dialogue in your class and ask class members to identify what American cultural characteristics are affecting the communication behavior of the American. Compare the class response with your own list of American characteristics used in the dialogue.

4

Understanding Others: Diversity of Cultural Patterns

Within the next hour 7,200 babies will be born. At the moment of birth, the infants will be more like each other than they ever will be again. Their differences will grow because each of them is born into a different family and into a different culture—into a way of living that has developed in a particular place over a long period of time. From birth onward, each child is encouraged to be ethnocentric—to believe that his homeland, his people, his everything is not only different but also superior to that of other people. The elders teach that the ways in which we do things are the natural ways, the proper ways, and the moral ways. In other places, they—"barbarians" and "foreigners"—follow a strange way of life. Ours is *the* culture; theirs is *a* culture.

Seymour Fersh

In the previous chapter we examined American culture as a basis for understanding others. Now, we turn our attention to other cultures and discuss two major themes: (1) how to become aware of other cultures, and (2) dominant patterns in other cultures.

Becoming Aware of Other Cultures

Approaches to Cultural Understanding

Much of our knowledge and understanding of other cultures comes from our images of those cultures, which may not be accurate, since they must be filtered through our own culture before they are meaningful to us. Three aspects of perception contribute to this problem: projected cognitive similarity (see p. 61), stereotyping, and ethnocentrism.

We often develop images of other cultures from incomplete and biased sources. Because we have seen pictures of tribal Africans in the *National Geographic,* watched old Tarzan movies, or toured Africa via the African Safari ride at Disneyland, we may have internalized images of all Africans wearing leopard skins, carrying spears, piercing their noses with bones, and living in grass huts. Although some Africans do or have done some of these things, it is not typical. These false images understandably upset and distress our African friends. A letter in the *Los Angeles Times* from the Director of the National Museum of Tanzania reflected this distress: "Disneyland artists and technicians have done an excellent job of perpetuating the myths about my continent. They have ignored the arts and civilizations of the 'jungle' people....I suppose it would distort the American image of Africa to have included representations of the high civilizations that have flourished in Africa."[1]

We often are influenced by our own ethnocentrism. We believe that our culture is the best, the most advanced, and the most correct. Ethnocentric views are not necessarily wrong or invalid. "In some ways the ethnocentric view of life is 'right'; the patterns of responses that evolved in a particular place may make relatively good sense—for that particular people and place."[2] But ethnocentric awareness can help us realize that what we see in another culture is largely our subjective view of that culture. We must learn to accept the idea that what we may view negatively according to our cultural biases may be valid in another culture.

Many of the ideas that most influence a culture are hundreds if not thousands of years old. Moses, Confucius, Buddha, Christ, and Mohammed, for instance, had profound influence on cultural thought. Yet their ideas as expressed in such sources as the Torah, the I Ching, the various Sutras, the Bible, or the Koran do not give us a detailed view of how their ideas have been incorporated into a society. We must examine the institutions in a culture in order to gain an understanding of their influence.

Differences between what cultures hold ought or ought not to be or which form of salvation is worthy or not worthy of attaining permit us to grasp points of conflict that may require mediation before effective communication can take place. By examining differences, we also can determine what a culture considers to be the nature of life and the purpose of life. These can differ vastly from one culture to another as well as from one geographic region to another. For some people, the nature of life is continual drudgery, pain, and suffering; life is to be tolerated rather than enjoyed. In other cultures and regions we may find that life is full of anticipation and discovery, a continual process of growth with ample opportunity for comfort and enjoyment. For some, the purpose of life is the task of controlling nature and of accumulating resources for self-pleasure and benefit. For others, the task of life may be to discover God's will or to develop scientific laws that explain the universe. As intercultural communicators, our concern with the nature and purpose of life is a matter of cultural homogeneity. The more widespread and accepted a particular view toward the nature and purpose of life within a culture, the greater the degree of cultural homogeneity and the easier it is for us to understand and to predict individual views and reactions within that culture.

Another factor related to homogeneity is that every culture has racial, ethnic, and other minority problems. Every country that has imported laborers, skilled workers, and professionals to work on its farms and in its industries, businesses, and schools is faced with this problem. Frequently, when others are imported as workers, they are not seen as equals by the local culture. West Germany, for instance, has imported almost three million workers from Italy, Greece, Turkey, Yugoslavia, and other European countries. But the majority of native Germans do not consider the foreign workers their equals. We find a similar problem in Iran and other Middle East oil producing countries. American and European workers who have been imported because of their knowledge of petroleum technology frequently are looked upon as inferiors or as intruders by local people. African countries also have numerous ethnic problems whose antecedents lie in tribal culture and identities. This problem has been compounded in such countries as Kenya and Uganda because they have imported sizable numbers of white skilled workers and managers who have become a sometimes elite minority disliked by the black majority.

Coupled with the minority problems common in most cultures we find sexism, which in many respects resembles racism. The effect of sexism on human relationships and role expectations is an important factor in understanding other cultures. Women's liberation is a popular concept primarily in the United States, and we must remember it is unique and not typical of the rest of the world. There are educated and aware women in other countries that support the idea of sexual equality, but they are not in a position to implement their wishes. Recent events in Iran show us just how fragile women's rights are and how rapidly they may dissolve.

Learning about Other Cultures

In our search for cultural understanding, we must assume "that a culture can be viewed as a body of knowledge, namely, that it is something that is knowable and can be learned to a greater or lesser extent in much the same way as any other body of knowledge is learned."[3] But, learning about another culture is not easy. At the very least we must make a prolonged and in-depth study which includes the culture's art, history, philosophy, social organization, social relationships, language, value systems, and level of technical development. It requires a great deal of time to reach below the surface of a culture and grasp the intricacies, nuances, and deep structures that escape casual observation. This task obviously is quite beyond our limitations in this book. But, we can learn how to study other cultures and become sensitized to a vast array of intricate cultural variations and to many important cultural dimensions that affect intercultural communication.

Success in our search for cultural understanding lies in knowing where to obtain useful and adequate information. Of major importance to us are the traditional tools of anthropologists which include traveler's reports, vital statistics, textbooks, opinion polls, and comparative studies of official ideologies. In addition, students from cultures of interest frequently attend school in this country. These international students can be a rich source of information, and they usually are willing and often eager to share their knowledge and experiences with people who are interested in the visitor's culture.

Yu-Kuang Chu offers six useful suggestions for learning about other cultures.[4] First, be wary of stereotypes. They function as shortcuts in our perceptual processes and provide us with easy guides to action. Although some stereotyping is unavoidable, many popular notions may be entirely false or be sweeping oversimplifications. Even when a stereotype is valid, it will not apply to every individual within a culture. It may be what is called a rare-zero differential. This is the tendency for us to identify a rare trait as a dominant trait because we do not find it in any other culture. For example, "some (but not all) Quakers use 'thee' for 'you' in their form of in-group address. Since no other group of people does so, this custom is called a 'Quaker trait.' "[5] When we observe this trait, there is a tendency for us to assume it is widespread and typical rather than rare and atypical.

Second, seek the common humanity of people and avoid emphasis on extremes, such as the differences between Western and non-Western cultures that perpetuate such popular but false notions that

Orientals, being mysterious and inscrutable, are not as human as we are. We also must avoid the opposite tendency to assume falsely that Western systems such as democracy or capitalism will work in foreign cultures. Avoiding these extremes allows us to seek that common humanity in which all people share the same problems in life for which they develop different solutions.

Third, recognize a different scale of values in non-Western cultures. Value systems can differ significantly. Non-Western cultures may embrace social stability over social change and group solidarity over individual freedoms in contrast to dynamic Western society and values. This stability and solidarity can manifest itself in marriages arranged by parents, respect for the aged, and punishment of a group for crimes of an individual.

Fourth, through education, develop human empathy and active concern for other people. This form of education can be seen as "a process continuously extending human sympathy and understanding in time and space—for one's immediate family through the community and nation to the world and from the present backwards to the remote past and forwards into the future."[6] In this manner we can learn to see human problems on a world scale and to develop a feeling for ethical problems on an international level. From this time and space perspective we also can learn how numerous cultures have contributed to the sum of human civilization, and how Western culture is indebted to other cultures. Arab scholarship, the Judeo-Christian tradition and ethic, and the Chinese invention of gunpowder, paper, and the compass have been fundamental influences on our Western culture.

Fifth, study the interrelationships between language and culture. Language is closely involved with feeling, thinking, and acting. The study of non-Western language presents us with insight into the culture that uses that language. For instance, when we hear someone say "pardon me," we normally respond with "surely," "certainly," or "of course." The Chinese, on the other hand, respond with an expression such as "not at all." We recognize the thing for which pardon is being sought and forgive it. The Chinese are more circuitous and wish not even to acknowledge the error. Both are examples of being polite, but in their own culturally defined way.

Finally, study non-Western cultures to see their richness of human thought and life. If we become better acquainted with other cultures, we naturally will reduce ethnocentrism. The discovery of non-Western art, philosophy, and literature can reveal a whole new fabric of delight as we study humanity from different perspectives.

Although cultural learning may sensitize us to other cultures, we must remember that we tend to assume our culture is superior. If we do not develop an alertness to this assumption, we will continue to judge other cultures by our own cultural standards and our learning will be of little use. We must evaluate others in their own contexts. For instance, most American newspapers are factually correct but contextually false when they report about cow worship in India. Few Americans realize the practical importance of cows to the Indians. They give milk, provide dung for fuel, and deliver other cows as well as bulls, which may be neutered and become oxen, which are the main work animals in India.[7]

Location and History

The location of a culture is an important factor that helps shape its orientations, because geo-political characteristics help determine behaviors and perceptions. The chewing of coca leaves by South American Indians has become an activity within their culture due in part to the influence of location. The numbing effect of the coca leaves helps the Indians live in the extreme altitudes of the Andes where cold and a reduced oxygen supply make life extremely harsh and uncomfortable. Coca leaf use then becomes a cultural pattern of behavior that helps people cope with their environment and location.

Location is also politically significant. Some cultures, because of their political boundaries and physical features, have had long histories of conflict that have become manifest in their attitudes, values, and perceptions. Turkey, for instance, because it straddles the Bosporus strait—the narrow water connection between the Mediterranean and the Black Sea—has long been fighting with Bulgaria, Rumania, and the Soviet Union as well as Syria and Iraq. The years of conflict in this area have had a profound effect on Turkey's perceptions of and attitudes toward these other countries.

As we know, every culture develops according to its unique history. Some histories are similar, but none are the same, even if they involve the same events. The winners and losers of wars experience the same event, but as the outcomes differ, their histories also differ.

Cultures also undergo unique experiences that lead to different developments. We in the West, for instance, have had the direct experience of the Christian tradition, which has helped shape our values and moral precepts. Indian culture was influenced by Buddha, and Chinese culture was influenced by Lao Tzu and Confucius. Each of these experiences has led to the development of different cultural patterns.

The vital factor for us to remember as intercultural communicators is that each culture has its own history, which produced a unique set of experiences resulting in different developments. These developments in turn have been culture's attempts to provide solutions to problems that were unique to a particular people in a unique time-space period. At the time the solutions were developed, they were the best that could be developed by the people at their time and in their place.

Dominant Patterns in Other Cultures

In Chapter 3, when we looked at dominant American cultural patterns, we followed a culture-specific approach. Now, as we turn to examine other cultures we will use a culture-general approach. Our goal here is to see how dominant patterns in other cultures differ from American patterns and how these differences can lead to intercultural communication problems. We will use the same categories of cultural patterns used in the analysis of American patterns, that is, world view, activity orientation, time orientation, human nature, the perception of the self, and social organization.

World View

As we have already noted, world view refers to the outlook or image we have concerning the nature of the universe, the nature of humankind, the relationship between humanity and the universe, and other philosophical issues or orientations that help us define the cosmos and our place in it. These orientations are tied directly to the historical, philosophic, and religious dimensions of a culture. Through the interaction of these and countless other events, culture provides people with a view of themselves, the rest of the world, the universe, and their relationship to them. We can see such an influence in the historical view of the Chinese that China is the center of the world.

World view often is ethnocentric. We would expect as a culture develops and acquires its self-image that it should see itself as the best, as the model for others. World view, however, goes beyond ethnocentrism and manifests itself in the psychological, sociological, and technical aspects of a society. It influences social organization, the use of tools and instruments, situational behavior, and language. In short, when we say that people belong to a particular culture, we are saying that they share common world views.

As we did in our analysis of world view in American culture, we here will consider the individual and nature relationship, science and technology, and materialism. In the discussion and examples that follow, we will see how the world view of cultures can differ.

The Individual and Nature Relationship. World view specifies the relationship of humankind to the universe. The nature of this relationship can be one of subjugation where people are helpless and at the mercy of nature. It can be a working relationship where people live in harmony with nature. And, as we saw in American culture, a third view holds that humans can exercise control over nature for their own benefit. Human control of nature is a relatively recent view and is found primarily among highly technical Western cultures.

The subjugation view is found primarily among primitive cultures where everyday life is an on-going struggle merely to survive. Extreme climatic conditions, scarcity of food and water, and a limited level of technological development put primitive cultures at the mercy of nature. Hence, nature is seen as an active, often capricious, force beyond human control that must be appeased. Such views lead to volcano worship, sun worship, and the like.

The cooperative view is widespread and prevails throughout most of the world. Closely tied to the cooperative view of humankind's relationship with nature is respect for the environment. Many Eastern cultures as well as American Indian cultures consider nature a divine creation in which the spirit of God resides. Nature and all living things, therefore, are sacred, and no one has the right to destroy or be the master of nature. This view is the basis for such cultural prohibitions as that against the eating of meat. When all livings things are seen as sacred, it naturally follows that killing animals for food is an act against nature and the destruction of the sacred.

These differences in conceptualizing the relationship between humanity and nature result in different frames of reference for perceiving and understanding human goals, attitudes, and behaviors. In intercultural situations, we can find ourselves in conflict with others who do not share our views about how to relate to nature. There are areas of conflict throughout the world as well as within the United States where technological Western cultures attempt to modify nature for their benefit. A case in point is the current conflict between the dominant American culture and some American Indian tribes who object to widespread strip-mining of coal because it results in the disfigurement of the earth. The two groups may fail to understand or even to see each other's point of view because their frames of reference are so different.

Science and Technology. The level of scientific achievement and technical accomplishment in a culture is not so much a single dominant pattern as it is an effect of many dominant patterns. Cultures that are not activity oriented and tend toward passive acceptance of the world as being in accordance with God's wishes remain relatively unsophisticated in many aspects of scientific and technical development. This is not to imply that non-Western cultures lack science or technology. On the contrary some of the world's leading scientists come from India, China, Japan, and other non-Western cultures.

The impact of technology, however, is related directly to the world view orientations prevalent in a culture. We in the United States and other Western cultures have embraced science and technology to provide solutions to our problems and to increase our pleasures and comforts. Other cultures do not hold science and technology in this position of importance because they conflict with social structure and traditional values. Modern technology often is related to large enterprise. Tractors are a marvelously efficient means of tilling the soil, but to be utilized effectively, they require large fields. The farmer who works five acres to feed his family could not benefit from a tractor because its costs of acquisition and operation are not compatible with small family farms. In terms of values, the reverent feelings many non-Western people have toward the earth would be violated by the use of impersonal machines to till and otherwise work the soil.

Science is based upon a set of epistemological assumptions—assumptions about how we gain knowledge. During the course of human development, cultures have developed varying epistemologies that have become very much a part of their world view. Whether science develops in a culture, to what extent it develops, and how it is accepted and employed is determined in part by how a culture generally believes it acquires knowledge.

In contemporary Western culture, knowledge is gained primarily by empirical means. This is the basis of science and technology, and it assumes an ability to observe and to measure phenomena in order to understand and to explain them. Competing with empiricism in Western cultures—and currently enjoying some popularity among humanistically oriented groups—is intuition. This is knowledge that comes from within oneself, the form of knowing called feeling. Advocates of intuition believe that empiricism is unreliable. They suggest that true knowledge can come only from within one's self.

In non-Western cultures, other ways of viewing and knowing the world have evolved. Hindus believe that even intuition is subjective and that true knowledge comes through meditation. This is seen as the mastery of the self over the mind which makes true knowledge more important than intuition. Buddhists believe the goal of knowledge is absolute reality, which cannot be found through the senses. Because sensory perception implies a dual relationship between the perceiver and the objects of perception, Buddhists, like Hindus, believe sensory perception is undependable. The objects of perception are dynamic and constantly changing and our perceptions of them are illusory and have no permanent reality. Their existence is purely relative. According to Buddhist thought, sensory perception, therefore, is subjective and the basis of all the ills of the world.

Mahayana Buddhism holds that knowledge is of three types: illusion, relative knowledge, and absolute knowledge. Illusion comes through the senses; it is not subject to verification by objective reality and critical judgment. Relative knowledge comes from the belief that all things are relative and conditional, that nothing can claim absolute existence. Absolute knowledge is free of illusions and assumptions. It is truth. Since all three stages are seen as necessary, one leading to the other, Mahayanists do not look down on science or religious beliefs. They believe that science alone is insufficient, but it is a step toward absolute knowledge.

Islam, contrary to other religious views, holds that the world is totally real. It is one of two realities: the divine and the created. Allah, the divine, created the world and everything on it for the pleasure of humankind. World reality is available to all persons, but the divine reality is revealed to only a few as an act of kindness by Allah.

Contrary views about how people obtain knowledge contribute to the diverse views cultures have of themselves and of their places in the universe as well as decisions about attitude and action. When people who rely on different sources of knowledge attempt to reach cooperative decisions, they may find that they disagree about the need for action let alone what action is proper.

Materialism. Materialism is a dimensional cultural orientation that ranges from non-material to material. As we saw in the last chapter, American culture is highly material; Americans believe they have a right to material well-being. This view does not prevail in most of the world. Only in a very few cultures has material well-being for everyone even been a possibility let alone any kind of reality.

Most of the people of the world live in cultures where material well-being is not considered a right or even a possibility. Those who are well-off usually are members of a social elite for whom wealth and material well-being is a birthright or the result of political rank or position. The sheer size of populations and the short supply of necessary resources lead to world view orientations that shun the material and instead enshrine natural beauty and aesthetic development. The prevailing view toward well-being may be contentment in being alive and having the minimal necessities of food, water, and shelter to maintain life.

These non-material views tend to produce ingrained cultural attitudes and values that may seem quite strange to people from Western material cultures. What produces happiness and contentment for others may be viewed by people used to a high level of material well-being as backward, underdeveloped, and unsophisticated. It may lead to questions about how can these people live without cars, televisions, refrigerators, and hand-held calculators. And the reply may be something like "who needs them?"

Activity Orientation

We saw in Chapter 3 how activity orientation describes human activity in terms of Being, Being-in-Becoming, and Doing. We also noted that in American culture the dominant pattern is Doing or goal directed activity measurable by external standards. Many non-Western cultures, however, emphasize Being-in-Becoming orientations in which activity contributes to the development of the self as an integral whole. Different activity orientations lead to different notions of activity and work, efficiency and practicality, and progress and change.

Activity and Work.   Activity orientation is expressed within cultures by the way in which people seek goal attainment through activity and work. Westerners tend to believe that through their deeds and acts they can cause things to happen. Eastern people may be more content with waiting for events to happen rather than trying to cause their occurrence. While Western people are prone to actively pursue truth, many Easterners more commonly share the view that truth will present itself when the time is appropriate. How different views toward work and activity manifest themselves in different cultures is reflected in the following anecdote:

> If you ask a Hindu why he got only ten bags of corn from his land while nearby farmers got much more he would say it was the wish of God. An American farmer's answer to the same question would be: "Hell, I didn't work hard enough."[8]

The Hindu's explanation that it was God's wish is indicative of a passive activity orientation. And the American's perception of not having worked hard enough reflects a maximum Doing activity orientation.

Activity also is directly associated with such variables as aggressiveness. In general, Western cultures are aggressive, persistent, and competitive. Eastern cultures generally tend toward passiveness embracing cooperative behavior. These differences may have a negative effect on intercultural communication. When Easterners interact with Westerners, the active, aggressive manner of a Western person may be interpreted as arrogance while the passive acts of an Eastern person may be viewed as timidity and weakness. Such misinterpretations can lead to wrong conclusions about the natures of the people involved.

We earlier stressed the American tendency to dichotomize work and play. This is a uniquely American view not shared in most other cultures. Work and play become interwoven, and this orientation allows for relaxed attitudes toward work. Work often is taken casually and becomes mixed with personal lives. The difference in values, norms, and expectations concerning work can create serious problems in intercultural communications for Americans when the distinction between work and play is absent.

Efficiency and Practicality.   Non-Western cultures frequently have a very different view than Westerners of efficiency and practicality. These concerns usually are secondary to aesthetic and ritualistic aspects of society as well as to interpersonal relationships and group rather than individual orientations. Direct goal accomplishment in these cultures may be subordinated by concerns for collective approaches to problems and tasks. In such cultures as the Japanese, decisions may be made through protracted highly ritualistic interactions among many people. In these interactions, direct approaches to the problem are avoided; the conversations constantly seem to skirt the issue at hand. But, eventually everyone knows when the decision has been reached and what it is even though it may never have been stated explicitly.

Progress and Change.   American culture is well known for its future orientation and positive evaluation of progress and change. In non-technological societies, there is greater emphasis on the present or the past than on the future. Many American Indian cultures, for instance, are concerned primarily with the present. Indians, of course, are aware of the past and anticipate the future, but what is important to them is the "now." Other cultures are tied to the past. In Korea, ancestor worship is common, and reverence for old age and its accompanying experience and wisdom is common to many traditional cultures. In addition, in many cultures, the ways of the past are valued highly, and attempts to induce change for the sake of "progress" are met with resistance. In intercultural settings, differences in the view toward and value of progress and change can cause many difficult problems.

Time Orientation

Time orientation is another dominant pattern subject to cultural variation. Every culture must deal with the conceptions of past, present, and future. But they can differ greatly over which aspect is predominant. The past, as reflected in custom, tradition, and the way it always has been done, is more important to Easterners than to Westerners.

Time orientation is also concerned with how people schedule their time and the importance they place on being punctual. Western people's lives are controlled by schedules and time slots. Few Eastern cultures are concerned with punctuality. Time of arrival is also an issue affected by a culture's time orientation. When asked "what time should we come to dinner?" the American tends to give two forms of response. If the invitation is sincere, the American specifies a particular time. In other circumstances, the response "anytime" will be used to designate a noninvitation that has been given only to be polite but is not intended to produce an actual event. On the other hand, in traditional Greek culture, villagers use the term "anytime" quite literally to mean the invited guest will be welcome *any time*. The Greeks believe that placing a limit on when a guest can come would be an insult to someone who is important enough to be invited to dinner.

Human Nature Orientation

In Chapter 3 we looked at the goodness, rationality, and mutability of human nature as they manifest themselves in American culture. Now we will see how these dimensions of human nature function in other cultures.

Goodness of Human Nature.   Contrary to the dominant American orientation that humankind has an essentially evil but perfectible nature, many non-Western cultures assume human nature to be essentially good or a mixture of good and evil. Since cultures that view human nature as being essentially good are quite limited, we will concentrate on the good-and-evil orientation.

Most Oriental cultures hold humanity to be an intricate part of the universe, which is seen as an infinite system of elements and forces in balanced dynamic interaction. Two of the forces present in the universe are good and evil. Since humanity is part of the universe, these forces also are naturally present in humankind.

Eastern Taoist tradition tells of the interrelated forces of Yang and Yin, which from a Western perspective can loosely be seen as the forces of good and evil. These forces, present throughout the universe, also are present in all humans. Yang and Yin are cyclic; they go through natural periods of balanced increase and decrease. Periodic increases in Yang are accompanied by corresponding decreases in Yin. This is followed by an opposite cycle in which Yin increases while Yang decreases. This view of the good and evil nature of humanity extends to the position that people cannot eliminate evil because it is a natural and necessary part of the universe. To go a step further, both forces are necessary because one is not discernible without the other. Good can only be recognized against a background of evil, and evil is only recognizable against a background of good. The elimination of evil, therefore, is not desirable—even if it were possible—because without evil humanity could not recognize good.

The differences between American and non-American views can pose problems in intercultural encounters because of the different values, attitudes, and behaviors these orientations can produce. The American view is active; it leads to goodness-producing behavior that actively seeks to eliminate evil. Non-American views, on the other hand, are more passive; they recognize the cyclic effect of good and evil and realize that in due time evil quite naturally gives way to the force of good. For humankind to interfere with the natural cyclic process of the universe is both foolish and a waste of time.

Rationality of Human Nature. In most instances involving intercultural communication, the participants possess and follow rational thought processes. Although there are cultural groups who subscribe to what we might call mystical or occult approaches to knowledge, these people primarily are members of small fringe groups in a society or are members of primitive cultures.

When considering modern cultures, almost everyone would agree that their culture follows rational processes and that human nature, if not essentially rational, possesses a rational dimension. However, the image or concept of rational is subject to cultural variation. As we use the term here, it refers to reaching logical and valid conclusions from the information at hand and from the metaphysical assumptions prevalent in the culture. To understand the rationality in any culture, we must understand the premises upon which it is based. American and European cultures tend to follow a system of logic based upon Aristotelean principles. Other cultures follow such principles as Yang and Yin. Awareness of the principles, premises, and assumptions present in other cultures enables us to understand that people from other cultures who do not readily grasp our line of reasoning are not necessarily being irrational.

Mutability of Human Nature. We previously recognized the American view that human nature can be changed. This view, however, is not universal; in some cultures people believe that human nature is a part of the total universe and that while it shows individualized or cyclic change, in the long run it remains generally constant. This difference in view leads to differences in how social institutions function within various cultures. The American view sees social institutions such as schools, churches, and government agencies having a role of changing and improving human nature. Other cultures see the role of institutions to develop the human to its potential but not seek change in the nature of humanity.

Perception of the Self

Although the self is a very important concept in American culture, it is not as central in many non-Western cultures. As in American culture, the perception of self in other cultures helps define the concepts of individualism and self-motivation.

Individualism. The concept of self is in part defined by a cultural dimension bound by individualism and collectivism. All cultures reflect a dominant pattern that specifies the cultural location of self within this dimension. In most non-American cultures, the group is the primary social entity. Russian communes, Israeli kibbutzes, and other social collectivities give primary emphasis to the group and to group needs rather than to individuals. Soviet society places strong emphasis upon the group or collectivity, deriving its conception of the relationship between the individual and the state from communist doctrine. Under this doctrine, the individual has little significance except within the context of the group, which provides him with the necessities of life in return for certain obligations, which the individual undertakes to assist in the support and maintenance of the group. In another view of the self, many Oriental cultures hold that the task of the individual is to deny the importance of the self so that the ego does not impose upon others nor interfere with an individual's pursuit of life. Many elements of Buddhist philosophy are concerned with teaching devotees the proper mental states in which the ego is lost.

Self-motivation. Self-motivation is tied very closely to the concept of self and is related directly to individualism. As we saw in the preceding chapter, high levels of self-motivation are distinctly American.

In cultures where the group is favored over the individual, self-motivation in the sense of individual development and success is also minimized. This does not imply that people in collective-emphasizing cultures lack motivation to work or to achieve. On the contrary, people in collective environments can be affected by a collective spirit and be very industrious and hardworking. The difference is the goal direction of the work. Americans tend toward development of the self often at the expense of the group or others while people in collective emphasizing cultures devote themselves to group goals often sacrificing self for group benefit. In these non-American cultures, competition is minimized because there is little or no emphasis placed on individual striving and success.

Social Organization

This cultural pattern refers to the patterns of social relationships in a society, to the hierarchical system, and to the organization of a society or social group. The structure of a culture manifests itself in many ways. In India, the distinguishing form of status is caste. In the United States, it is skin color with a color bar still existing in most Western cultures. In another instance of structure, the United States makes a distinct separation between religion and state. Other cultures combine the two systems integrating them in the conduct of state affairs.

Social organization also specifies levels of a society and freedom of movement, if any, between the levels. This hierarchy frequently has its legitimizing basis in references to ancient books and prophets. Although Western cultures have well-defined hierarchies, there is a prevailing belief—substantiated by occasional examples of accomplishment—that through industry and hard work one can move freely to higher levels upon one's own merit. Social status in Eastern cultures is more static with birth position tending to predict status.

Social class and caste systems often lead to social prejudices that separate members of cultures. Children learn from their parents that they are superior or inferior because of where they live, their skin color, or their caste. A child's experience when growing up in a particular level of society helps to determine the roles it will play and the communication style it will use as an adult. More static cultures tend to have greater respect for persons of high status because of the limited social movement. Western cultures have less culturally based respect for status or station because of the greater mobility between social levels and the idea that any one can attain high status.

Another aspect of social organization is the number of groups to which one belongs. Americans tend to be joiners, to be members of many groups based on form or activity. The depth of commitment to these groups and their members is very weak, and memberships and people move freely from group to group. In Eastern cultures, people belong to only a few groups, and it is virtually a lifetime commitment.

Social organization also specifies roles for members of a culture. In non-Western cultures it is generally true that the woman's role is to serve the man. This often includes doing hard physical work and subordinating herself to the man. In Western cultures—even in the face of

99

the women's movement—the general relationship is one in which women are treated much like children: weak, immature, less intelligent, and more emotional. In South African tribal cultures, women generally are responsible for the cultivation of land and the raising of crops. Men keep the livestock. Children raise poultry and, when old enough, herd goats, sheep, and finally cattle.

Within the structure of most non-American societies are two dominant forces. These are the family and religious institutions.

Family.   The core of any culture is its family structure. This unit probably varies more among cultures than any other variable. Yet within cultures, the family unit has the smallest variation. We can therefore use the family as a foundation for cross-cultural comparisons.

A major function of the family is to socialize new members of a culture. As children are raised in a family setting they learn to become members of the family as well as members of the larger culture. The family provides the model for all other relationships in society. A first task in this process of socialization is to teach the child "proper behavior." This ranges from learning where to defecate to how to hold properly one's fork, spoon, or chopsticks. Expressions of affection are a part of proper behavior and the child learns very early how to expect and to express affection.

Through the observations and modeling of the behavior of other family members, children learn about the family and society including the values of the culture. When a child hears its parents levy criticism against some individual, group, or institution, it learns to believe that people have the right to levy such criticism. In democratic cultures, the child learns the right of the individual to express himself and the freedom to criticize. In most authoritarian cultures the child is impressed with the limits of such expression.

Young family members also learn how to be adults by observing and playing the roles of adults. In Asian countries, children find the father is the head of the family and his authority is accepted by everyone in the family. The male child learns authoritarianism by acting as his father does. The female child, likewise, learns to be subservient by emulating her mother.

Family structure and their inherent relationships and obligations are a major source of cultural difference. Eastern families tend to be extended. People live in family compounds or in other communal arrangements, and the individual's primary obligations are toward the whole family. In India, for example, when a couple are married, they most likely will live with the family of the husband in what is called a joint family. The couple's adjustment to and acceptance by the husband's family and village is essential to a successful Indian marriage.

Western families tend to be nuclear. Immediate families live in units that are physically separated from other relatives. Loyalties and obligations are limited primarily to the immediate family. Personal gain and intrafamily competition are encouraged. Social and legal systems legitimize equal opportunity, equal access, and personal independence.

The influence of family structure, organization, and relationships is felt strongly in intercultural communication. The family influences strongly the values, beliefs, behaviors, and expectations of its members. As these differences come in contact with one another in intercultural contacts, the conditions for confusion, misunderstanding, and conflict are present and active.

Religious Institutions.   Religion plays an extremely influential role in people's lives. This fact was dramatically demonstrated in Guyana by members of the People's Temple. *Church* as we use the word refers to all religious institutions be they Christian, Islamic, Hindu, Buddhist, Jewish, Shinto, or any other. Our concern is with the effects of institutionalized religion on the lives of people. As religions vary from culture to culture, churches differ and thus exert a variety of influences.

The church is a primary source of values, customs, and beliefs that are taught to children by both parents and priests. These influences are closely associated with the written teachings of the Bible, the Koran, the Torah, the various Sutras, the I Ching, and various Confucian, Taoist, and Shinto teachings. Religious beliefs, embodied in the church, affect one's values deeply and mostly unconsciously.

Religious influences pass beyond family structures and influence the entire fabric of society. Business and politics, as well as individuals and households, are subject to religious influence. This influence in business and politics is both unconscious, in terms of values and ethical considerations, and conscious—attending church enhances prestige in the community and helps in business or politics by projecting an image of high ethical standards.

In some cultures the influence of a church is enhanced by the declaration of an official religion. Unlike the United States where great pains have been taken to ensure religious freedom and separation of church and state, many countries have an official religion—Islam in Pakistan, Saudi Arabia, and Iran, Judaism in Israel, Catholicism in Ireland, and the Church of England in England. State policies are shaped by the teachings of the religion and by the religious leaders in these cultures. Frequently the priest or other church leader is the community opinion leader. They teach the people whom to vote for, what products to buy, and what social values to accept and to reject.

The political impact of religious views is obvious. The Catholic church maintains diplomatic ties with many nations where the Vatican ambassador is accorded the same prestige and influence as national diplomats. Religious views on social issues are very apparent, and politicians, whether elected, appointed, or otherwise placed in power, are wise to heed the voice of the church.

In many cultures the church or temple is the center of social activities. This is particularly true in rural areas where the church may be the only place where social life takes place. In large urbanized areas, the role of the church as the center of social life is diluted by the competition of secular centers.

A variety of holidays and festivals are found in different cultures that permit religions to reinforce their values and teachings. Christmas, Easter, and Buddha's birthday present such occasions. Symbolic representations of religious values are prominently displayed in public places, which reinforces these values.

In order to see how religious philosophy, traditions, and values can differ between cultures, we will make a brief examination of Zen Buddhism. Zen is concerned with the development of complete awareness. Salvation comes through development of this awareness, and anything that is an obstacle to it must be avoided. "In Zen, anything that interferes with the freedom of the individual experience is abhorred. Dualistic reasoning, subject-object duality, and attachment to form are all considered to hinder a free experiencing of reality by their constricting effects on awareness and openness to experience."[9]

Zen approaches these obstacles by what is called *no-thought*. In this process the mind functions on its own, free from thoughts about the environment, objects of consciousness, ideas of good and bad, and established forms and practices. No-thought avoids the intermediate effect of such thoughts on behavior. Zen teaches that behavior should follow from a spontaneous functioning of the organism. In such a state of a free mind, we are capable of marvelous deeds.

Trust in one's own experience and intuition is a main teaching of Zen. Through intuitive processes one obtains an indirect perception of the deeper meanings and possibilities inherent in all things. As reality may be something other than the words or concepts we use to describe it, we can only get to it by intuitively focusing our minds and allowing them to work on their own.

In contrast to Western traditions of dualism where from Aristotle we hold that anything is either A or not-A, Zen denies this dualistic thought. In brief, Zen provides a way of perceiving the world that utilizes intuition and the direct experiencing of reality. This achievement is called *satori*, which literally means enlightenment. *Satori* is a difficult state to obtain, characterized by a full participation in reality.

Summary

In this chapter we discussed some of the obstacles to learning about other cultures, such as projected cognitive similarity, stereotyping, and ethnocentrism, and gave some suggestions for helping to overcome these obstacles. We also discussed the importance of location and history to cultural development and then examined some dominant patterns in other cultures, with respect to world view, activity orientation, time orientation, human nature orientation, perception of the self, and social organization.

Notes

1. Fidel T. Masao, "Letter to *The Times*," *Los Angeles Times,* 23 April, 1979, part II, p. 12.

2. Seymour Fersh, "Observations Through the Cultural Looking Glass" in Seymour Fersh, ed., *Learning About People and Cultures* (Evanston, Ill.: McDougal & Littell, 1974), p. 35.

3. John E. Walsh, "Thoughts About 'Thought and Expression' in Culture and Learning" in Richard W. Brislin, ed., *Topics in Culture Learning,* vol. 1 (Honolulu: East-West Center, 1973), p. 3.

4. Yu-Kuang Chu, "Six Suggestions for Learning about Peoples and Cultures," in Seymour Fersh, ed., *Learning About Peoples and Cultures* (Evanston, Ill.: McDougal & Littell, 1974), pp. 51–55.

5. Gordon W. Allport, *The Nature of Prejudice* (New York: Doubleday, 1958), p. 97.

6. Chu, pp. 53–54.

7. Fersh, p. 35.

8. K.S. Sitaram and Roy T. Cogdell, *Foundations of Intercultural Communication* (Columbus, Ohio: Charles E. Merrill, 1976), p. 51.

9. Emanuel M. Berger, "Zen Buddhism, General Psychology and Counseling Psychology," in Paul Pedersen, ed., *Readings in Intercultural Communication,* vol. 4 (Pittsburgh: Society for Intercultural Education, Training and Research, 1974), p. 15.

Additional Readings

Bochner, Stephen. "The Mediating Man and Cultural Diversity," in Richard W. Brislin, ed., *Topics in Cultural Learning,* vol. 1. Honolulu: East-West Center, 1973.

Chu, Yu-Kuang. "Six Suggestions for Learning about Peoples and Cultures," in Seymour Fersh, ed., *Learning About Peoples and Cultures*. Evanston, Ill.: McDougal & Littell, 1974.

Condon, John C. and Fathi S. Yousef. *An Introduction to Intercultural Communication*. Indianapolis and New York: Bobbs-Merrill, 1975.

Fersh, Seymour, ed. *Learning About Peoples and Cultures*. Evanston, Ill.: McDougal & Littell, 1974.

Mead, Margaret. *Culture and Commitment: A Study of the Generation Gap*. Garden City, New York: Natural History Press/Doubleday, 1970.

Prosser, Michael H. *The Cultural Dialogue: An Introduction to Intercultural Communication*. Boston: Houghton Mifflin, 1978.

Sarbaugh, L.E. *Intercultural Communication*. Rochelle Park, N.J.: Hayden Book Company, 1979.

Sitaram, K.S. and Roy T. Cogdell. *Foundations of Intercultural Communication*. Columbus, Ohio: Charles E. Merrill, 1976.

Concepts and Questions

1. How can we best become aware of other cultures?

2. What are the six most significant things to know about another culture before trying to communicate with members of that culture?

3. How can we apply Chu's six suggestions for learning about cultures? Can you think of other ways of learning about cultures?

4. What significant roles do location and history play in the development of a culture?

5. What are the differences between an individual-oriented and a group-oriented culture? How might these differences affect intercultural communication?

6. How do differing religious viewpoints affect a culture's world view?

7. How might differences in orientations toward work and play affect intercultural communication?

8. What influence does the family unit have on how children learn a culture? How do differences in family structure affect intercultural communication?

Exercises

1. List the ten most important cultural characteristics of a foreign culture with which you feel familiar. Try to determine how you learned

these characteristics. Check the accuracy of these characteristics by discussing them with (a) someone from that culture, and (b) some American who has recently lived or worked in that culture. Did you learn some new things about the culture from your discussions with these two types of persons?

2. Talk with a foreign student from a country less familiar to you. Try to learn about the major cultural patterns of this culture. What difficulties did you experience in understanding this culture? Did you feel that you were often comparing that culture with your own? Did you experience some ethnocentrism?

3. Interview some faculty members who have worked abroad. Ask them to identify the most important factors about the foreign culture that facilitated their work abroad and the most important factors that inhibited their work. Try to identify the relationship between the facilitators and inhibitors. If you find it difficult to see any relationships between these factors, ask someone from that culture to explain to you how these factors are interrelated.

4. Ask a social studies teacher at a junior high school in your community: (1) what foreign cultures are included in the social studies curriculum, (2) what books are used for teaching about these foreign cultures, (3) what audio-visual materials are used for teaching about these cultures, and (4) what training did the teacher receive about the foreign cultures. Write a brief report about the teaching of foreign cultures at this junior high school along with some suggestions to improve it.

5. Read a few news articles about a particular foreign country. Try to determine what you learned about the culture of the foreign country involved. Now try to read more about the culture of this particular country. Reread the same articles. Did you notice any difference in your level of comprehension and appreciation between the first and second reading? Did your cultural knowledge facilitate your understanding of the news articles? What are the implications of this experience for Americans interested in learning about international events?

5

Intercultural Perception: Differing Images

> Members of different cultures look differently at the world around them. Some believe that the physical world is real. Others believe that it is just an illusion. Some believe everything around them is permanent while others say it is transient. Reality is not the same for all people.
>
> K. S. Sitaram and Roy T. Cogdell

We now will examine the influence that one's perception of the world, its people, things, and events has on intercultural communication. Understanding and appreciating differences in perception are crucial if we are to improve our ability to get along with people of other cultures. We must understand the workings of perception in general before we can see its relationship to culture. We will begin, therefore, with an introduction to perception theory as a basis for understanding the relationship between culture and perception.

Fundamentals of Perception

The Role of Perception

Perception is the process by which we maintain contact with the world around us. Because we usually are capable of hearing, seeing, smelling, touching, and tasting, we can sense our environment; we can be aware of what happens outside of us. In actuality, what we do is create internal images of the physical and social objects and events that we encounter in our environments.

Everything we sense impinges on us in a form of raw energy: what we see is light transmitted to us in the form of electromagnetic radiation; what we hear arrives in the form of differential air pressures. Our taste and smell are the result of various molecules coming in contact with our mouths and noses, and what we feel or touch is really various forms of energy pressing on our bodies. These energies carry no inherent experience for us. Experience, as we speak of it here, is each of us making sense out of our environment through the development of structure, stability, and meaning for our perceptions. This development involves internal operations that we perform by converting these impinging energies into electrochemical, neurophysiological impulses that we route through our nervous system to our brains, where we convert them into meaningful experiences.

These internal perceptual operations are learned. We are born with the physical apparatus essential to perception just as we are born with the physical capability for walking. In both cases, though, we must learn how to do it. We must learn to create personal experience out of the various energies that we encounter.

Structure. If we close our eyes, turn our heads, and open our eyes, we experience immediately a structured and organized environment. At any instant our world appears as coherent and ordered. We are able immediately to have an image of our environment whether it is through an individual perceptual channel or some combination of channels. The social and physical objects and events we encounter are not perceived as jumbles of reflected or vibrated energy; they instantly have size, shape, texture, tone, intensity, as well as many other characteristics. Our image of our environment is the outcome of our selves being actively engaged in information processing, which includes the selection and categorization of inputs. We give structure to the stimuli of our external world by translating raw stimulus energies into structured experience. We develop this structure-forming capacity by learning categories into which we force the external stimulation.

We do not all use the same categories for classifying our environment. Our categories are dependent on our past history, language, and culture. Although some categories are widespread and well agreed upon within a particular social community, they are never universal. The physical energies that will be transformed into the category house, for instance, differ considerably from an Eskimo resident of the Alaskan tundra to a Hollywood movie star living in Beverly Hills, to an Arab nomad living in the desert of Saudi Arabia. Consequently, the category that emerges from these energies will vary considerably from one locale to another, and so will the internal mental image of what constitutes a home.

Social or physical objects may fall into various structures depending on our immediate needs. Function, for instance, may serve us as a category. When we are buying a new pen, we may have a particular category that includes specific color, size, shape, ink color, writing quality, and other such attributes. But, when we are in a hurry to write down an important telephone number, a pen, a stubby dull pencil, or a piece of chalk all may simultaneously fit the immediate functional category of writing implement.

Two other important aspects of categorization are stereotypes and prejudices. Because they are so very important to intercultural communication, we will postpone discussion of them until the end of this chapter.

Stability. Our structured world of perceptions has endurance. We do not see it as a constantly changing jumble of sights, sounds, odors, tastes, and pressures.

Even though the inputs that provide our perceptions vary, our world remains fairly constant. As we move closer to someone, we tend not to notice the apparent change in their size, unless, of course, we come eyeball-to-eyeball. Through experience, we know that a person's height is constant, and we, therefore, keep them constant in our image even though the size of the image focused in our eye changes with distance. If we move closer to a sound source, we only notice changes when we have moved a considerable distance closer. Moving throughout our house, we internally keep the sound of music coming from our radio constant, even though it changes as we approach or move away from the radio. Even though our sensory organs are quite sensitive, we are capable of internally smoothing out moderate changes in input so the outside world appears constant. We cannot, however, smooth out wide variations; gross differences will be apparent, and if the stimulus changes we may notice the change.

Meaning. The notion of meaning refers to the fact that our structured and stable perceptions are not isolated from one another, but are related over time. If they were not, then every perceptual input would be new; we would constantly be in a state of surprise, and nothing would ever seem familiar.

Meaning develops from past learning and experience within a framework of purposive activity. We learn to develop rules for the purposes we seek to accomplish. Using these rules we operate as active stimulus event processors; we categorize events and relate them to past and present events. We become active problem-solvers in the pursuit of meaning for our environment. And, we eventually learn to give meaning to our perceptions that makes sense in relation to our past experiences, to our present actions and purposes, and to our anticipations of the future.

An essential property of meaning is a linguistic coding system. Through our language facility we are able to take the raw materials provided by external stimulation and produce meaning by naming and defining their categories. Eventually, we learn to code linguistically our experiences so that we can recall them, manipulate them, share them with others, and relate them to other experiences through our use of words that represent our experiences and come to stand for them. Meaning, then, becomes tied to our language facility, and depends on our use of words to describe it.

Perception, as we can see, is an active, internal process. It is what communication theorists refer to as proactivity, and it can be defined as "the process through which we become aware of our environment by organizing and interpreting the evidence of our senses."[1]

Dimensions of Perception

What we have seen so far is that the perception of our physical and social environments is an internal operation where we take stimulus energies as they arrive and process them through our nervous systems and brain until we create structure, stability, and meaning for them. Our description has been one of internal operations that must take place without regard to how they occur. For us to understand how we develop structure, stability, and meaning for external energies, we must consider two fundamental aspects of perception: the *physical* (organizing) and *psychological* (interpreting) dimensions. These two dimensions, working in conjunction with one another, are responsible for our perceptual outcomes, and a knowledge of them gives us a picture of how perception takes place.

Physical Dimensions of Perception. Although the physical dimension is an important phase of perception, for our purposes it is the initial phase and offers us the least amount of help in our search for improved intercultural communication. We shall, therefore, examine only briefly a few concepts.

The physical dimension of perception describes our acquisition of information about the outside world. This initial stage includes the energy characteristics of stimulation, the nature and function of human receptor mechanisms (eyes, ears, nose, mouth, and skin), and the transmission of sense data through the nervous system to the brain. As we can see, this stage is basically concerned with the external world and with our neurophysiological, electrochemical representations of it.

When a stimulus arrives via the senses, it must reach the brain so it can be converted to a usable form. The physical phase of perception has the job of beginning that conversion. What the human body does, on the neurophysiological level, remains fairly constant from one person to another and from one culture to another. All people have essentially the same anatomical and biological mechanisms that connect them with their environments, and the differences that do exist between one person and another are inconsequential when compared to the differences that exist in the psychological stage of perception.

Psychological Dimensions of Perception. Our individual make-up (personality, intelligence, education, emotions, beliefs, values, attitudes, motives, etc.) has much more impact on how we perceive our environment and how we behave in regard to it than does our physical handling of stimuli. It is during this phase that we create structure, stability, and meaning for our perceptions and put our own unique personal touch and interpretation on the outside world. Our psychological make-up enables us to tinker with and even fictionalize our views of the world.

We are bombarded constantly by incoming messages. At this moment some of the following information might be headed for our brains: the words we now are reading, the room temperature, the feel of the chairs we are sitting on, the feeling of the pens in our hands, the sight of a small bird sitting on a tree limb, the ticking of our clock, the sunset outside our window, the workmen mowing the lawn outside, the tapping of our feet, the taste of the gum we are chewing, and possibly the smell of smoke from our cigarettes. These are but a few of the countless signals arriving at our brains simultaneously and waiting to be processed—waiting to be given meaning. We do not and cannot process all arriving message stimuli. Rather, we select some of them to pay attention to and we ignore the others.

We obviously cannot attend to all messages in our environment. We must be selective. Our selections normally are made unconsciously in fractions of seconds. The decisions we make about what will arouse and hold our attention and hence receive meaning are related directly to our culture. In most instances we have learned as individuals and as members of a particular culture what is important and to what we will pay attention. This cultural influence on the outcome of perceptual process was demonstrated in a classic study by James Bagby. Mexican children and children from the United States viewed, for a split-second, stereograms in which one eye was exposed to a baseball game while the other was exposed to a bullfight. In the main, the children reported seeing the scene according to their culture; Mexican children tended to see the bullfight and American children tended to see the baseball game.[2] The children made certain selections based on their background; they tended to see and to report that which was most familiar, expected, and culturally related, and to ignore the other. This is known as selectivity.

Selective Perception

Because selectivity is such an important part of perception, we will explore three closely related ways in which we selectively perceive our world: (1) selective exposure, (2) selective attention, and (3) selective retention.

Selective Exposure. We often avoid perceiving particular aspects of our environment simply by not putting ourselves in a position to encounter them. Similarly, we also may deliberately look for situations in order to perceive certain things. Examples of both of these phenomena, selective nonexposure and selective exposure, may help us understand their nature.

In a research study on selective exposure, subjects who had just bought new cars were observed and their reading habits noted. The question was, did the subjects read only the advertisements touting the car they had purchased or did they also read ads for cars they had considered initially but did not buy? The results revealed that people who had just bought a new car did, in fact, selectively expose themselves to ads about the car they bought far more than to ads for the rejected cars. They sought out and exposed themselves to information that would reinforce their decision to buy a particular car.[3] The selective avoidance of certain types of information also seems equally likely, but experimental evidence of this point is scant. Our own experience, however, should bear this out. For example, if we know someone who has bad news or will cause us trouble, do we actively seek out that person? How many of us have not hidden from our father, at least once, when we were a child, knowing he would be angry when he got home? When a person arrives at our door to sell us something or to talk about a particular political candidate, are we not more likely to talk with the person if he or she is selling something we wish to buy or is supporting a candidate we favor? Clearly, all of us selectively expose ourselves to some messages and situations and avoid others.

We not only physically expose ourselves to certain messages and avoid others, but in a given context we are selectively *vigilant* or *defensive* toward certain cues or types of information. From the variety of information available to us in the environment, because we desire to receive only certain cues, we are more sensitive to them. Similarly, as there also are cues we do not want to receive, we are less sensitive to them; indeed, we often try consciously to ignore them. For example, when an actress reads the reviews of her latest film, she will probably have a perceptual set to seek positive reinforcement (increased vigilance for positive information) and a perceptual set to filter out negative information (increased defensiveness to negative information). In other words, she will more likely admit statements of praise to her consciousness and avoid admitting statements of negative criticism. Both forms of perceptual behaviour are forms of selective exposure.

Selective Attention.   We can all remember having been very hungry and found ourselves focusing on the food words and pictures in a movie, or been worried about an exam and viewed everything in relation to the subject area in which we were being tested, or anxious about a family member's health and noted only the medical shows on television. We were giving selective attention to just one piece of our environment. At any time in any given environment, we are more or less tuned to specific types of information. We listen more acutely to certain segments of a conversation, speech, or newscast than we do to others. As a result of our being tuned in to a specific type of information, we are quite likely to become senders of messages relative to that information. A dieter, for example, may become very sensitive to food commercials on television and may yell at his or her partner, "Turn that damn TV off." Why do we selectively attune to some stimuli and not to others? Very simply because we have to. Our environment is far too vast and complex for us to attend to more than a small portion of it; we cannot pay attention to everything. Although we may seem to pay attention to many things simultaneously, there is a large body of scientific evidence that suggests we can only pay conscious attention to one thing at a time, but that we can shift our attention at the rate of about five times per second. This rapid shifting ability gives us the illusory sense of stimultaneous attention, but actually we are limited to about 300 perceptual items each minute. And, considering that we return to various items frequently each minute—we can hardly miss an entire minute of a concert and be paying attention to it—we cannot attend to very much at one time. Because our environment is vast, complex, and dynamic, we lack the perceptual ability to be fully aware of it. Since we are limited in this way, a relevant question is: Which psychological factors determine selective attention and how is it determined? Among the many factors are four that are influenced strongly by culture that stand out as being particularly important: *needs, training and experience, expectations*, and *attitudes*.

The most basic psychological factor in selective attention is *individual need*. Earlier we recalled a situation in which we were very hungry and attended to food-related cues in a movie. This example illustrates how our need levels direct our perception. The need (hunger) directed our attention toward cues with need satisfaction potential and away from others that lacked this potential. There are many psychological needs that can cause our attention to be directed toward select aspects of our environment. Four of our most common needs are independence, sex, social approval, and achievement. These develop within us for a variety of reasons, and our culture plays a dominant

112

role in their development. All things being equal, we tend to perceive and respond to these particular needs because they are a part of our cultural heritage. A few examples will help clarify this point. In the United States independence is a compelling need. Consequently many parents and grandparents are sent to live in convalescent and retirement homes to protect the independence of the children. In Japan, however, where independence is not so important, parents and grandparents are encouraged to live with their children. Even the need for achievement is perceived differently in some cultures. The U.S. Army in Vietnam often had trouble making the native tribesmen see the need to fight. For us victory is a sign of achievement; this was not a need shared by all Vietnamese. When they looked at the fighting, they perceived something quite different. Their culture had simply prescribed a different hierarchy of needs.

Individual *training and experience* also cause us to focus our attention on one object rather than another. We may remember having taken a class from an English composition teacher who could spot immediately a misplaced comma or from a mathematics teacher who could see an arithmetic error at fifty paces. Because of their training, both teachers selectively attended to certain types of information. In addition to our training, both personal and cultural experiences may also result in a particular pattern of selectivity. For example, our personal past history may have included experiences that placed a high priority on clothes and personal appearance. Hence, when in an interaction, we will tend to select out and to perceive messages about appearance. As noted earlier, members of a culture also have had experiences that contribute to their specific selection of cues in the environment. An individual who is a member of a culture that stresses neatness, as do the Swiss and German cultures, will quickly select messages in the environment that reflect unsightliness.

Our *expectations* also might cause us to focus on or to ignore particular types of cues. If we expected a person to be kind, while our friend expected him or her to be unfriendly, we might attend to cues indicating friendliness and our friend would selectively attend to those indicating the opposite. Since we are both likely to find cues that prove we are right, each of us probably will arrive at the conclusion we expect. And, if we later discuss the interaction with our friend, we may feel perplexed wondering how our friend could arrive at such an obviously incorrect conclusion. As we shall see later, this form of selectivity is a major cause of ethnocentrism.

Our culture gives us many of our perceptual expectations. Our expectations about time, for example, reflect our culture, and this helps determine how we anticipate the manner in which others treat and respond to the clock. Cultures view time in a wide variety of ways. Americans tend to value it highly as something to be saved and not wasted. Hence, we expect people to be prompt in their appointments and to work efficiently. Other cultures do not value time in this manner. What is of value is the immediacy of experience. Being on time has no real meaning, and a statement like "I'll meet you at two o'clock" may mean that one intends to see the other some time that afternoon. When we operate within our cultural expectations, we may become upset, uncomfortable, and defensive because we have trouble predicting what will happen next. Our normal expectations about the future are invalid, and we are in the dark.

Our *attitudes* also will make us selective in our attention. Attitudes are inclinations and tendencies to respond in predetermined ways toward people, objects, and ideas. They are learned and hence usually reflect our culture. Like many items within our culture, attitudes are built over a period of time, and although they are fairly consistent they are subject to the same changes that characterize other aspects of perception.

In directing our attention, we tend to focus on those features in the environment that reinforce our existing attitudes. We see and hear what we are disposed to see and hear. If we deem intelligence important, we are apt to pay more attention to persons we deem intelligent than to those we view as somewhat dull. Even our attitudes toward women influence how we perceive them. In countries such as Saudi Arabia or Turkey, where women still occupy very traditional roles, they will be perceived and responded to quite differently than are women in America. And even in the United States where the role of women is undergoing rapid change, many people who still hold traditional attitudes respond negatively to women who espouse such notions as equal rights and affirmative action.

For a variety of psychological and situational reasons, we selectively attend to certain cues and not to others. Selectivity is necessary because we cannot handle all the stimuli that arrive at our brains for processing. Communicators, knowing this, try to present their messages in ways designed to attract and to maintain a receiver's attention. Given the number and importance of our needs, training and experience, expectations, attitudes, and the characteristics of stimuli, it is somewhat surprising when we do all pay attention to the same message stimulus.

Selective Retention. Some information is perceived, processed, and then forgotten, since we cannot retain all message stimuli we process. As a general rule, we retain information that is pleasant, favorable to our own self-image, fosters cognitive consistency, or is likely to be needed at a later time. For example, if we listen to a speech by a politician we like and he makes seven points (five of which we agreed with and two of which we disagreed with) it is likely that we will remember most of the points of agreement and few of the points of disagreement. Do we remember the names of any of our elementary school teachers? If we do, we probably liked those teachers and worked well in their classrooms. If we meet people at the bus station, are we more likely to remember their names if we believe we are going to meet them again, or if we believe we will never see them again? We all selectively retain information, and our selectivity operates generally to protect our psychological state—we remember what we want to remember and conveniently forget those things that might damage our self-image or cognitive consistency.

We have already noted that perception and culture are inseparable. For the full cycle of the perception process to take place, we must not only receive data but must respond to that data in light of our unique backgrounds. As has been stressed throughout this book, culture is a predominant part of our backgrounds. In order that we can better understand perceptual processes, we must sharpen our analysis and now focus on the direct relationship between culture and perception.

Perception and Culture

Culture and Perceptual Processes

The stimulation of sensory organs by environmental energies, the conversion of these energies into neurophysiological impulses, and their transmission to the brain are physical capacities everyone shares regardless of culture. But, when it comes to what we make of these impulses, "cultural factors may provide some of the meaning involved in perception and are, therefore, intimately implicated with that process."[4] The specific influence culture has on perceptual processes is difficult to calculate. Whether personal experience or cultural background is responsible for perceptual variations is often impossible to determine. A person's view of manhood may stem from having watched John Wayne movies as a cultural experience or from his father telling him that all animals experience pain and pleasure and, therefore, he should never hunt or use a gun. As we can see, it is difficult to know whether culture or personal experience formed this perception of manhood unless we know the individual concerned. In most instances, a combination of both elements contributes to one's view of reality. Because our interest primarily is intercultural communication, we shall consider individual personalities briefly, and then we shall spend the bulk of our time focusing on cultural aspects of perception and how they affect intercultural communication.

115

An important phase of perception involves our giving meaning to the objects and events in our environment. Objects and events can vary considerably in their ability to elicit meaning, and the meaning extended varies according to the individual and the individual's culture. Although identification and naming is a part of meaning attribution—often referred to as the objective part—there also is a subjective aspect. When encountering a tree, almost everyone agrees on the objective part of meaning, but what a tree means to any unique individual varies according to that individual's experiences and culture. Thus, a vegetarian who sees a slice of raw meat might become ill or find the object unsavory, while a meat eater can hardly wait to place the specimen on a barbecue. Each one attaches a personal subjective meaning to the object. Although the object is outside both of them, they have learned and internalized different personal meanings and responses for the external world.

The behaviors that follow from perceptions also are learned. Again, we might find the vegetarian turning away in disgust (an overt behavior) while the meat eater's mouth is watering in anticipation (another overt behavior). Turning away or licking one's lips are culturally learned expressions of disgust or anticipation.

This example is an extreme case for the sake of illustration. All perceptions, reactions, and behaviors by different people to the same stimulus object are not as divergent as that just described. Indeed, they often are quite similar, and the differences can be very hard to detect. We must keep in mind, however, that all individuals do have specialized and unique differences that force them to perceive the external world in highly personalized fashions. And, the greater the differences between people, the greater the disparity in their perceptions is likely to be. Consequently, two people with similar experiences tend to share a similar view of the world. Conversely, as was the case with the meat eater and the vegetarian, dissimilar backgrounds can call forth vastly different responses to the same object or event.

Culture, by exposing a large group of people to approximately similar experiences relative to other cultures, often has the effect of being a unifying force in the perception of the environment. A culture that values kindness above all else, for example, will perceive acts of violence differently than will a culture that stresses a survival-of-the-fittest orientation toward life. To one group a harsh word may be a violent act while to the other group a knife or a gun may be a common object used on a daily basis. The members of a culture share common experiences and, therefore, learn common behavior patterns. Through this cultural learning, they come to share common perceptions. Individual differences within a culture tend to be considerably less variable than differences that occur between cultures.

The amount of difference within a culture depends, in part, on the culture in which those individual experiences occur. A very diverse culture such as that found in the United States will produce much wider variation than will a small, geographic bound, narrow culture such as that which would be found in a monastery where neophytes enter as children and remain for their entire lives. Diverse cultures also will tend to develop smaller subcultures that share much of the pervading general culture but also take on characteristics unique to the group forming the subculture.

The intercultural communicator normally is confronted with people who do not share his or her perceptions of the external world, and who may respond to that world in a manner that is often hard to understand. The more diverse the cultures, the more bizzare the behaviors may appear. In England, for example, a person with good manners is perceived as someone with nonaggressive behavior in an interpersonal setting—someone who does not speak to strangers. In other cultures, such as the Arab, Italian, or Jewish, aggressive behavior during interaction is normal and, consequently, is perceived as highly desirable while a reserved attitude is a sign of bad manners. Even our nonverbal actions can be perceived differently from one culture to another. In the United States it is not uncommon to see men without their shirts walking in the streets or eating at public restaurants. In Hong Kong, on the other hand, shirts are never taken off in public places. The meaning attributed to a shirtless person is quite different in Hong Kong than in the United States. To many Chinese, a semi-dressed person in public is uncouth.

There is also research that demonstrates that cultural factors create differences in visual inference. Two people could disagree over a single event or an object because they actually perceived it differently. Disagreement about an event can occur within a culture as well. Who caused an accident, or which team played the hardest are typical events over which witnesses can and often do disagree. Our individual psyches cause us to see that which fits in with our personal perceptual sets. In these instances no amount of talking will alter the fact that two people, viewing the same external happening, "saw" two different events.

Many times cultural backgrounds influence the inferences people draw from a perceptual event. Take, for instance, a tree limb covered with snow breaking off a tree and falling to the ground. Two observers may rightly agree the event occurred, and they may describe it in identical objective terms. But, when asked to specify the cause of the limb breaking, which is the drawing of an inference from a perception, the two people might differ considerably. We, from the United States, would probably respond matter-of-factly that the limb broke because it was weak. Yet, a Taoist might say the limb broke because it was strong. Here is a clear-cut case of culture influencing the inferences that are drawn from perception. To the American, things break because they are weak or lack strength—everyone knows that: it is a cultural truism. Yet, to the Tao mind, that which is strong is weak, and that which is weak has strength. Because the tree limb was strong, it could not bend to the weight of the snow. Thus, the snow continued to accumulate until the limb could bear no more and it broke. Had the limb been weak, it would not have broken because it would have bent under the weight of the snow and allowed the snow to fall off before its weight became unbearable. Thus, for the Taoist, the limb broke because it was strong and could not bend or give.

Cultural influence on social perception can even operate on a very subtle level. In China, for example, the use of red ink in a letter means that the letter writer is unhappy with the idea being communicated or with the person to whom the letter is directed. Although the color red is perceived by the Chinese differently than by other cultures, this same color does have special meaning in cultures other than the Chinese. We in the United States, for instance, use red ink to indicate financial loss or an overdrawn checking account.

Culture and Perceptual Attributes

The influence of culture on perception processes is so pervasive that there seems to be very little agrement as to what specific areas of our perceptions are and are not touched by cultural experiences.

"Among these aspects are the cultural relationships of perception to language, art forms, belief, and personality factors. We could add thought-patterning and intelligence in general."[5] In addition can be added recognition and retention, the perception of space, illusions, physiognomic perception, and the perception of emotion. We will take a brief look at a few of these specific items to further highlight the inseparable issues of culture and perception.

Language. Although language will be dealt with specifically in the next chapter, it will be discussed here briefly as a way of demonstrating the fusion of language and culture as a part of perception. The central idea of the Sapir-Whorf hypothesis (see p. 49) is that language functions not simply as a device for reporting experience, but also, and more significantly, as a way of defining experience for its speakers. Meanings are "not so much discovered in experience as imposed upon it, because of the tyrannical hold that linguistic form has upon our orientation in the world."[6] What obviously is being suggested by this analysis is that our language and our culture work in tandem to shape our perceptions of reality. In short, a culture's language habits help to select and to define that culture's world.

Simply stated, a culture has no need for words or phrases for things that are not part of the environment or important in the environment. We name and we use what we see and what we think about. This is apparent in the words that are used to name the group of stars in the northern hemisphere that we in the United States call the Big Dipper; in other parts of the world it is known as the Big Bear or as the Big Plow. And, the phrase *bodysurfing* has no cultural value if that experience is not part of the culture's environment.

Recognition.   Another aspect of the interdependence between culture and perception is the influence culture has on what we learn to recognize. A vivid example of this influence of culture on recognition was revealed in the Bagby studies with children mentioned earlier. (See p. 110.) Even though both groups of children experienced equal exposure to the bullfight and baseball scenes, the Mexican children recognized the bullfight most frequently and the American children recognized the baseball game most often. The influence of the children's cultures on what they recognized was reflected in their perceptions.

Values.   Because perception deals with developing both objective and subjective meanings for people, events, and objects, a culture's hierarchy of values influences the perceptions of the people in that culture. Native American Indian cultures value age and the wisdom and maturity of thought that accompanies it. As a result, they have a long history of respecting and venerating their elderly. Contemporary American society tends to value youth. This value orientation is evident in the way we perceive people's age and in the myriad ways in which we attempt to camouflage our age through such devices as hair transplants, face-lifts, exercise, and wrinkle removing cream. When members of each culture are confronted with an aged person, their perception will reflect their values, and hence be different.

A similar case can be made for a culture's perception of the female members of that culture. Where a culture places its female members in its value hierarchy will affect how the woman is seen and will govern her behavior and the behavior of males toward her. In India, for instance, women are much lower in the value hierarchy than men. As a result, it is not uncommon for women to eat their meals separately after the men have been served and completed their meal. The cultural value system determines how women are seen, and it also prescribes their appropriate behavior. As long as women behave within the limits of the cultural value system, they will be perceived positively. If they were to behave contrary to their cultural values, they would be perceived differently and quite likely dealt with harshly. This same perceptual activity can be seen to some extent in the United States culture. The behavior of women who are seeking passage of the Equal Rights

Amendment has been upsetting to the value system of many men and women in the United States, and the way in which the ERA supporters are perceived and evaluated is directly related to the values of the perceivers.

A member of a culture that does not value language will not be aware of the nuances of language patterns and vocabulary, while a culture that deems language to be significant will produce individuals who are keenly cognizant of even the most subtle differences in speech, vocabulary, and pronunciation. Specific cases linking values to perceptions could fill an entire book, but for our purposes it is not the examples that are salient, but only the idea that what a culture believes to be important (or unimportant) will affect perception.

Space.   A recent news magazine carried a story telling how many Englishmen were troubled by the behavior of some of the Arabs who were living in London. It seemed that, among other things, the English, who instinctively queue up (line up) for all occasions, were bothered by the manner in which Arabs crashed into lines and disregarded the straight and rigid order of those lines. Here is a vivid example of how different cultures perceive the use of space—including personal space. The English value personal space very highly; members of that culture respect that space by following various conventions for the use of space—such as queueing up. The Arabs, who view space quite differently, respond to lines in what the English perceive to be an uncivil manner. Whether it be lines, space, distances, or shapes, each of our cultures has taught us how to perceive, evaluate, and give meaning to the various dimensions of our environment.

Person Perception.   Person perception is that aspect of social perception where we evaluate and give meaning to the people in our environment. " . . . the observer's needs, values, prejudices, hopes and expectations all exert a powerful influence on the activities of observing the other person and formulating conclusions concerning his nature, or structure."[7] The impact of culture on person perception ranges from the perception of friends to the judgment of beauty. To many Americans, a man wearing a plain gold chain around his neck might be perceived as "cool" or "with it," but that same object worn in China might be viewed as a ridiculous and ostentatious adornment. In our culture a beautiful woman or handsome man is generally slender, muscular, well-groomed, neat, and has no unusually obvious features (other than perhaps breasts in the case of women). Yet in other cultures plump people are perceived as beautiful while slender people are perceived as being sickly and unhealthy. Even the International Weight Watchers diet organization has to take culture into consideration. When the organization offers members their correct weight goals, they take into account how a particular culture perceives stoutness. Each country has a different set of standards and goals that the organization deems the correct weight for one to be attractive.

Emotion. Although there are many universal emotions (love, surprise, fear, anger, disgust, contempt, etc.), the display of these emotions, what motivates display, and how the emotions are perceived, are colored by our cultural experiences. We may, for example, have some difficulty in interpreting the fact that the Chinese scratch their ears and cheeks as a sign of happiness, while widening of their eyes constitutes a sign of anger. Even depression may be manifested differently among various cultures. There are countless other variations in emotional expression as we shift from culture to culture. We will say more about this in Chapter 7 when we discuss nonverbal communication.

Stereotypes and Prejudices

Through our perceptions, we create stability, structure, and meaning for the environment. We learn to name things and to develop categories whereby we may easily identify environmental objects and events and so fit them into our existing structures and meanings. As a means of category development, we learn stereotypes and prejudice.

Stereotypes and prejudice are interrelated concepts. Usually they occur together. A person holding stereotypes about a group also tends to have some prejudice toward that group. Stereotypes and prejudice are learned behaviors that tend to be self-perpetuating. Both affect intercultural perception and other aspects of intercultural communication, and both are affected by intercultural contacts. Let us examine briefly the meaning of stereotypes and prejudice, how they originate and persist, and how stereotypes and prejudice affect and are affected by intercultural communication.

Meaning of Stereotypes and Prejudice

Stereotypes.   What do we mean by stereotypes? What are some common examples of stereotypes? We have often heard stereotypes such as "blacks are lazy," "Jews are shrewd," and "American Indians are alcoholics." Each of these stereotypes involves a belief about a group of people, about a category. Also, each of these beliefs is an oversimplified, overgeneralized, or exaggerated statement. Some of these stereotypes might be totally false, some might be based on half-truths or might have a kernel of truth. Thus, *stereotypes are overgeneralized,* *oversimplified, or exaggerated beliefs associated with a category or group of people.* The holders of such beliefs are construed to be relatively rigid in their adherence, and the beliefs are often emotionally colored. A stereotype is not identical with a category; it is rather a fixed idea or belief that accompanies the category. ". . . the category 'Negro' can be held in mind simply as a neutral, factual, nonevaluative concept, pertaining merely to a racial stock. Stereotype enters when, and if, the initial category is freighted with 'pictures' and judgments of the Negro as musical, lazy, superstitious, or what not."[8]

The principal difference between stereotyping and social classification or *sociotyping* done in the social sciences is that stereotyping is an emotionally rigid process whereas sociotyping is a scientific process. The sociotype of a group or social category is flexible, and probabilistic, and it is revised as new data become available. For instance, when communication scholars compare self disclosure patterns of males and females, it is done on a statistical basis, the object being to ascertain the distinguishing characteristics of males and females, if any. Statistical generalizations for males and females are developed. Such statistical generalizations about a social category are called sociotypes. If our research showed that females are more self-disclosing than males we would consider this generalization to be a sociotype rather than a stereotype.

Stereotypes vary along several dimensions. First, they might vary in terms of their *direction*—favorable versus unfavorable. When people from countries that place a high value on hard work, ambition, and honesty say that Americans are hardworking, ambitious, and honest, they are expressing their positive stereotypes of Americans. Even for a given group (e.g., the Negro), a person may hold some positive and some negative stereotypes. Second, stereotypes vary in their *intensity*—how strongly a person believes in a given stereotype. For instance, "Negroes are very lazy" is a more intense or stronger stereotype than "Negroes are somewhat lazy." Third, stereotypes vary in their *accuracy*. Some stereotypes are totally false, some are half-truths, and some are only partially inaccurate. A common misconception about stereotypes is that they are always totally false or totally unfounded in fact. Although some stereotypes may be totally false, many stereotypes develop from a sharpening and overgeneralization of facts. Stereotypes may have a kernel of truth. For instance, it is historically true that certain Jews favored the crucifixion of Jesus. The stereotype sharpens this fact until the entire Jewish group in modern times becomes known as "Christ killers." Finally, stereotypes vary in their specific *content*—specific traits attributed to a group. All people do not hold the same set of stereotypes for a given group. Some white Americans for instance might view black Americans as lazy, superstitious, and happy-go-lucky, while other white Americans might view black Americans as religious, musical, and militant. Although there are some widely-shared stereotypes, there is considerable variation in the content of stereotypes for various racial, ethnic, and national groups in a large society like America. We also should remember that stereotype content changes over time.

Prejudice.   What is prejudice? How is it different from stereotypes? By derivation and connotation the term prejudice implies an advance judgment or prejudgment. In this sense prejudice would refer to judgment of a person before acquaintance with him. But prejudice is a special kind of prejudgment. Prejudgments become prejudices only if they are not easily reversible when exposed to new knowledge. A prejudice, unlike a simple prejudgment or misconception, is actively resistant to all evidence that would unseat it. We tend to become emotional when a prejudice is threatened with contradiction. Thus the difference between ordinary prejudgments and prejudice is that prejudgments are not rigid and can be rectified without emotional resistance. In the case of prejudice, the advance categorical judgment about a group or a member of that group is highly rigid and is difficult to modify. We define *prejudice as a rigid attitude toward a group, based upon erroneous beliefs or preconceptions.* This definition suggests the following characteristics of prejudice: (1) Prejudice is a categorical attitude, that is, it is an attitude toward a group or category of people, not toward a particular person. Interpersonal attitudes are irrelevant unless they are influenced by the group membership of the persons involved. If one's attitude toward another person is conditioned by the group membership of that person, then prejudice is involved. (2) Prejudice entails erroneous beliefs or preconceptions. It is based on oversimplified, overgeneralized, exaggerated, or erroneous ideas about a group of people. It is based on stereotypes rather than sociotypes, scientific facts, or factual evidence. Because of this, prejudice usually tends to be a misjudgment, that is, an inaccurate judgment about a group or a person belonging to that group. In this sense, it is an unfair, irrational attitude. (3) Prejudice is an emotionally rigid attitude. A prejudiced person is unwilling to modify or change his attitude even when the group or individual does not correspond to the preconceived image of the group. In this sense also, it is an irrational attitude. The emotional factor associated with its rigidity contributes to its irrationality.

The primary difference between prejudice and stereotypes is that prejudice is an *attitude* whereas stereotype is a belief. Like any other attitude, prejudice may involve a large number of beliefs or belief systems that form a relatively coherent cluster to produce a specific prejudiced attitude toward a group. Usually the belief system comprising a given prejudiced attitude includes many stereotypes about the group but the prejudice may also include other beliefs, values, attitudes, and elements to provide it coherence, rigidity, permanence, and emotional tone. Further, the belief system has a way of slithering around to justify the more permanent prejudiced attitude. The process is one of rationalization—of the accommodation of beliefs to attitudes.

Prejudice, like stereotypes, varies in terms of direction and intensity. It can be either positive or negative. We usually think of prejudice as a negative attitude toward a group, and in the absence of any qualification, the conventional meaning is intended in this book. It is this negative prejudice that seems to produce the most social friction. However, positive or love prejudice cannot be ignored entirely, because a favorable attitude toward one group is frequently associated with a hostile attitude toward some other groups. A positive prejudice toward the in-group and negative prejudice toward the out-group is the familiar pattern. Likewise, prejudice varies in terms of intensity. Some individuals hold much stronger prejudice against a group than others. In this sense, positive or negative prejudice could be viewed on a continuum ranging from very low intensity to high intensity of prejudice. Usually stronger stereotypes produce stronger prejudice.

Prejudice is expressed in many ways, which can be classified as five main types of overt expressions, depending upon the intensity of prejudice. (1) Antilocution—talking about one's negative attitudes, feelings, opinions, and stereotypes about the target group—is done mostly with friends but sometimes with strangers. (2) Avoidance leads the individual to avoid members of the disliked group, even perhaps at considerable inconvenience. (3) Discrimination—here the prejudiced person makes detrimental distinctions of an active sort; he undertakes to exclude all members of the group in question from certain types of employment, residential housing, political rights, educational or recreational opportunities, churches, hospitals, or from some other social privileges. Segregation is an institutionalized form of discrimination, enforced legally or by common custom. (4) Physical attack—under conditions of heightened emotion, prejudice may lead to acts of violence or semiviolence; for instance, an unwanted Negro family may be forcibly ejected from a neighborhood, or so severely threatened that it leaves in fear. (5) Extermination—lynchings, pogroms, massacres, and the Hitlerian program of genocide mark the ultimate degree of violent expression of prejudice.[9] Thus we find that stereotypes lead to prejudice and prejudice in turn leads to various types of overt behaviors. Each of these five types of overt expressions of prejudice has implications for intercultural communication. Also, these overt expressions of prejudice provide raw materials for further stereotyping and prejudice among various racial and ethnic groups. Now let us examine how we develop stereotypes and prejudice and how they are perpetuated over time.

Origin and Perpetuation of Stereotypes and Prejudice

How do we acquire stereotypes and prejudice? We are not born with them. They do not suddenly appear through instinct. Stereotypes and prejudices are learned just as other beliefs and attitudes are. They are learned and acquired in several ways. First, we learn stereotypes and prejudices from our parents, relatives, friends, and others with whom we interact frequently. Just as we learn language, values, attitudes, and beliefs from our family, teachers, and friends, so do we tend to adopt their stereotypes and prejudices for or against different racial, ethnic, and national groups. This tendency to develop stereotypes and prejudices through the experience of others is particularly strong when one has not had sufficient personal experience with the members of the group in question. Earlier it was stated that antilocution was a common form of expressing one's prejudice. Such antilocution among family members, like-minded friends, and others provides a fertile ground for developing stereotypes and prejudices.

Second, we also develop stereotypes and prejudices through personal experience. Having interacted with one or two members of a different racial, ethnic, or national group, we generalize to other members of that group a trait or series of traits that have impressed us. Once we have formed an impression about a group, we condition ourselves to look for these characteristics in future encounters with members of that group, and through selective perception we find those traits and thus we continue to reinforce and strengthen our stereotypes. These stereotypes provide the raw material for developing prejudice toward the group. Usually it is easier to develop stereotypes and prejudices about groups that have distinct, visible traits such as skin color, physical appearance, and race. The visibility of traits of a group aids immensely in the process of categorization and in developing prejudices and stereotypes about it. In this sense, cultural pluralism is a factor in developing stereotypes and prejudice. Since cultural pluralism implies coexistence and encouragement of distinct racial, ethnic, and cultural groups within a society, and these groups often have distinct visible traits, it has the potential for categorization, stereotyping, and prejudice. Individuals who do not believe in cultural pluralism are very likely to view distinct cultural traits of out-groups as justification for holding negative stereotypes and prejudices about such groups.

Finally, we learn stereotypes and prejudices through the mass media. Books, newspapers, magazines, motion pictures, radio, and television present us with oversimplified generalizations and stereotypes about most groups in our society. Each of us can think of many stereotypical roles portrayed for various racial and ethnic groups in mass media. Over a long period of time, these images begin to have lasting impact on our own image of these groups. Although there is a growing recognition of the problem of stereotyping in our mass media, and some attempts are being made to reduce stereotyping in the media, textbooks used in schools and mass media still are major contributors to developing stereotypes and prejudice about racial, ethnic, and national groups.

How do stereotypes and prejudice perpetuate and survive? As stated earlier, stereotypes and prejudice are rigid, emotional, and highly resistant to change. Once formed, they tend to persist. They tend to perpetuate by various selectivity processes: selective perception, selective interpretation, selective retention, selective recall, and selective relay. Stereotypes and prejudice structure our perception in such a way that we selectively perceive only those stimuli in a given situation that are consistent with our existing "pictures in our heads." Consciously, and more often unconsciously, people tend to notice and be impressed with facts that fit their preconceived images. If you have certain stereotypes about blacks, for instance, these stereotypes will affect your perception and other cognitive processes during your interaction with blacks, unless you are careful about your selectivity processes. One has to make a conscious, deliberate attempt to overcome these selectivity processes. Mass media are especially susceptible to selectivity processes because people can perceive and interpret whatever they wish to; no one is there to point out that you have selectively perceived a wrong message. The "All in the Family" television program tended to reinforce existing stereotypes and prejudices and have very little effect in terms of changing them. In interpersonal encounters, it is possible to correct misperceptions caused by selectivity processes, if at least one of the two persons notices such misperceptions.

Relationship between Stereotypes, Prejudice, and Intercultural Contacts

Stereotypes and prejudice affect intercultural contacts in many ways. First, stereotypes and prejudice can prevent intercultural contact from occurring. If we have strong negative stereotypes and prejudice, we may choose to live and work in settings that minimize the chances of contact with persons from disliked groups. Second, stereotypes and prejudice tend to produce several negative factors during an intercultural encounter that seriously affect the quality of interaction. The selectivity in our perception and interpretation produced by stereotypes and prejudice induces distortion and defensive behaviors. Defensive and superficial communication reduces chances of further meaningful interaction, which in turn can lead to reinforcement of stereotypes and can become a vicious circle of negative communication. Finally, if the stereotypes and prejudices are very intense the prejudiced person might engage in active antilocution and discrimination against the disliked group, which can easily lead to confrontation and open conflicts. Antilocution and discrimination between racial and ethnic groups create a negative climate for intercultural contacts and can have lasting effects for future communication between the members of groups involved.

Contacts between hostile groups can sometimes help in overcoming problems created by stereotypes and prejudice. It would be naive to assume that any intercultural contact will destroy stereotypes and prejudices. However, there is growing evidence to suggest that intercultural contacts do produce change in beliefs and attitudes and thus can affect stereotypes and prejudices. The direction of change depends largely upon the conditions under which contact has taken place. There are several favorable conditions for intercultural contacts: equal status, supportive social climate, intimate rather than superficial contact, a pleasant or rewarding outcome, and shared participation in functionally important activities or development of some common goals.[10] These are general guidelines and cannot guarantee that a given intercultural contact under these favorable conditions will definitely destroy stereotypes and prejudices. Much will depend on the individuals involved in the intercultural encounter. In summary, it can be said that intercultural contact is a necessary but not sufficient condition for destroying negative stereotypes and prejudices.

Summary

Perception is the mechanism by which we convert the various environmental energies that impinge upon us into meaningful experience. This experience comes through the development of structure, stability, and meaning for our perceptions. Structure gives our world order and coherence while stability provides constancy and endurance. Perceptual meaning refers to the fact that our perceptions are not single, isolated events but are an ongoing image of our immediate environment in relation to past experiences and future expectations.

Perception has both physical and psychological dimensions that work in conjunction with one another. The physical dimension performs organizing functions and is described in terms of electrochemical neural activities. The psychological dimension involves data interpretation and is related to our personalities, intellects, education, emotions, beliefs, values, attitudes, motives, and the like. This psychological dimension, influenced chiefly by individual experience

127

and culture, has far greater impact on our constructions of reality than does the physical dimension.

Our perceptual activity is selective because there are more environmental stimuli than we can possibly attend to. This selectivity functions in terms of exposure, attention, and retention. We tend to expose ourselves to those stimuli we prefer and to avoid those we dislike. We also tend to pay attention to and remember those stimuli of interest to us and to ignore or forget the others. Selective exposure, attention, and retention are to a large degree influenced by our cultural experiences.

Perception and culture are inseparably related across at least eight dimensions: culture and perceptual processes, culture and perceptual attributes, language, recognition, values, space, person perception, and emotion. Because of these relationships, culture plays an instrumental role in determining how we interpret our world, how we judge, evaluate, make sense of, and create our social reality.

Finally, perception is influenced by stereotypes and prejudices. Stereotypes are images we have of whole groups of people based on lack of knowledge or inadequate observations. Prejudice refers to a usually negative evaluation of individuals because they have membership in some racial or ethnic group. Stereotypes and prejudices usually predispose us to act toward members of other cultures in ways that inhibit meaningful intercultural communication.

Notes

1. Jerome Kagan and Ernest Havemann, *Psychology: An Introduction* (New York: Harcourt Brace Jovanovich, 1968), p. 154.

2. James W. Bagby, "A Cross-Cultural Study of Perceptual Predominance in Binocular Rivalry," *The Journal of Abnormal and Social Psychology* (1957): 331–34.

3. D. Erlich, et al., "Post-decision Exposure to Relevant Information," *Journal of Abnormal and Social Psychology* 54 (1957): 98–102.

4. Harry C. Triandis, "Cultural Influences upon Perception," in Larry A. Samovar and Richard E. Porter, eds., *Intercultural Communication: A Reader*, 2d ed. (Belmont, Calif.: Wadsworth, 1976), p. 119.

5. Michael H. Prosser, *The Cultural Dialogue: An Introduction to Intercultural Communication* (Boston: Houghton Mifflin, 1978), pp. 198–99.

6. Edward Sapir, "Conceptual Categories in Primitive Languages," *Science* (1931): 578.

7. Sidney M. Jourard, *Personal Adjustment* (New York: Macmillan, 1970), p. 313.

8. Gordon W. Allport, *The Nature of Prejudice* (New York: Doubleday, 1958), p. 187.

9. Allport, pp. 14–15.

10. Yehuda Amir, "Contact Hypothesis in Ethnic Relations," *Psychological Bulletin* 71 (1969): 319–42.

Additional Readings

Allport, Gordon W. *The Nature of Prejudice.* Garden City, N.Y.: Doubleday, 1958.

Amir, Yehuda. "Contact Hypothesis in Ethnic Relations." *Psychological Bulletin* 71 (1969): 319–42.

Gordon, Milton M. *Assimilation in American Life: The Role of Race, Religion, and National Origins.* New York: Oxford University Press, 1964.

Klineberg, Otto. *The Human Dimension in International Relations.* New York: Holt, Rinehart & Winston, 1964.

Martin, J.G. and C.W. Franklin. *Minority Group Relations.* Columbus, Ohio: Charles E. Merrill, 1973.

Moore, J.W. and A. Cuellar. *Mexican Americans.* Englewood Cliffs, N.J.: Prentice-Hall, 1970.

Rich, Andrea L. *Interracial Communication.* New York: Harper & Row, 1974, Ch. 2.

Schneider, O.J., A.H. Hastrof, and P.C. Ellsworth. *Person Perception.* Cambridge, Mass.: Addison-Wesley, 1979.

Simpson, George E. and J. Milton Yinger. *Racial and Cultural Minorities: An Analysis of Prejudice and Discrimination,* 4th ed. New York: Harper & Row, 1972.

Concepts and Questions

1. How does your cultural background affect your perception of persons from different racial, ethnic, and cultural backgrounds?

2. What could be done to overcome various selectivity processes that operate in intercultural settings?

3. How do we form stereotypes? What could be done to prevent the formation of stereotypes of various racial and ethnic groups?

4. What is the role of mass media in formation and perpetuation of stereotypes and prejudices?

5. Under what conditions do stereotypes lead to prejudice? Under what conditions do prejudices lead to discrimination?

6. What types of intercultural contacts destroy stereotypes and prejudices? What is the effect of forced school busing on stereotypes and prejudices?

7. What type of persons are most likely to develop stereotypes and prejudices against various racial minorities? What are some implications of this knowledge for appointing persons to decision-making positions in organizations devoted to the welfare of minority groups?

8. What is the relationship between culture and perception?

9. Give an example of the influence of needs, training and experience, expectations, and attitudes on perception for different cultures.

Exercises

1. Attend some event involving persons from several countries. Identify the main material and non-material cultural elements manifested in the behavior of people from one or two foreign cultures. What do these elements mean to you? Compare your meanings with the meanings of natives for the same cultural elements. Why did these perceptions differ?

2. Keep a diary of situations where you could recognize the influence of your cultural background upon your perception of (1) foreign cultural objects, (2) foreign persons, (3) persons of different racial or ethnic groups.

3. Conduct a brief survey in your class to find out the most common stereotypes of (1) blacks, (2) American Indians, (3) Mexican-Americans, and (4) white Americans. In what ways are these stereotypes similar? How do they differ? Why?

4. Interview some teachers of integrated schools in your area, especially those teaching social studies courses. Ask their perceptions of the role of school integration in dealing with the problems of stereotypes and prejudice among various racial and ethnic groups in the area. Ask their suggestions for improving human relations among various racial and ethnic groups in school settings. Compare

the perceptions and suggestions gathered from school teachers with the concepts presented in this chapter.

5. Watch a movie or television program showing the problems of stereotypes and prejudice in this country. Write a brief paper explaining the impact of this movie or TV program on the public's perceptions, stereotypes, and prejudices concerning the racial or ethnic groups involved in the program being analyzed.

III

Interaction:
Verbal
and
Nonverbal
Messages

6

Verbal Messages

Words can arouse every emotion: awe,
hate, terror, nostalgia, grief. . . . Words
can demoralize a man into torpor, or
they can spring him into delight. They
can raise him to heights of spiritual and
aesthetic experience. Words have
frightening power.

Colin Cherry

One of the most difficult and persistent problems we find in intercultural communication is that of language differences. In this chapter, we will concentrate on questions that deal with the relationship between language and culture and how it influences communication and understanding. Our examination will begin with a brief look at the general nature of language.

The Nature of Language

Language may be both verbal and nonverbal. The spoken and written forms of language we all use are called verbal language. But all of us also use a wordless language. This is called nonverbal communication, and it employs such wordless behavior as facial expressions, gestures, mannerisms, use of space, and orientations to time. This nonverbal language form is a very crucial part of human communication, and it will receive full attention in the next chapter.

Any verbal or nonverbal language uses symbols that stand for or represent various concrete and abstract parts of our individual realities. These symbols in turn are governed by rules that tell us how to use them in order to best represent our experiences. We are able thereby to share symbolically our experiences with others and to achieve various levels of mutual understanding, at least among members of a particular language using community.

There are many language forms and not all of them use words as symbols. Mathematics, for instance, is a language; it has symbols and rules that tell us how to use the symbols. Computers use special languages: COBAL, FORTRAN, and BASIC are three commonly used computer languages that also use sets of particular symbols according to specific rules. Even music has a language. Dots are used to represent musical tones, and there are rules that tell how the dots are to be set down in order to represent various musical forms. Our concern, however, is not with computer and music languages, but with humankind's principal form of communication: words. Consequently, in this chapter, language refers to words.

The most common form of verbal language that we use is the one with which we are most familiar: spoken language. Written language is merely a convenient way of recording spoken language by making marks on paper or some other suitable surface. If we recall our history, we will remember that before paper was invented, language was recorded on clay tablets, papyrus, copper sheets, and many other surfaces that permitted humanity to record and store knowledge for future use and for transmission to future generations.

For most of us, English is our primary language. It consists of symbols (words) and rules (grammar and syntax). But, so also do Spanish, Swahili, Chinese, German, and French. If we study another language, we soon discover that not only are the words different, but so are the rules. In English, we live in a *house*. In Spanish, we live in a *casa*. In English we show the possessive form by use of an apostrophe and say Mary's house. In Spanish, the rules do not permit using an apostrophe to form a possessive. So, in Spanish, we learn to say *casa de Maria* or *house of Mary* to form the possessive.

Language: Symbols and Sounds

One of our most unique characteristics as humans is our faculty and capacity to have sounds and marks serve as substitutes for things and feelings. That seemingly effortless process in which we all engage is at the very core of being human. Over a period of millions of years we evolved the anatomy necessary to produce and to receive sounds, and within a much shorter span of time created a system whereby those sounds took on meaning by standing for things, feelings, or ideas. This evolution has led to the development of a four-part process that enables us to use sounds to our advantage. We have learned to receive, store, manipulate, and generate symbols. It is these four steps, working in combination, that in part set humankind apart from other animals. The extent to which we use language is one of our most singular features.

Our sense of vision and hearing equip us with nerve endings that allow the outside world to become part of our personal life-space. Once these sights and sounds that symbolize our external world enter the body, they become electrochemical stimuli and travel by means of our nervous system to our brain. Upon reaching the brain, they are translated into meaning either to be responded to at once or to be stored for later use. (In a sense, learning involves our giving meaning to new stimuli.) At any given instant we can retrieve many of these stored symbols and arrange and manipulate them in any manner we desire. Our ability to engage in this manipulation phase affords us the luxury of being able to say what we want to say when we want to say it. For here in this final stage of our language ability, we can generate words for other people as well as receive them. The messages we receive and store become source material for new messages we manipulate and generate.

These four interrelated steps describe the faculty of language: an ability that allows us to take sounds produced by other people and give them meaning so they become symbols representing something in our environment. In essence, we have learned a form of shorthand; we have learned to use words as symbols in order to represent all parts of our social and physical environment.

Spoken language is the most extensive and adaptable symbolic medium we possess. We use symbols to represent things: objects, feelings, or ideas. The symbols used in communication are the products of human activity; people simply invented sounds to name things. In a rather arbitrary way, a piece of wood with lead in the middle became a *pencil*. Because symbols are arbitrary and only represent things, they can have several, sometimes diverse, meanings. This one-to-many symbol-referent relationship comes about as people apply their personal meaning to a particular symbol. If, for instance, someone says, "It's a very black day," this phrase can elicit a host of interpretations as we attempt to form a connection between what the sender intended "very black day" to mean and what we normally believe the symbols to mean. The term "very black day" could refer to any set of conditions ranging from the degree of cloud cover and visible sunlight to internal psychological states of despair and depression.

How We Acquire Language

It is generally agreed that children learn to talk as they learn to walk. Long before a single word is uttered, children learn to influence people around them through partly symbolic behavior. Prelinguistic behavior such as crying and arm movements introduce children to how they can influence others and thereby gain a degree of control over their environments. When children cry, people appear; if they hold out their arms, someone picks them up. Children learn to get things and to get things done through this form of behavior.

A child's first words do not form sentences. Its first vocabulary normally consists of nouns—names for objects and things in the child's immediate life space. Mama, dada, dog, and milk are common examples of first word-named objects. This early stage of naming things in the child's environment reveals two important links between language development and communication. First, a child begins to label things in its surroundings in order to make some sort of sense out of what it perceives. This is a natural development because all of us seem to feel more comfortable when we are around what we know, and naming things is a way of knowing. Second, meanings for various feelings, objects, or ideas are learned. A child's experience leads it to learn that words have meaning. A child, therefore, quickly learns unique internal responses (meanings) for dada, mama, dog, and milk. Another child having different experiences when being introduced to these same items would develop different internal responses and consequently have different meanings for them. A child who has been bitten by a dog will have internalized a different meaning for the word *dog* than will a child who has only met a warm, friendly, happy puppy.

The next stage in language development comes when a child begins to combine words. First it links two words, then three, and so on. A child no longer says, "milk," but rather, "John milk" or "more milk," then, "John drink milk."

Around the age of three a child learns in very subtle ways about grammar and correct speech. As this new awareness is incorporated in language behavior, a child begins to use proper grammatical structure. Instead of saying, "John want milk," he says, "May I have some milk?" By this stage in a child's life it can produce and respond to around 900 words. As we can see, there is a snowball effect inherent in learning to speak. The more a child is spoken to, the more it will learn to speak. As in most human endeavors, practice leads to proficiency.

The Importance of Language

It is through language that we reach out and make contact with our surrounding reality. And, it is through language that we share with others our experiences of that reality. If we survey a normal day we will soon see that we use words for a variety of reasons. Even the first few minutes we are awake might find us using language for some of the following purposes.

"Good morning!" Here we use words as a way of becoming united with the world outside our skin, as a means of keeping in touch with other people.

"Let me tell you about the horrible dream I had last night. . . . I was almost eaten alive by a giant toad." In this case, we use words to share an experience. We even use words to get support from other individuals so that we might feel better. This example also demonstrates how we employ words so that we can deal with the *past*, so that we can talk about something that has already happened.

"Please pass the salt and pepper." In this instance words are used so that we can exercise some control over the *present*. We each seek to have an effect on our environment, to influence many of the daily situations in which we find ourselves. Words, and how we manipulate them, permit us to make those alterations through symbolic transactions with others. We use words to persuade, to exchange ideas, to express views, to seek information, or to express feelings as we maintain contact with other people.

We also use words to form an image of the *future*. "Well, I guess I've got to go to work now. I've an important meeting with Jane today, but I dread seeing her as I know she's going to be angry about the changes I'm going to make in her work schedule." Here we see how our word-using ability allows us to predict and to describe the future. Although our pictures of the future are not always accurate, at least language enables us to think about, talk about, and anticipate the future.

In these four examples we have seen a few of the ways in which we manage words when taking part in a communication act. The widespread use of words, however, is only one reason why language is important. It takes on additional significance when we reflect on its impact. We manipulate others, and they in turn manipulate us by language. A single word or an entire sentence can often regulate our thinking and color our perceptions. For example, most veterinarians are offended when they are called "vets." They believe that this word better describes a former member of the armed forces than someone who has a doctor's degree. And the next time you hear a debate on abortion, notice that one side will talk about the rights of "the unborn child" while the opposition refers to a "fetus." Even the word *girl*, if used to refer to a woman, can arouse emotional responses.

When we move from single words to sentences, the influence of words is even more apparent. Notice how the words used in these two fictitious newscasts influence the picture we have of the actual events:

NOVEMBER 1

Newscast 1:   Police riot in Florida—24 students injured

Newscast 2:   Three police injured in breakup of beach drug party

NOVEMBER 2

Newscast 1: CIA attempt to assassinate Latin American leader uncovered

Newscast 2: Communist coup thwarted in Latin America

NOVEMBER 3

Newscast 1: Supreme Court affirms defendant's right to counsel

Newscast 2: Convicted murderer gets off on technicality

NOVEMBER 4

Newscast 1: Parole found more effective than prison in reducing repetition rate

Newscast 2: 60% of parolees return to prison

NOVEMBER 5

Newscast 1: Increase in crime rate slowed last year

Newscast 2: Major crimes up 14% last year[1]

Another vivid instance of the ability of words to color our perceptions was recently reported in the newspapers: At least nine persons were injured and nine were arrested as 1500 black and white students of a Pensacola, Florida high school fought with guns, rocks, and tree limbs over whether the school's athletic teams would be called the Rebels or the Raiders. The emotional connotations aroused by those two words were sufficient to inflame racial prejudices and to replace rational discourse with emotional violence.

Language plays a paramount role in our daily transactions as senders and receivers. Our own day-to-day activities provide the best evidence of the importance of our ability to use language.

Thus far we have examined language as a means of communication between people. Another main function of language is self-communication or thinking. In thinking we use words silently, but in much the same way we use them in interpersonal communication. During intrapersonal communication, words remain within us; they are not shared with others. Nevertheless, the purpose and function of words remain identical: words help us to understand and to make sense out of reality.

The ability to communicate with others is not only dependent upon our language faculty, it is also dependent on there being enough commonality of experience between people that the words they use mean, basically, the same things. The wider and more divergent the language communities from which people come, the more difficult mutual understanding becomes. Thus, when the young man from England tells his girl friend that he "will knock her up at noon" he is not making a

139

sexual reference as American English would tend to indicate; he is specifying the hour at which he will meet her for their date. Although both British and Americans speak English, they come from different language using communities, and they may not always understand each other.

As we might surmise by now, there is much more to the study of language than the little just described. Language has a vast number of social, philosophical, and psychological dimensions that are far beyond our needs in an introduction to intercultural communication.

Language and Meaning

As children most of us asked our parents, "What does that word mean?" Chances are we asked that question many times, and perhaps still ask it on occasion. This question reflects the way we view language. It suggests that we tend to look for meaning in the word itself. But we err if we think that words have meaning. It is more accurate to say that people have meaning and that words stir up meanings in people. We can all have different meanings for the same word. Take the word *grass*, for instance. To one person it might mean something in front of the house that is green, has to be watered, and must be mowed once a week. To another person grass may mean something that is rolled in paper and smoked. There is no "real" meaning in this example *because every person, from their own personal background, decides what a symbol means*. People have similar meanings only to the extent that they have had similar experiences or can anticipate similar experiences. Witness how various backgrounds and experiences can alter meanings. If our past experience is in professional baseball, a *rope* is a line drive. If our background is in the rock music world, *monster* is not something ugly or evil, but rather a very successful record. And, finally, isn't it likely that we and a physician respond differently to the symbol *cancer*?

A word, then, can elicit many meanings. Linguists have estimated that the 500 most often used words in the English language can produce over 14,000 meanings. This diversification of meanings suggests that words not only mean different things to different people, but also that words mean different things at different times and in different contexts. Take the word *love*. It often is used to denote a strong personal feeling of attachment; yet in the context of a tennis game, love means that no points have been scored. Think of the variety of meanings that each of the following words can call up: trip, pot, fix, fuzz, bread, chicken, swinger, pad, and tough. The simple fact is that we have many more ideas, feelings, and things to represent than we have words to represent them.

Language and Culture

The relationship existing between language and culture should have begun to emerge from our discussion of language acquisition and meaning. Both language acquisition and language meaning are directly related to our experiences. These experiences are unique to each of us not only because of the differences we encountered as individuals while we were growing up and learning to use language, but also because of what our culture has exposed us to. In short, each of us learns and uses language as we do because of both our individual and cultural backgrounds.

Language is composed of the following four ingredients: (1) a structured system of (2) arbitrary vocal sounds that (3) a collection of people have learned to use as a means of (4) labeling and cataloging the things, processes, and experiences of their environment. Language and culture are inseparable. Both are learned and serve to transmit values, beliefs, perceptions, norms. The idea that culture and language work in tandem contributes to the fact that our experiences and our world view are also interdependent.

It is obvious that our culture teaches us to name what is practical, useful, and important. We learn to name what is around us. In a general sense, the important things in our environment take on specific names while the less important things have more generalized names that must be modified through additional words to become specific. The French boy, consequently, can name and talk about various types of wine, while the youngster growing up on a farm in Iowa may well be able to offer ten different words that describe plows. We have all repeatedly heard the example of how the Eskimos have countless words for *snow*. And in the Arabic language there are hundreds of different words for the camel and all of its parts. For the Eskimo snow is extremely important and so crucial to life that each of its various forms and conditions is named. The same is true for the desert nomad whose life depends on camels. In English-speaking cultures, snow and camels are far less important and the single words *snow* and *camel* usually suffice for our needs. When our needs become more specific, however, we can make up longer phrases to meet these needs: "corn snow," "fine powder snow," "drifting snow," "big camel," "cantankerous camel," et cetera. There is, as we can see, a connection between the words a culture selects and the ideas and things of that culture. Each culture presents to its members, in conscious and subconscious ways, through words, the ideas and concepts that the culture transmits from generation to generation.

Language becomes linked to the influence of culture on perception because part of our perceptual activity involves the determination of

141

meaning for our environment. As language is often used to symbolize our environment, all of the perceptual concepts that we discussed in the last chapter also apply to language insofar as they help us to understand how meaning for words is developed. The influence of culture goes far beyond the mere naming of objects or things although this does provide a simple and obvious example to use.

It is a well-established fact that the structure of a language frequently reflects a culture's major themes. The primacy of hierarchical status in Japanese culture is clearly reflected in the Japanese language, which uses grammatical structures to define the various social statuses of conversational partners. And, as an indication of the strength of these language structures, cultural themes of Meiji-era Japan are still dominant in social communicative behavior of many Japanese-Americans even though English is the language of communication.

Our language must also enable us to deal with thoughts, feelings, and ideas as well as objects for which we have developed names. And, language must deal with and allow us to express and to develop meaning for the various value dimensions our culture establishes for thoughts, feelings, ideas, and behaviors. It is culture that leads to different interpretations and reactions to language. The statement, "we stopped on the way home from class last night and had a couple of beers," most likely would be taken by American students only to be a description of past acts and would probably receive a neutral evaluation or perhaps a slightly positive evaluation. But this same statement, if made by two Moslem students in Saudi Arabia, would receive a tremendously negative reaction because of the Islamic prohibitions against drinking alcohol. The influence of culture is pervasive and far exceeds the differences that occur between individuals within any given culture. This relationship is explained in greater detail when we examine the relationship between language and reality.

Language and Reality

"Every language is a special way of looking at the world and interpreting experience—concealed in the structure of each different language are a whole set of unconscious assumptions about the world and life in it."[2] Language not only describes perceptions, thoughts, and experiences, but it may determine and shape them. The Navajo's use of a verb-orientation form not only contributes to language problems, but may force both groups to attend and ignore entirely different things. More simply, what we think about and how we think about it is a function of the language we speak, and the language we speak is a function of what we think about and how we think about it. And both, thinking and speaking, are functions of culture.

Foreign Languages and Translation

The translation of one language into another is far more complex than most people believe. "Most people assume that text in one language can be accurately translated into another language, so long as the translator uses a good bilingual dictionary."[3] Unfortunately, languages are not this simple, and direct translations in many cases are difficult if not impossible because: (1) words have more than one meaning, (2) many words are culture-bound and have no direct translations, and (3) cultural orientations can render a direct translation into nonsensical results. There also are unique difficulties when one works through an interpreter.

Language translation is not only difficult, it can be inept and have extreme consequences. Near the end of World War II, after Italy and Germany had surrendered, the Allies sent Japan an ultimatum to surrender also. Japan's premier announced that his government would *mokusatsu* the surrender ultimatum. *Mokusatsu* was an unfortunate word choice because it could mean both *to consider* and *to take no notice*. The Premier, speaking in Japanese, apparently meant that the government would consider the surrender ultimatum. But, the English language translators in Japan's overseas broadcasting agency used the *to take no notice* meaning of *mokusatsu*. Consequently, the world heard that Japan had rejected the surrender ultimatum rather than that Japan was considering the ultimatum. This mistranslation led the United States to assume Japan was unwilling to surrender and the atomic bombing of Hiroshima and Nagasaki followed. Quite possibly if the other meaning had been selected in the translation process, the atomic bomb would not have been used in World War II.[4]

Of course, the atom bomb might still have been used on Japan for various political reasons, or it might have been introduced later during the Korean war. But, this example does serve to illustrate vividly the difficulties that can be found in foreign language translation and to demonstrate the seriousness of consequences that can follow inept translation of words with multiple meanings.

A second major difficulty in translation is dealing with words that have no direct translation. Word meanings come from social experience; some are intranslatable, at least in part. *Peace* has various meanings for peoples of the world according to their conditions, time, place; so does *war*. The meanings that we have for words are based on shared experiences. The ability of a word to convey or elicit meaning depends on culturally informed perceptions by both source and receiver as message processors. When we lack cultural equivalents, we lack the words in our vocabulary to represent these experiences.

Another difficulty found in translation lies in obtaining a concept match. By this is meant that when a concept is stated in one language it does not lose or change meaning in translation. For instance, in Mexican Spanish, there are at least five terms that indicate agreement in varying degree: *me comprometo* (I promise or commit myself), *yo le aseguro* (I assure you), *si, como no, lo hago* (yes, sure, I will do it), *tal vez lo hago* (maybe I will do it), and *tal vez lo haga* (maybe I might do it). This agreement concept ranges from a durable agreement that everyone recognizes to agreement being unlikely. The problem, of course, is to understand the differences between *me comprometo* and *tal vez lo haga* in their cultural sense so that a correct version can be rendered in another language. If, for instance, we are rendering English translations of these Mexican Spanish terms, we could expect all sorts of misunderstandings and confusion to arise if we simply translated each of these phrases of agreement as "OK."

Language translations frequently produce misunderstanding or incomprehensible translations due to cultural orientations reflected in the language. For instance, the *Quechua* language of Peru uses orientations to past and future that are the opposite of those found in the English language. In *Quechua*, the past is visualized as being in front or ahead of us because it can be seen. The future is visualized as being behind us because it cannot be seen. This is just the opposite of Americans who speak of the past being behind them and the future being ahead of them. If this aspect of cultural orientation were not known or if it were ignored, it could lead to incomprehensible translations about time, the past, and the future. It might even imply that people must look behind them if they are to be able to see what normally lies in front of them.

A final problem of language in translation arises when it is necessary to work with a professional interpreter. Proper use of an interpreter can enhance our ability to communicate with people of other cultures, but misuses of an interpreter can lead to serious consequences.

A good interpreter needs highly developed special skills. An interpreter must be able to translate a message so that others understand it as though it had not been translated. This means that the interpreter be skilled not only in understanding the words of the language being translated but the emotional aspects, thought processes, and communicative techniques of that culture as well.

The effective use of an interpreter requires the establishment of a three-way rapport. Rapport must exist between the speaker and the interpreter, between the speaker and the audience, and between the interpreter and the audience. This is an extremely difficult state to obtain because of the complexity of translation in real time. Consider what an interpreter must be doing simultaneously. When the speaker says a phrase, the interpreter must listen to that phrase. While the speaker says the next phrase, the interpreter must not only be translating the first phrase, but must also be listening to the second phrase. Then while the third phrase is being said, the interpreter must remember the first phrase, be interpreting the second phrase, and listening to the third. This procedure goes on and on throughout the process of the message delivery. And, it requires that the interpreter be able to remember not only what has just been said, but what may have been said several minutes ago because the interpretation of the latest words spoken may reflect a reference to what was said several minutes earlier. Learning to help an interpreter can make speaking through an interpreter a much easier experience. Meeting an interpreter in advance and going over a list of difficult words or phrases that will be used can be a big help by giving advance opportunity to consider a proper translation. Using an interpreter can be a difficult intercultural communication problem, but with experience and proper use of the interpreter, the problem can be minimized and the outcomes very rewarding.

In intercultural communication situations where people speak different languages or come from different primary language using communities, there are many communication problems that can arise if advance steps are not taken to prevent them. This problem exists to a lesser degree, however, when we encounter unfamiliar language codes as they are used by subcultures and subgroups within a larger cultural context. This is the last area of concern in our study of language and culture.

Subcultural Language Codes: Argot

Mike: What's happenin' mellow?

Bill: Hey man, last night after Ken split from his crib, some dude ripped off his box and all of his bad jams.

Mike: Anyone see the cat?

Bill: Yeah, the gray broad downstairs said he had a Deuce and a Quarter. Hope they bust him, man.

Mike: Right on, brother.

Bill: If Ken meets him he says he'll be trumpin' not rappin'.

Mike: I can dig it.

Bill: You got it . . . Hey! Cribbin' at Skeet's. Wild gig at his brick last night till the head breakers came.

Mike: Oh yeah. Any stallions?

145

Bill: No stallions. Met a fine pearl. Tacked down some honky jive and iced me.

Mike: What's goin' down with Skeet?

Bill: He's goin' oreo. A real Doctor Thomas.

Mike: Hear his lady's a mighty fine hammer.

Bill: You heard jive. She's a bugger bear.

If this conversation cannot be understood, it is probably because the argot is strange and unfamiliar. Briefly, the dialogue represents a conversation between two blacks who are good friends. Their conversation tells of their friend Ken's record player (box) and records (bad jams) being stolen. It also goes on to explain their hope that the thief will be caught (busted) and that if Ken should meet the thief he will beat him (trumpin') rather than talk to him (rappin'). They also mention a party where there were no attractive women (stallions) and discuss another friend, Skeet, who is beginning to assume value orientations and behaviors of the whites (goin' oreo). A rereading of that brief conversation will demonstrate to those of us who do not know the code that in many ways the words could be a foreign language.

Subculture languages adhere to one of the same basic assumptions about language as major cultural languages. Our use of language, and the meanings we assign to various words and phrases are learned. Our culture has taught us the meaning for the word *tachometer*. In Vietnamese, however, there is no such word, and hence no culturally agreed-upon meaning. The word *bird* for most of us means a flying, feathered animal. This simple word takes on a variety of meanings when employed by people with different experiences. To the badminton player it is a shuttlecock, for the baseball player it is a fast base runner, and to the rock musician it is an attractive woman. What this rather simple example points out is that as cultural experiences differ, so will the meanings people assign to words.

One way to gain insight into any subculture or subgroup is to examine its use of language. Things of the world about which we have little knowledge usually take on added significance and appear real once they are given specific names. This general process of naming, which is a universal characteristic, is part of our cultural inheritance. Through manifest and subtle ways the people around us not only help us learn the labels for things, but they teach us to name experiences and feelings. Often these experiences mirror a point of view or a lifestyle different from the one found within the dominant culture. When this happens, naming assumes added dimensions. People who are members of a subculture or subgroup not only share membership and participate in their social and cultural communities, they also share

146

modes and styles of verbal communication. In fact, groups that do not demonstrate a special language seldom are considered a subgroup or subculture. Subgroups and subcultures, then, can be examined in terms of their language, values, and behavior. This method of analysis recognizes that experience and language work in combination.

In the case of subcultures that are far removed from the main culture, we find language frequently takes on added significance. For example, in subcultures that are identified as primarily consisting of deviant behavior, the language patterns of that subculture may well develop into an *argot*. This "deviant behavior" takes on a variety of forms. Prisoners, for example, who have become deviants by breaking the law, have an argot. Hobos and vagabonds, not criminals by most standards, also are removed from the main culture, and hence they too have an argot. The important point for us is to know that argot is language usage limited to a particular subgroup or subculture whose members are outside the dominant culture. The understanding of an argot is vital to the understanding of a subculture or subgroup, since

> Argots are more than specialized forms of language, they reflect a way of life. . . . They are keys to attitudes, to evaluations of men and society, to modes of thinking, to social organization and to technology.[5]

Argot, then, is but one way in which language and behavior are linked together. And "because vocabulary is a part of language that is most immediately under the conscious manipulation and control of its users, it provides the most accessible place to begin exploration of shared and disparate experiences."[6]

Functions of Argot

A number of significant and real needs are satisfied by a subculture's use of a specialized linguistic code. First, "argot aids the counterculture in providing a means of self-defense."[7] Because many subcultures function in a hostile environment, members of the subculture use argot as a device for communicating with each other in a manner that makes it difficult for outsiders to understand or detect the code. The European Jews' use of Yiddish during harsh periods of discrimination is an obvious example of argot as a means of defense. There are, however, even more subtle and contemporary instances to be found. Prostitutes, because they are engaging in an illegal profession, also must use language for concealment. Consequently, not only the sexual acts themselves must be concealed, but discussion of the acts also must be camouflaged to avoid arrest. Argot is used for this purpose. The following might be a typical conversation between a prostitute and her pimp. "I have a steak if you're interested. I tried for some lobster but couldn't get it." Translated—*steak* means a client who will pay fifty dollars to be with the prostitute. A seventy-five dollar client is often called *roast beef,* a *lobster* is someone willing to pay one hundred and fifty dollars, while a three hundred dollar client is labeled *champagne.* Other argot or code terms for self-protection include cab, nunnery, parlor house, and sporting house for bordello.[8]

A second major function of argot is to assert a subculture's solidarity and cohesiveness by a uniform learned language code. Occasionally there even is a degree of secrecy associated with the use of argot. A sense of identity and pride are associated with the realization that you are part of a group that has developed its own private language; a bond forms among those members who understand the code. Homosexuals who know *AC-DC* (bisexual), *bill* (a masculine homosexual), *Black Widow* (a person who takes love mates away from other gays), and *chicken* (a young gay male), are privy to an argot that is unique to a particular group. The tramp and hobo are set apart from the main culture, yet they can feel a type of in-group solidarity because they have learned that a *yap* is a new comer, a *tool* is a pickpocket, a *paper* is a railroad ticket, to be *oiled* is to be intoxicated, and to *lace* is to punch.[9]

The third function of argot is to help establish groups as real and viable social entities. During the 1960s, for example, when people began taking drugs as a way of life, they gathered at specific locations and immediately developed what was to become known as the "San Francisco drug language." As these individuals became more than a group of people simply taking drugs, they evolved a rather elaborate glossary of terms—terms that helped transform them from a collection of people into a subgroup. Some of their terms were *Bernice* for cocaine, *hay* for marijuana, *heat* for police, *pipe* for a large vein, *roach* for the butt of a marijuana cigarette, *octagon* for a square person, *lightning* for achieving a *high*, and *head* for a heavy drug user.

Subgroup and Subcultural Experiences and Argot

A subculture's or subgroup's use of language, the words they select and the meanings they have for those words, offer us insight into the experiences of that subculture or subgroup. We cannot be members of all the subcultures with whom we are going to come in contact. By examining the language of various subcultures and subgroups, however, we can develop some appreciation for them.

The link between language, culture, and experience is predicated on one of the premises we examined as part of the Sapir-Whorf hypothesis. It held that we name (label) those ideas, concepts, and feelings that we find in our environment. Because culture helps determine and shape our surroundings, it plays a crucial role in deciding

148

what experiences we learn to name. In many subcultures and subgroups, the name given to the experience clearly demonstrates how subcultures and subgroups perceive and interact with the dominant culture. Some examples will help clarify this point.

The prostitutes' attitudes toward the main culture are most evident in their use of the argot word *trick*. In the argot of this subculture a client is referred to as a trick, or a sexual act for pay as a trick. The hidden meaning of the word, and for the prostitute the joke being acted out on society, is that the woman is getting paid for what she ought to be doing for free. Or stated yet another way, the client is literally playing the fool—he is being tricked.

Most other subcultures also have argot words that help describe their perception and attitude toward the dominant culture—words that are often uncomplimentary. In the subculture of carnivals, for example, the *slum* is used to refer to the cheap prizes and merchandise that people are willing to pay for when they go to a carnival. The rock music subculture shows its condescending and patronizing attitude by using the word *bubblegum* to describe the teeny-bopper set—for them, the lowest common denominator in rock music. And prisoners talk of their attitudes when they use the word *hit* to mean a rejection of parole.

Attitudes toward specific people in the environment of a subgroup or subculture also are reflected in their argot. The argot of the hard-core urban poor yields some of our best examples and even these few instances show how language and experience work in tandem. The words *lump maker* (for police) and *job man* (for social worker) tell us something about the contacts and relationships between these two segments of our society. One word for baby in this subgroup is *pea pusher*. This is not a very loving term, but it helps us understand some of the perceptions of the hard-core urban poor. If one is truly poor it is difficult to be enthused about adding a new person to an already financially overtaxed family.

Lawyers are yet another group that have been labeled by various subcultures and subgroups. These labels, like most argot terms, tell us something about the contacts between lawyers and subgroups. Carnival workers call them *patches*, and prostitutes refer to them as *oilers*.

The experiences named in argot also help us understand something about daily life in subcultures and subgroups. Drug and prison communities afford us numerous instances. Because most drugs are taken illegally, the police are a major concern in the life of this community. Hence, there are a variety of names that refer to police—the man, fuzz, heat, nabs, Feds, and narcs. For the person in prison, hómosexual activity is a common occurrence; therefore, the argot reflects that particular aspect of prison life. *Jockers* are aggressive homosexuals, and a *jail-house punk* is someone who becomes a homosexual while in prison.

Insight into a subcommunity's perception of society in general also can be gained by an examination of argot. For example, because the hard-core poor usually have jobs centering around manual labor, they refer to all work as a *sweat job*. Once they are fortunate enough to secure an automobile, which enables them to drive to a better job, they call their car *bread and butter*.

In the subculture of delinquency argot is employed to help talk about the activities faced by members of a specific and unique group. For instance, *burn* is to be shot with a gun, *a hustle* is any illegal means of making money, and *Mr. Pierce* is a switchblade knife.

There are a number of important points we should like to make as we conclude this section on subcultural language codes. First, the words that make up an argot are constantly changing. The change is usually so rapid that it makes many argot words and phrases out-dated in a very short period of time. The maintenance of in-group secrecy is an important reason for the short-lived nature of the words that compose the argot of a subculture. If the dominant culture learns the code, or if the code filters into middle-class vocabularies, as is the case with much of the black argot, then new words must be invented. Many times the new words are intended to deliberately mislead the dominant culture. This was the case when blacks used *bad* for the very best, *blade* for Cadillac, and *stallion* for a tall attractive woman. Because members of dominant cultures tend to latch on to and incorporate subcommunity argot into the main culture's language, argot undergoes a constant and rapid updating. Many of the examples used here may no longer be in use by the time this book is read.

A second characteristic of argot is that many of its words and expressions are regional. Homosexuals in one area of the country may not know all the words used by members of that same community who live in other parts of the United States. And, blacks who live in Los Angeles use many expressions that are unfamiliar not only to blacks who live in Detroit but to blacks who live in San Diego (just 100 miles away) as well.

Summary

Language and its relationship to culture is a major variable in intercultural communication. We have seen through our examination of language, its acquisition, and its cultural relativity, how it shapes our perceptions, thoughts, and feelings. We also have noted some of the problems inherent in situations where the speakers use different languages or have different primary languages. Problems of language translation revealed how confusion can arise through inept and inappropriate translations, and we have looked at the difficulty of working with an interpreter. Finally, we have looked at the concept of argot as it is used by subgroups that are in conflict with the main culture. In all of this detailing of language, the issue of nonverbal communication has purposely been avoided. In the next chapter we will look at this form of communication and see how closely it is related to verbal communication.

Notes

1. Stephen W. King, *Communication and Social Influence* (Reading, Mass.: Addison-Wesley, 1975), p. 26.

2. Clyde Kluckhohn, "The Gift of Tongues," in Larry A. Samovar and Richard E. Porter, eds., *Intercultural Communication: A Reader*, 2d ed. (Belmont, Calif.: Wadsworth, 1976), p. 109.

3. Peter Farb, *Word Play* (New York: Alfred A. Knopf, 1974), p. 197.

4. Farb, p. 198.

5. David W. Maurer, "The Argot of the Dice Gambler," *Annals of the American Academy of Political and Social Sciences* 269 (1950): 119.

6. Edith Folb, "Vernacular Vocabulary: A View of Interracial Perceptions and Experiences," in Larry A. Samovar and Richard E. Porter, eds., *Intercultural Communication: A Reader*, 2d ed. (Belmont, Calif.: Wadsworth, 1976), p. 194.

7. Andrea Rich, *Interracial Communication* (New York: Harper & Row, 1974), p. 142.

8. Larry A. Samovar and Fred C. Sanders, "Language Patterns of the Prostitute: Some Insights into a Deviant Subculture," *ETC: A Review of General Semantics* (Winter, 1977): 34.

9. Irwin Godfrey, *American Tramp and Underworld Slang* (Ann Arbor, Mich.: Bryphon Books, 1972), pp. 12–13.

Additional Readings

Blubaugh, J. A. and D. L. Pennington. *Crossing Differences: Interracial Communication.* Columbus, Ohio: Charles E. Merrill, 1976, Ch. 6.

Farb, Peter. *Word Play.* New York: Alfred A. Knopf, 1974.

Hoijer, Harry, ed. *Language in Culture.* Chicago: University of Chicago Press, 1954.

Kantrowitz, Nathan. "The Vocabulary of Race Relations in a Prison." *PADS* 51 (1969).

Keller, J. J. *Intercommunity Understanding: The Verbal Dimension.* Washington, D.C.: University Press of America, 1977.

Kirch, M. "Language, Communication and Culture." *Modern Language Journal* 57 (1973): 340–43.

Lerman, Paul. "Argot, Symbolic Deviance and Subcultural Delinquency." *American Sociological Review* 32 (1967).

Samovar, Larry A. and Richard E. Porter, eds. *Intercultural Communication: A Reader,* 2d ed. Belmont, Calif.: Wadsworth, 1976, Ch. 4.

Watzlawick, Paul. *How Real is Real?* New York: Random House, 1976.

Whorf, B. L. *Language, Thought and Reality.* Cambridge: MIT Press, 1967.

Concepts and Questions

1. What is meant by the phrase "language influences how we shape our view of culture"?

2. What is meant by the phrase "words are only symbols"?

3. How do we decide what a symbol means? What is the influence of culture on this process?

4. Why is foreign language translation so difficult? Give some examples that demonstrate this difficulty.

5. Are you familiar with any subcultures or subgroups that have their own argot? What are some of the words and meanings of that argot?

6. Can you think of some examples where the argot of a group reflects the unique experiences, values, and lifestyle of that group?

7. Can we ever really learn the language of another culture? Why?

Exercises

1. Ask an instructor of English as a second language (ESL) for permission to attend a few classes in which foreign students are learning conversational English. Try to distinguish which of the students' difficulties are linguistic problems and which, if any, are culturally-based. Talk with some foreign students. What language problems did you experience in: (1) understanding the foreign student, and

(2) communicating your ideas to the foreign student? How could the quality of communication in such a situation be improved?

2. Ask your instructor to invite foreign students from several countries to your class. Ask the foreign students to tell briefly the purpose of their study program, their adjustment experiences in this country, and their hobbies or interests. Identify the five most important language problems experienced in understanding and communicating with the foreign students. Did you notice any relationships between language and culture in this communication experience? How did you overcome the language problems in this setting?

3. Find two bilingual persons using the same foreign language and English. Ask one of them to describe some common interest topic to the entire class in the foreign language (e.g., Spanish or Arabic). Ask the second bilingual person to simultaneously translate the message into English for the class. Ask the first bilingual person to tell the message in English. Compare the English messages presented by these two bilinguals to check their accuracy, information loss, change in emphasis, and other translation-related problems discussed in this chapter. If possible, record the two English messages and use these recorded messages to do a more accurate comparison and analysis.

7

Nonverbal Communication: The Other Code

I am convinced that much of our difficulty with other people in other countries stems from the fact that so little is known about cross-cultural communication. . . . Formal training in the language, history, government, and customs of another nation is only the first step in a comprehensive program. Of equal importance is an introduction to the nonverbal language which exists in every country of the world and among the various groups within each country. Most Americans are only dimly aware of this silent language even though they use it every day.

Edward T. Hall

At last, after four years of college we are about to embark on our first employment interview. We know the importance of making a good impression, so we pay particular attention to every detail of our physical appearance. After showering we look in the mirror and decide to trim our beard. However, as we reflect further we conclude that the beard must go. So, for the first time in three years, a razor touches our face. At the same instant we mutter something about the fact that people will do anything for a job. Now the after-shave lotion is splashed on so that we will smell as good as we look. Then we select a freshly ironed shirt, one that matches the new suit and tie. On with the shined shoes, retrieve the new thin briefcase, and we now are ready to present ourself.

At precisely eight-fifteen we knock lightly, yet decisively, on the door marked Vice President of Personnel. From inside a voice responds "Please come in." We enter. Behind a large oak desk sits the vice president—a middle-aged woman in mod clothes! She smiles, we return her smile, and she motions us into the room. After a few brief seconds, during which we look at one another, she walks over and offers her hand. We remember to grip it firmly as a sign of control and self-confidence. We hold on for just the right amount of time and then release her hand. With a nod of her head she invites us to sit down. The interview is about to begin.

This hypothetical episode demonstrates some of the many and subtle ways in which nonverbal communication touches our lives. In our little drama the interviewer may well have read meanings in our punctuality, grooming, apparel, smile, handshake, briefcase, and after-shave lotion. We in turn could have inferred meanings from the vice president's punctuality, grooming, and apparel. We often are unaware of information of this kind. Yet most communication researchers agree that in normal face-to-face interaction only about 35 percent of the *social content* of a message is conveyed by words. The rest is transmitted through nonverbal behaviors.

> Many, and sometimes most, of the critical meanings generated in human encounters are elicited by touch, glance, vocal nuance, gesture, or facial expression with or without the aid of words. From the moment of recognition until the moment of separation, people observe each other with all their senses, hearing pause and intonation, attending to dress and carriage, observing glance and facial tension, as well as noting word choice and syntax. Every harmony or disharmony of signals guides the interpretation of passing mood or enduring attribute. Out of the evaluation of kinetic, vocal and verbal cues, decisions are made to argue or agree, to laugh or blush, to relax or resist, to continue or cut off conversation.[1]

Nonverbal communication clearly plays an important role in our lives. Consciously and subconsciously, intentionally and unintentionally, we send and receive nonverbal messages. In addition, we make important judgments and decisions based on these messages. We make judgments about the quality of relationships existing between people partly on the basis of their nonverbal behavior. In our Western culture, for example, the distance between communication partners leads us to draw inferences about the closeness of their relationship. If one partner moves away from the other, we may infer that the relationship has ended at least for the moment. Another clue to the quality of a relationship is afforded by the amount, type, intensity, and location of touching. Various zones of our bodies are reserved for certain people. A shifting or avoidance of these zones could be one way of communicating.

We also make judgments about the emotional state of people by observing their nonverbal behavior. If we see a man with clenched fists and a grim expression, we do not need words to tell us that he is not exactly happy. If we hear people's voices quaver and see their hands tremble, we probably infer that they are fearful or anxious, despite what they might say to the contrary. Most of us place heavy reliance on what we see as the outward signs of inward feelings.

We make judgments about the meaning of verbal messages in light of accompanying nonverbal cues. If the two kinds of communication contradict each other, we often become dubious. When people say they feel fine but look ill, we may ask them to explain the apparent contradiction. We really never know what is going on inside the other person, but taking into account both the verbal and the nonverbal data enables us to make realistic guesses.

Studying Nonverbal Communication

Nonverbal Communication Defined

Since the central concern of this chapter is to examine how and why we communicate nonverbally, and with what consequences, we begin with a definition of nonverbal communication.

Nonverbal communication involves all those stimuli within a communication setting, both humanly generated and environmentally generated, with the exception of verbal stimuli, that have potential message value for the sender or receiver.

By specifying stimuli that have potential message value we approach nonverbal communication from a point of view that reflects how the process really works. Messages are more than just words and movements. Hence we will view nonverbal messages as all of those stimuli inherent in face-to-face situations to which communicators can attach meaning.

Our definition also permits us to include unintentional as well as intentional behavior as part of nonverbal communication. The preponderance of nonverbal messages are, in fact, sent without our ever being aware that they have meaning for other people.

> The expressiveness of the individual (and therefore his capacity to give impressions) appears to involve two radically different kinds of sign activity: the expression that he *gives* and the expression that he *gives off*. The first involves verbal symbols or their substitutes which he uses admittedly and solely to convey the information that he and the other are known to attach to these symbols. This is communication in the traditional and narrow sense. The second involves a wide range of action that others can treat as symptomatic of the actor (communicator), the expectation being that the action was performed for reasons other than the information conveyed in this way.[2]

An important limitation in our definition restricts nonverbal communication to stimuli operating in a communication setting or context where two or more people are interacting. While granting that works of art, ballet, architecture, and the like, do possess message value for viewers, they belong to nonverbal communication only to the extent that they operate in a communication transaction between persons in face-to-face situations.

Nonverbal Communication: Guidelines and Limitations

Since the popularization of nonverbal communication there has been an explosion of information and books available to the general public. Much of this information tends to distort rather than clarify the role of nonverbal messages in human interaction. Although there is ample and reliable information on the subject, most popular writers feel compelled to offer the type of information that makes clever and witty cocktail chatter. This sort of approach tends to give a misleading picture of what nonverbal communication is all about. Many of the distortions contribute to a superficial study of this important subject. The intercultural setting, because of its added complexities, magnifies these errors. As a preface to our discussion of nonverbal communication, therefore, we must become alert to some of the hazards and dangers of engaging in a shallow study of this vital communication component.

Overgeneralizing is perhaps the greatest danger when discussing nonverbal behavior. We act as if all people, groups, regions, nations, et cetera, are alike. Admittedly people are alike in many ways, but there also are subtle and elusive differences. Variations in subgroups, subcultures, educational and occupational levels, as well as individual differences, should alert us to be very tentative in drawing our conclusions. It is possible to generalize about nonverbal communication, and some general assertions about nonverbal messages will follow. What we are proposing, however, is that we become aware of the issues and problems that arise out of the exceptions and variations. Our generalizations should be based on a sufficient number of cases. When we read that most Arabs perceive and use space differently than do Americans, we must be aware of the problems of overgeneralizing. On the other hand, when our reading, travel, and the research on the topic warrant such a conclusion, we should make it.

A second danger of superficial information is that some nonverbal behaviors occur with some degree of regularity within a culture while other actions are not part of a culture's everyday repertory. The fact that the "Kayan males of Borneo grasp each other by the forearm, while a host throws his arm over the shoulder of a guest and strokes him endearingly with the palm of his hand,"[3] might be interesting, but

157

in most instances it is not the kind of information we need to remember as students of intercultural communicaiton.

A third danger in studying nonverbal communication stems from the fact that we often are guilty of making the differences more important than they actually are. Is it crucial, for example, to know that in Thailand people often say hello to their friends by lifting their hands to their faces and placing their thumb below their chin and the index finger against the forehead? Again, this type of information might be interesting, but does it help us in our day-to-day interactions? We must keep returning to this important question: What difference makes a *significant difference* in the communication situation? This fixation with differences often keeps us from focusing on cultural similarities. One culture may bid farewell by waving the hand up and down while another simply cups the hands, yet by being aware of the total context and what has just happened, we can ascertain the intended meaning.

Finally, there is the danger of forgetting that nonverbal behaviors seldom occur in isolation. Although we may examine isolated and individual nonverbal messages, in reality they are part of the entire communication context and process. We send many nonverbal cues simultaneously, and these cues normally are directly related to spoken language.

Functions of Nonverbal Communication

Our nonverbal behaviors perform a variety of functions during interaction. Five rather specific functions of nonverbal communication can be identified: first impressions, relational messages, affect, self-presentation, and manipulation of others. It will be helpful to look briefly at these five functions so that we can learn to identify them as they operate during an encounter.

> A natural starting place for studying the communicative functions of nonverbal cues is first impressions since our first reactions to others supply the framework, within which all the other nonverbal functions operate. Those first judgments color our perceptions of everything else that follows.[4]

The narrative at the beginning of this chapter demonstrates the importance of first impressions as a basic function of nonverbal communication.

The second function, relational messages, are the nonverbal cues people send each other that help to explain how they like each other, themselves, and the relationship they are in. We offer people this type of information in many forms. We position and space our bodies as a means of signaling who we want to include and exclude from our conversations. We use body orientation and space to show friendliness and affection. And we smile, touch, nod, and the like to communicate our feelings about what is going on and how we feel about it.

Affective, or emotional states as they are often called, also are communicated by nonverbal cues. Our emotions are reflected in our posture, voice, facial expressions, and eyes. Be it fear, joy, anger, or sadness, we express these emotions and feelings to others and they in turn attach meaning to them.

Fourth, we use nonverbal elements as one way of presenting ourselves to other people. We manipulate a host of nonverbal cues as we try to influence what others think of us. The car we drive, the clothes we wear, the smile on our face are messages that we send others to help them decide who we are and whether they wish further contact with us.

Finally we manipulate nonverbal symbols, either consciously or unconsciously, to alter the thinking and behavior of others. Our nonverbal actions often influence how others will act and how they will think. We use nonverbal elements just as we use words to affect how people feel and even what they might learn.

Verbal and Nonverbal Symbol Systems

In the preceding chapter we saw how verbal symbols (words) were used to represent experiences, ideas, information, and feelings. As has already been indicated, nonverbal symbols perform many of the same functions. Although the systems parallel each other in certain areas, they are different in many respects. To better understand the workings of nonverbal codes it will be helpful to examine those similarities and differences. In addition, we will look at those situations where the two systems work in tandem.

Similarities

The most obvious similarity between verbal and nonverbal communication is that they both employ a *sign-symbol system*. As pointed out in Chapter 6, in the case of oral communication, we use a culturally-agreed-upon set of words we call language. The sounds we produce, or the marks we make on paper, are intended to stand for something. In this sense, a word is only a symbol *standing for* a thing or idea in reality. The words, "our black dog Buddy," are only symbols we employ to represent the dark, furry creature that we own. This same process of symbolization applies to nonverbal communication. If we kiss someone (tactile comunication) we like, that symbol (kiss) is only a representation of our internal state. It is an attempt on our part to share a feeling or an idea, just as words were used to share something about a black dog named Buddy.

These two systems are alike in still another way. They *are the product of an individual.* Whether we speak, point, touch, or move, we are still generating an action that someone else can use as a message. It matters little at this point in our analysis whether or not the symbol was intentional or unintentional. The idea is that we, as senders, produced a symbol, be it word or movement.

Our next similarity might well be a corollary of the first two, but it is worth developing in some detail. In both verbal and nonverbal communication, *someone is attaching meaning to a sign or symbol we have produced.* If we say "turn to the right," the consumer of the message will attach meaning to our words and move in a certain direction. If we point to the right with one hand and motion with the other, here again the receiver will attach meaning to our efforts (pointing, motioning) and move in a certain direction. Even our example of a kiss or a certain smell embodies this idea of attaching meaning.

Differences

One important difference is that many nonverbal behaviors are governed by biological necessities. For example, a boy might be out hiking with his girl firend when a rattlesnake appears on the trail. Wanting to act out his culturally accepted role of masculinity he tries to disguise his fear. He cannot, however, tell his hands to stop trembling, his knees to cease knocking, or his voice to return to its normal octave. Verbal communication, on the other hand, is governed by a rather rigid set of man-made rules and principles concerning such areas as syntax and grammar. We consciously decide when to talk, yet we have little control over winking and blushing.

Nonverbal communication can be used as international, intercultural, and interracial language. This is an important consideration for our analysis. Whether in the United States, China, or South America, people seem to have the same general meaning for a smile. This cannot be said for verbal messages. Our verbal language systems are used by a culture for specific in-group meanings.

We are all aware that in nonverbal communication we can, whether intentionally or unintentionally, indicate multiple events simultaneously. This is because we are able to cause separate movement in many parts of our bodies at the same time. For instance, we can give off signals inviting or rejecting others by employing different movements and motions with our hands and arms. We also can smile at the same time as if feeling good while tapping our fingers as an act of nervousness. In using verbal messages we must indicate events successively.

Nonverbal communication is learned early in life. An infant, soon after birth, is able to make some sense out of both the quantity and quality of contact its body experiences. A baby also responds to smiles and waves early in its life. Our use of verbal communication is learned much later in life. We have to develop a certain degree of socialization before we can employ word-symbols as a device for communication.

There are many who suggest that nonverbal messages can be more emotional in their appeal than can verbal. For example, telling a group of people that you have an injured kitten for whom you must find a home, would not have the same impact as having them see and hold the kitten.

Combinations

In most communication encounters nonverbal behaviors work in combination with the verbal. We will explore briefly some of the more common ways in which these two systems merge.

In many instances our feelings are given added tenor by having our nonverbal behavior *accent* our verbal. By means of words we can tell a loved one of our feelings. We can gently squeeze our partner's hand, or smile, as a way of accenting and punctuating what we are trying to communicate. Verbal and nonverbal systems also work in combination by allowing us to *repeat* a message. We can, by using words, inform someone that "the library is south of this building." We can repeat this same message by pointing south.

Our nonverbal actions can also *complement* our verbal expression. We might tell a friend we are sorry that we can't lend him the money he wants. The believability of our story is complemented by a facial expression demonstrating our regret. The same point could be made by our turning out our empty pockets.

There might also be occasions when our nonverbal behavior is a *substitute* for our verbal. We could, as many cultures do, express our reverence for a situation by remaining silent. Instead of saying "I am very moved by this experience," simply let our silence speak for us.

There are even instances, while working in combination with the verbal elements, that our nonverbal actions *contradict* our words. We might tell a friend that we are relaxed and at ease during a particular situation, while at the same time our hands are trembling, our eyes are rapidly blinking, and our face is becoming wet with nervous perspiration. Though we can only speculate, there does appear to be an apparent contradiction.

Nonverbal Communication and Culture

Having been introduced to the topic of nonverbal communication in rather broad terms, we now are ready to examine the relationship between nonverbal messages and intercultural communication. This relationship is obvious if we stop and reflect on the idea that both culture and nonverbal communication are *learned, passed on, and involve shared understandings.* Both represent what a collection of people have deemed important enough to codify and transmit to the members of that group.

When viewed in this light we can see why culture and nonverbal communication are inseparable. For example, by living and growing up in the United States our culture has taught us to greet people by shaking hands, yet in most Oriental countries people have learned to bow as a means of expressing this same idea. Nonverbal communication and culture are also inseparable because we learn them the same way. As has been said throughout this book, most of what we call culture was transmitted on the affective rather than the cognitive level.

Many of our nonverbal behaviors are culturally learned. For example, all people learn how to present themselves to other people, but in our culture we disclose self by the way we dress, how we move, by the objects that we possess, and the like. We are a rather outgoing people. In Japan, however, people have learned that it is a sign of weakness to disclose too much of themselves by overt actions. One is taught very early in life that touching, laughing, crying, or using a loud voice in public are not part of the accepted communication ritual.

Our culture not only teaches us our nonverbal actions but also what in our environment serves as a stimulus for those actions. In a sense, both cause and effect are culture-bound. For instance, "food regarded as a delicacy in one culture brings out expressions of disgust in another."[5]

The past few paragraphs have suggested that culture and nonverbal communication work in tandem on a variety of levels. On one level, cultural constraints help shape and control emotional expression. On another level, our cultural attitudes toward emotions help determine their expression.

The relationship between culture and nonverbal communication is important to us for a variety of reasons. First, by understanding basic patterns of nonverbal expressions within a culture we are able to gather clues regarding the underlying attitudes of that culture. We have already seen that nonverbal communication is highly revealing of basic cultural traits because of the fact that a large part of nonverbal activity is governed by unconscious habit. No one, for example, ever sat you down and told you that the palm-back V-sign (made with index and middle finger) meant victory or peace. But by use and by habit that sign takes on an automatic meaning in the American culture. However, there are other cultures where that same sign simply means "two." And in some regions that sign is sexual insult. In most cases these meanings were learned without our ever being aware of it and are hence habitually employed. To understand those habits is often analogous to understanding that culture.

Nonverbal behavior patterns also can provide us with information about a culture's value system. A good example of the connection between values and nonverbal communication might be seen in a culture's use of time. Persons from identifiable Doing-oriented cultures (such as the United States) tend to regard an absence of words as a waste of time, a period when "nothing is happening." For those who can be characterized as a Being or Being-in-Becoming culture, silence in conversation has a positive value—it is essential to self-fulfillment and to an awareness of the here and now.

The study of cultural nonverbal behaviors also can assist us in isolating our own ethnocentrism. For example, we might be more accepting of a person's use of space if we were to realize that this usage is based on cultural characteristics that reflect something of the user and the culture.

When applying our understanding of nonverbal behavior to interpret the meanings of a person from another culture, we should keep three things in mind. First, when we focus on one particular form of nonverbal communication we must not forget that in an actual conversation a number of nonverbal messages are being transmitted simultaneously. The speaker's facial expressions, movements, clothes, eye contact, and the like, as well as his words, combine to form the message that is received. Second, it would be impossible to describe and list all of the nonverbal messages found in all cultures. But, if we sample a few of the more common nonverbal messages found in the intercultural context we will gain a general understanding of the types of things we should be alerted to. Third, it is important to understand our own behavior as a prelude to understanding the actions of others. With this concept in mind, we will see examples of North American nonverbal behaviors in each of the categories discussed in the remainder of the chapter.

In discussing the types of nonverbal messages, we shall look at those messages produced by *the body* and those that grow out of the use we make of *space, time, and silence.*

Body Behavior

General Appearance and Dress. From hair sprays to hair pieces, from reducing diets to muscle-building courses, from false eyelashes to blue contact lenses, we show our concern for our general appearance. Because of our desire to look better, multi-million dollar industries thrive. And who is able to calculate the price we all pay in mental anguish over our personal appearance?

Reflect for a moment on some of the ways we make judgments based on another's personal appearance or dress. When deciding whether or not to strike up a conversation with a total stranger, we are influenced in part by the way that person looks. We make inferences (often faulty) about another's intelligence, or social status, or profession from cues provided by their appearance. We complain that some fellow student who didn't work any harder than we did got a higher grade because of his or her greater attractiveness. Or we say someone else got the promotion we deserved just because we were overweight. There was even a newspaper story recently that talked about a young man who said he lost his job because he had too many freckles. A line on the employment folder noted: "Excessive noticeable freckles."

Appearance is so important that we communicate differently around people who are handicapped. Even people's clothing influences our judgments about them. Every occupation has its official and unofficial uniform. Every change of any significance, be it birth, entering school, graduation, getting a job, marriage, or even death, requires a different set of clothes. Ask yourself how you respond to someone in a suit versus someone in overalls or an apron. Some department stores have found that individual sales go up when the male sales staff wear a shirt and tie instead of casual clothes. In one study customers in a department store failed to notice shoplifting when it was being carried out by people in suits and ties, yet watched and reported the pilferage when the subjects were dressed as "hippies."[6] In ways that are both rational and irrational, we react to people's dress and personal appearance.

In intercultural communication, dress and personal appearance are manifested in two ways. First, *standards for general appearance are subject to cultural variations.* Second, *our personal response to the other person is influenced by dress and appearance.* Each of these ideas has significant impact on the intercultural encounter.

We have already seen that judgments regarding dress and appearance are culturally based. In America, for example, we tend to value the appearance of the tall, slender woman. But in some European countries such an appearance signals weakness and frailty; heavier women are regarded as much more desirable. Within the same country different races usually have contrasting standards for the judgment of beauty. Even the regard we place on uniforms is rooted in a culture's value system. In Mexico, for instance, uniforms are a popular mode of dress. The police, the military, school children, and anyone else who gets the opportunity enjoys wearing a uniform. There are, however, other countries where the culture has a different view of uniforms. In Israel, as a reaction to Nazism, uniforms are very unpopular. Americans are often shocked when they see a group of Israeli soldiers dressed in everything from short pants to tee-shirts that say "The Rolling Stones."

The influence of culture on appearance and dress is often so subtle that we tend to overlook its significance. Even within subcultures and subgroups, nonverbal communication has nuances that help define them. Prisoners are a good example. Members are often identified by appearance and clothing. New arrivals to a prison became members of "clinic" classification and could be categorized by their blue denim jumpsuits, which were in sharp contrast with the brown shirts and trousers that helped identify the other inmates.[7]

Cultures, as we have seen, teach their members what to value in appearance and dress, and these standards shift from culture to culture. We now move to the second issue and examine the ways our culture has conditioned us to respond to other people.

We all know from personal experience that the color of other people's skin or the shape of their eyes or nose influences how we behave around them. This influence is even more profound if the people are strangers. During our explanation of prejudice and stereotypes, we found that our perceptions of other people influence our communication with those people. We certainly are aware that whites generally respond differently to black-skinned people than to other whites. What we end up doing is allowing skin color and physical traits to reinforce our individual stereotypes.

We often allow appearance to be a nonverbal message that impedes successful intercultural communication. We must, therefore, be more tolerant of differences in dress and appearance. What you might consider a costume and quite garish is very likely the native dress of that particular culture. Whether it be high leather boots or tennis shoes, brown skin or white, we have learned to let these and other messages stand for a part of the other person. While admitting that this is an unavoidable part of perception, it is better to assign positive rather than negative meanings to these and other nonverbal symbols in the absence of contrary evidence. They are, in the last analysis, only cues that the individual gives off. *We* must decide the significance, or lack of significance, we want to assign to the cue.

Body Movements (Kinesics). In recent years books and articles on body language have focused our attention on the ways we use movement as a form of communication. The systematic study of body movement that attempts to formalize and to codify this behavior is called *kinesics*.

Kinesic cues are those visible body shifts and movements that influence communication. The study of kinesics attempts to examine how such things as slight head nods, yawns, postural shifts, and other nonverbal cues, whether spontaneous or deliberate, affect communication. This study is based, in part, on a number of assumptions about human movement and human behavior:

1. Every movement conveys information about the psychological and physical states of the person moving, regardless of that person's culture. This assumes that we never engage in random or meaningless movement. A yawn, wink, scratch, wave, or smile all have a purpose. Although we may not always be aware of the reasons behind our actions, we never perform any actions that are not related to some internal state. If this be so, it becomes crucial for us to understand movement if we are to understand communication.

2. Everyone can interpret body movements and use them for communication purposes. Just think of the numerous gestures and movements we utilize consciously in our daily contacts with others. We wave "goodbye" to the family, wave "hello" to our fellow workers, point at something we want at mealtime, shrug our shoulders to say "I don't know," shake our heads from side to side to say no, and down to say yes. Then consider all those movements we make without thinking—movements that tell others something about us. They infer that we are rested or weary, happy or sad, angry or placid, outgoing or retiring, partly on the basis of our movements.

3. Unconscious and instantaneous body movements refer to whatever is happening to us at that second. Our body is "talking" to the outside world at each moment of its existence, and movement is but one of its statements.

4. Communicative movements are those related to the presence of other people. They send messages or in some way make communication easier. Outward behavior changes around others, and the nature of the changes depends on the relationship to the other person(s). A man whose posture is normally slouchy, for example, might suddenly straighten up when an attractive woman enters the room.

With these assumptions of kinesics before us, we will examine a few of the more common body movements and the reactions they elicit. Since it has been suggested that we can make as many as 700,000 separate physical signs, any attempts to catalog them would be frustrating and fruitless. We shall limit our discussion, therefore, to a few movements that express our attitudes toward others, show our emotional states, and underscore our verbal messages.

We express our attitudes toward others in a variety of ways. In American culture, for example, we tend to show liking by facing each other directly instead of turning to one side. We offer a signal to the other person with our body. In this sense we not only show them we like and dislike, but we also use our body to notify the people around us who shall be included in our conversation and who shall be excluded. A positive or negative attitude toward a communication partner is also signaled by leaning toward or away from the partner. In our culture we have come to equate forward-leaning with a positive attitude (and in some cases, with an aggressive attitude).

Body movements may also indicate the intensity of an emotional state, particularly distress. A depressed mood, for example, seems to be revealed by fewer movements of head and hands, but many leg movements. Nervous states often are exhibited by fussing with objects, twisting rings on the fingers, rattling keys or coins in a pocket, or tapping and drumming with the fingers on the body or a table. The internal states and moods revealed by our body activity are often uncontrollable.

Finally, there are those movements that take place while we talk or listen. These are the actions we engage in as a means of highlighting or underscoring our verbal messages. Visualize, for example, the kinds of hand gestures you have seen people use when uttering such expressions as "come closer," "back up," "get that thing out of here!" Notice how people's bodies move when they listen to an exciting story. We use all parts of our body as a way of clarifying spoken language or of providing feedback to the words of others.

Each culture displays certain unique facts of movement and posture. The size and speed of gestures is one phase of movement that is culturally based. Jews and Italians, for example, are often quite animated. At times even our walk is related to our culture. Young whites seem to walk fast, while young blacks learn a slower walk that resembles a stroll.[8] Johnson further suggests that the "Black stroll" is so much a part of the culture that very young black males practice their walk in front of a mirror before they try it out in public. For them the walk is more than a means of getting from one point to another; it is an expression of an attitude—a nonverbal message. Even on the international level we can see how this simple act of walking shifts from culture to culture.

> European males sometimes seem effeminate to American tourists because when they walk, their posture and hand and arm movements are similar to the female walking patterns in our culture. On the other hand, Orientals often view American women as bold and aggressive

because they walk with a longer gait and more upright posture than do Oriental women.[9]

The use of hand and arm movements as a means of communicating also varies between cultures. In the United States, for example, "making a circle with one's thumb and index finger while extending the others is emblematic of the word 'OK'; in Japan it signifies 'money' (okane), and among Arabs this gesture is usually accompanied by a baring of teeth and together they signify extreme hostility."[10] In the United States we also have learned that waving the hand and arm up and down is a symbol for goodbye or farewell. However, if we wave in this manner in South America, we are apt to discover that the recipient of this gesture is not leaving, but moving toward us. In many countries what we use as a sign of parting is a gesture that means "come."

There are many other instances of how movements, either accompanying or replacing speech, are altered by our cultural experiences. To illustrate, in southern Italy and Yugoslavia, touching the ear denotes jeering at effeminacy. To Greek children the same gesture is a warning of imminent punishment. It is a superlative in Portugal, protection against the evil eye in Turkey, a sign of skepticism in Scotland, and refers to an informer in Malta, and a sponger in the Canary Islands.[11]

Many of our movements relate to an attitude that our culture has, consciously or subconsciously, taught us to express in a specific manner. In the United States, for example, we show status relationship in a variety of ways. The ritualistic nonverbal movements and gestures in which we engage to see who goes through a door first, or who sits or stands first, are but a few ways our culture uses movement to communicate status. In the Middle East status is underscored nonverbally by which individual you turn your back to. In Oriental cultures, the bow and backing out of a room are signs of status relationships. Humility might be shown in the United States by a slight downward bending of the head, but in many European countries this same attitude is manifested by dropping one's arms and sighing. In Samoa humility is communicated by bending the body downward. And we are all aware of the different gestures for derision. For some European cultures it is a closing fist with the thumb protruding between the index and middle fingers. The Russian expresses this same attitude by moving one index finger horizontally across the other.

Although a culture's value system has an influence on outward nonverbal expression, lack of movement also says something about a culture and its character. The English and the Japanese have been taught not to reveal outward signs of emotion; hence, members of these cultures display very few gestures in the intercultural situation.

When the English and the Japanese are compared with outward and gregarious cultures, such as the Italians and Jews, we observe opposite values regarding public behavior, and hence contrary displays of movement when interacting. In a sense, what we might call examples of the "general national character" are reflected in the nonverbal affective actions of all four cultures.

Posture and sitting habits also offer insight into a culture's deep structure. In the United States, where being casual is valued, people often fall into chairs and slouch when they stand. In many European countries, such as Germany, where lifestyles tend to be more formal, a slouching posture is considered a sign of rudeness and poor manners. The way we sit can also be a type of communication. For example, in the United States people seldom squat. Most places, both public and private, have facilities for sitting. At home, work, in Little League baseball fields, at parks and at bus stops we can count on a place to sit. Many countries, however, do not have places to sit and rest. In these areas squatting is as common as sitting. In fact, in some rural parts of Mexico squatting is employed more than sitting. The U.S. Border Patrol, being well aware of this cultural variation, uses the squat as a means of locating illegal Mexican aliens. The Patrol has spotter planes fly over the mountains of Southern California at low altitudes. From these elevations they can tell which group of campers are sitting and which are squatting. The assumption is that the squatters have entered the country illegally. Hence, the way they were sitting said something about the culture they were from. Even an act as simple as crossing one's legs when sitting has cultural connections. In parts of Russia, for example, a female sitting with her legs crossed is viewed as a prostitute.

Although we have focused on cultural differences, there are thousands of gestures and movements that are shared by people throughout the world. For example, gestures as obvious as pointing need no translation. One study even suggested that many of the nonverbal messages used in flirting and courting are the same all over the world.[12] And, it is very uncommon for women to stand or sit with their legs apart—regardless of the situation or the culture.[13] It is essential to keep in mind the idea that intercultural communication involves an understanding of the likenesses as well as the differences found in nonverbal communication.

Facial Expressions. At one time or another most of us have been intrigued by the way our reactions to other persons are influenced by their faces. The early Greek playwrights were keenly aware of the shifts in mood and meaning conveyed by facial expressions. They even used masks to demonstrate changes in each actor's character and attitude. In a sense, all of us are actors, putting on a variety of masks. To quote the poet T. S. Eliot, we "put on a face to meet the faces that we meet."

The mask analogy is a good one to keep in mind as we view facial cues. Earlier in this chapter we considered unintentional messages, saying that other people sometimes found meaning in our nonverbal behavior. This is especially true when applied to meanings elicited by facial cues. As part of our heredity each of us acquires a face—a mask, if you will. That face is part of us; it goes where we go. But it is capable of looks of happiness when we may not be happy, and expressions of sadness when we are not sad.

As has been mentioned, there are innumerable changes and alterations that we can make on our face, and of course there are those changes made by gravity and age. Some of these changes are micro-momentary expressions that are so fleeting they register on the subconscious level. Others are momentary—wrinkling the nose, biting the lips, sniffing, yawning, or grimacing. There are some that have a longer life—such as a smile or rolling the tongue inside the mouth. Even our wrinkles or our paleness communicates.

Women are quicker and slightly more accurate in their judgment of facial expression than are men. With practice, however, anyone can interpret facial expressions fairly accurately.

People are more apt to interpret facial expressions correctly if they take the communication context into account. The same facial expression may have different meanings at home, at an informal party, at work, or on a date. If we were shown a photograph of a person's face, with no hint of the context in which the photograph had been made, would we feel confident about guessing what the expression meant? Was joy or terror mirrored on that face?

The importance of facial expressions to communication is well established; however, the intercultural implications of these expressions are more difficult to assess. The reason for this difficulty centers on an academic debate. The core of the argument revolves around this question: Is there a nearly universal language of facial expression? The majority position posits that there are universal facial expressions— that people all over the world smile when they are happy or want to appear happy, and scowl when they are angry.[14] The other point of view holds that anatomically similar expressions may occur in everyone, but the meaning people attach to them differs from culture to culture.[15]

Members of all cultures display emotion, express intimacy, and deal with status. The particular form of display, however, does vary from culture to culture. Cultures vary considerably in the amount and variety of facial expressions they are willing to reveal to other people. Specific cultural norms usually dictate how, when, and to whom we show our emotions through facial expressions. The reason is simple: we learn the rules that govern the use of facial expressions during childhood, and they become habits, learned to the point of being automatic and outside of normal awareness.

Because emotional expressions are culturally learned, their display differs from culture to culture. In some cultures smacking your lips together is a sign of approval. Yet there are many cultures, the English for instance, where such an expression would be deemed in poor taste. In many Mediterranean areas, signs of grief or sadness are exaggerated. Yet in the United States, at least among middle-class white males, the display of this same emotion is neutralized. The Japanese, on the other hand, use laughing and smiling to mask anger, sorrow, or disgust.

The Chinese do not readily show emotion. Chinese children are conditioned to use the face to conceal rather than reveal emotion. Even if the internal states felt are similar, people from different cultures may not show similar facial expressions. Japanese and American subjects in one study revealed the same feelings of fear and disgust while watching stress-inducing films, but when discussing the films in a face-to-face situation, the Japanese manifested only neutral facial expressions.[16]

Eye Contact and Gaze. In drama, fiction, poetry, music, or in real life, eyes have always been accepted as a major source of communication. From Shakespeare's "Thou tell'st me there is murder in mine eye," to Dylan's "Your eyes said more to me that night than your lips would ever say," to the musical ballad "your lips tell me no, no, but there's yes, yes in your eyes," the eyes have held a strange fascination for us.

The number of messages we can send with our eyes is almost limitless. The quantity and quality of our interpersonal relationships are affected by our establishing eye contact, avoiding eye contact, looking downcast, shifting our eyes, squinting, staring straight ahead, or even closing our eyes. We have all heard some of the following words used in association with a person's eyes: direct, sensual, sardonic, expressive, intelligent, penetrating, sad, cheerful, worldly, hard, trusting, or suspicious. These words express judgments and decisions based on the nonverbal cues received from a person's eyes.

In group communication we spend between 30 and 60 percent of our time in eye contact with others. It is estimated that 10 to 30 percent of the looks have a duration of about one second. The frequency with which we engage others in eye contact is a sign of its utility for us. We may look at people to say, nonverbally, "I'm ready to communicate with you." Or we may look to discover how they react to something we have said. We may look at a group of persons to let them know, "I want to be included. I want to share in this encounter."

How often we use eye contact, and how intensely, is determined by a number of factors. Our need to interact, our physical proximity to one another, the people we are interacting with, the amount of competition from others, the intimacy of the topic of discussion, and the level of comfort or discomfort in the encounter are but a few of them.

Among the interesting discoveries that research has uncovered about how Americans use eye contact are the following: (1) We tend to look at our communication partner more when we are listening than when we are talking. The search for words frequently finds us, as speakers, looking into space, as if to find the words imprinted somewhere out there. (2) The more rewarding we find our partner's message to be the more we will look at him or her. (3) The amount of eye contact we try to establish with other people is determined in part by our perception of their status. Researchers claim that when we address someone we regard as having high status we attempt a modest-to-high degree of eye contact. But when we address a person of low status, we make very little effort to maintain eye contact. (4) We tend to feel discomfort if someone gazes at us for longer than ten seconds at a time. "Stare him down" apparently has some scientific foundation.

Practices unique to certain cultures abound in the use of eye contact and gaze. All cultures, however, use eye contact and gaze basically for the same reasons. We all need our eyes to see who we are with so that we can adapt our behavior as needed. Also, all people use eye contact as a means of signaling their desire to engage in communication. It is a way of saying, "Let us talk." Granting these and other cultural similarities, we are now prepared to look at a number of instances where the use of eye contact and gaze is altered by cultural experiences.

> To express hostility and disapproval of an authority figure, Blacks will stare and then quickly "roll their eyes" away from the authority, or "cut their eyes" toward the superior and keep them focused on this person. . . . Another kind of eye behavior common to the Black, Chicano, Native American, and Puerto Rican cultures is the avoidance of eye contact as a nonverbal sign of recognition and respect for the authority-subordinate relationship.[17]

This notion of avoidance often changes from culture to culture. In some Far Eastern cultures, for example, it is considered rude to look into another person's eyes during conversation. Arabs, on the other hand, because of their use of personal space, stand very close to their communication partners and stare directly into their eyes. For Arabs, the eyes are a key to a person's being, and looking deeply into another's eyes allows one to see another's soul. This explains why we have seen Palestine Liberation Organization Chairman Yasser Arafat wearing dark glasses indoors. He is hiding his eyes to prevent others from seeing deep into his being. Educated Englishmen consider it good manners to look directly into the eyes of the person they are communicating with. And in America, we are taught to "look them in the eye."

A culture's male-female relationship also influences eye behavior. In many Asian cultures it is considered taboo for women to look straight into the eyes of males. Most men, out of respect for this cultural characteristic, do not stare directly at women. This is in stark contrast to men in France who stare at women in public. Such a stare is an accepted cultural norm. In America this prolonged stare is often a part of the nonverbal code employed in the subculture of the homosexual. An extended stare at a member of the same sex is often perceived as being suggestive and a signal to approach.

There even are cultures and subcultures where pupil size is used as a nonverbal cue. It has been said that people dealing with Chinese jade dealers would have to wear dark glasses to shield their eyes from these astute traders, who were able to accurately read a person's pupil enlargement as a positive sign of interest. The same skill in reading pupil size has also been claimed by Turkish rug dealers.

Touch. Just as our words and gestures are messages carrying our internal thoughts and feelings, so touch, too, conveys messages. The meaning we assign to being touched, and our reasons for touching others, help us gain insight into the communication encounter, as Holden Caulfield so aptly pointed out:

> I held hands with her all the time. This doesn't sound like much, but she was terrific to hold hands with. Most girls if you hold hands with them their goddamn hand dies on you, or else they think they have to keep moving their hand all the time, as if they were afraid they'd bore you or something. [18]

Touch is the earliest sense to mature; it manifests itself in the late embryo stage and comes into its own long before eyes, ears, and the higher brain centers begin to work. Soon after birth, infants employ all of their other senses as a way of interpreting reality. During the same period, they are highly involved with the tactile experiences of other people. They are being nuzzled, cuddled, cleaned, patted, kissed, and in some cases breast-fed. In addition, they touch and explore themselves.

As we move from infancy into childhood in America, some significant changes take place that influence our use of touch. First, touch becomes less important than sound and sight as a message channel. People point to things and talk to children. Second, a type of socialization sets in; we learn whom to touch and where we can touch. Phrases such as "don't do that" and "that's not nice" become commonplace. Childhood desires to touch and be touched must be replaced by words.

By the time we attain adolescence, our culture has taught us the do's and the don'ts of touching. We can shake hands with nearly everyone, hug certain people, be intimate with still others, and make love to yet a smaller group. Whom we shall touch and when and where we can touch them is now generally clear to the adolescent.

The few existing studies on touching in North American culture have uncovered some interesting insights. For example, the meaning inferred from a touch is influenced by a number of factors. First is the state we are in at the time of the touch. If we are crying when someone touches us, it has a somewhat different meaning than when we are touched during a joyful or happier period. Second, our personal past history helps define the contact. If we have grown up associating touch with sexual activity, and have been told that sex is "evil," our reaction will be colored accordingly. Third, our perceived relationship with the toucher will influence the meaning we attach to the touch. Different meanings will be inferred when we are touched by a parent, friend, professor, or lover. In short, the person doing the touching and how you see him or her is a crucial factor. Finally, the location of the touch (arm, leg, breast), the relative pressure of the touch (firm handshake, soft kiss), the duration of the touch (momentary, prolonged), the relative temperature of the skin, whether the touch was active or passive (purposeful touching or accidental brushing), and the situation (two people alone or a crowded room), are all conditions that affect the meaning of the message. This last factor—the situation—is a particularly important one. There are a number of socially acceptable touches that we can use in public places: the full embrace, shoulder embrace, hand on shoulder, arm linking, hand in hand, head contacts, kissing (if nonsexual), and handshaking. Yet in private, the list of acceptable touches changes.

We need only watch the news on television or visit an international airport to see that there are major differences in intercultural contact. You could also ask yourself how readily you touch someone who has a skin color different from your own.

In most instances, our culture teaches us how to use and how to interpret tactile behavior. As children we grow up in different cultures and learn various roles and nonverbal activities that are associated with these roles.

> As a child matures . . . he learns that boys don't hold hands, but girls may. Or, if he grows up in many parts of Africa and the Middle East, he learns that male hand-holding is a perfectly acceptable sign of friendship. He learns who to kiss, where and when. [19]

We also can look at the Moslem who has learned about touch as an integral part of his culture. Moslems eat and do happy things with the right hand, but to touch another person with the left hand is a social insult; the left hand is reserved for toilet functions.

Earlier in this chapter we observed some differences in greetings —as diversified as kissing, embracing, licking, and staring. There even are cultural variations in the proverbial handshake. In countries such as Germany people shake hands at every meeting, and hence there are few modifications from situation to situation. However, in the United States the handshake is much more revealing. Handshaking can take the form of the limp palm, the firm grasp, or the sensual touch and stroke.

There is widespread agreement about a number of generalizations regarding touching and nontouching cultures. The English, British-Americans, and the Germans, for instance, are cultures that employ very little touching in public. In contrast, Hispanic-Americans and peoples of Eastern European Jewish descent represent cultures with a great deal of tactile experiences. The Italian, French, and Arab cultures also are highly tactile people.

The few studies that have been conducted on intercultural touching seem to support the observations and generalizations just mentioned. For example, in a study of Arab and American student interactions the only touching was among the Arab students.[20] In another study, it was "noted that the French in their mental hospitals deliberately encouraged touching including massage, whereas body contact in American culture is generally limited to such acts as pulse taking."[21]

As this last example demonstrates, even the location of a touch is altered by one's cultural experiences. Each culture has established its own definition for touching and has decided upon which zones of the body can be approached and which are taboo. For example, in Thailand the head is sacred and it is a sin to touch someone on that spot. For Muslims the shoulder is an approved zone, and it is used for hugging—a sign of brotherhood. In America the zones and types of touches are also defined. With unmarried opposite-sex friends, the kind and location of touch help determine the meaning of the touch. Strokes generally communicate warmth and sexual desire; pats indicate playfulness and friendship; while squeezes and brushes are generally ambiguous.

Subcultures also have established areas and various definitions for touching locations. In prisons, for instance,

> There are numerous nonverbal cues which when observed are attributed to homosexual intentions and interests. . . . A slap on the buttocks, acceptable on the playing field or in the gymnasium, may

have a different meaning when it happens in the block or more so in the cell.[22]

Homosexuals also seem to have another set of standards and rules for the using of touch as a form of communication. Those who have "come out of the closet" tend to be much freer about touching their mates than are most middle-class Americans. This appears to be true both in public and private.

These examples have shown that we employ touch as a form of communication, and it has been learned as part of our being a member of one group or another.

Smell.   While we can all grant that vision and hearing provide most of our messages, the sense of smell can also be a channel for eliciting meaning. Americans spend millions of dollars trying to change or cover up the way they and their surroundings smell. Body odors, including detectable breath odors and perspiration, and artificial fragrances (deodorants, perfumes, colognes, lotions, etc.) are especially influential in interpersonal communication.

Smell, like touch, is one of our more basic modes of communication. Most animals, for example, use odor as a means of ascertaining the presence of their enemies, attracting the opposite sex, marking their territory, and identifying emotional states. Human beings, even with all their perfumes, give off an odor when they are sexually aroused.

All odors can help or hinder communication. There are a number of elements that influence the meaning we give to a smell: (1) its strength in relation to competing fragrances and odors (French perfume versus an inexpensive after-shave lotion), (2) its distance from the other person, (3) the perceived relationship between the parties involved, (4) the context of the encounter, and (5) the past associations we have had with the smell.

A few examples will illustrate the role of smell in different cultures. In Bali, when lovers greet one another, they breathe deeply in a kind of friendly sniffing. The Burmese, Mongols, and Lapps smell each other's cheeks to say hello. In China, and in some other low-meat-consumption countries, it is felt that people from the United States produce an odor that is often offensive, an odor brought about by the large amounts of meat we devour.

We can assume from the above instances that there often are vast differences existing between cultures and their perception of odor. Americans represent the most blatant example of an anti-smell culture. In many other cultures smell is regarded differently. In some Arab countries, such as Lebanon, men like women to smell naturally. To the

Arab, good smells are not only pleasing, they are also considered to be an extension of the person:

> Olfaction occupies a prominent place in the Arab life. Not only is it one of the distance-setting mechanisms, but it is a vital part of the complex system of behavior. Arabs consistently breathe on people when they talk. However, this habit is more than a matter of different manners. To the Arab good smells are pleasing and a way of being involved with each other. To smell one's friend is not only desirable, for to deny him your breath is to act ashamed. Americans, on the other hand, trained as they are not to breathe in people's faces, automatically communicate shame in trying to be polite.[23]

Paralanguage. We have probably attended, at one time or another, the showing of a foreign film with English subtitles. During those intervals when the subtitles were missing we heard the actor on the screen uttering a strange language but probably received some sort of message just from the *sound* of his voice. Perhaps we inferred that the performer was expressing anger or sorrow or joy or any one of a number of other emotions. Maybe the sound of his voice led you to conclude that he was a hero or a villain. The rise and fall of his voice may have told us when he was asking a question or making a statement or issuing a command. Whatever the case, certain vocal cues provided us with information with which to make judgments about the character's personality, emotional state, and rhetorical activity. To be sure, we could only guess at the meaning of the words the actor uttered, but his voice told us a lot about him as a person.

Now, suppose we are watching an American film. Again, the actor's voice causes us to make judgments about the kind of person he is portraying. But because the actor speaks our language, his words have meaning for us, too. Yet their ultimate meaning for us depends heavily on how he utters them. Indeed, the way words are spoken adds an important dimension to the meanings we infer. The sound of a voice may be compatible with, and reinforcing of, the words uttered, or it may be sending separate, unrelated, or even contradictory messages. In any case, we can see the importance of the voice in human communication. As an advertisement in a recent news magazine stated, "Maybe his voice will give us a clue. Let's talk to him by long distance."

What we have just been considering is often referred to as paralanguage. It deals with the linguistic elements of speech—how something is said, not the actual message of the spoken words. Paralanguage is the acoustic behavior that accompanies, interrupts, or temporarily takes the place of speech. It accompanies speech by means of pitch, loudness, rate, quality, distinctness, and dialect. It interrupts with sounds of "uh," "umm," "uh huh," and the like. Paralanguage takes the place of the statement with instances such as "brr" for the statement "I'm cold." Looking at a few examples of paralanguage cues in our culture, and in others, will help us appraise its place in human interaction.

During speech we manipulate the pitch of our voice to impart varying shades of meaning to our words. In fact, these pitch variations, or inflections, are often crucial. For example, *now* may be uttered as a question by giving it an upward inflection. By reversing the inflection *now* becomes an answer. "Now?" "Now!" Speech without inflectional variation is akin to writing without punctuation marks. A person who speaks in a monotone—without pitch variation—deprives his listeners of important clues to the meaning of his words.

Obviously, we have to talk loud enough for our verbal message to be heard. But equally important is the way in which we vary the intensity level of our voice. Like changes in pitch, changes in loudness provide the speaker with an additional means of modifying his verbal message. Whether words are uttered softly, loudly, or moderately can greatly affect the way in which they will be interpreted. Normally, if we speak one word of a sentence at an intensity level different from the other words, that word stands out. Intensity change, then, is one means of emphasis.

The loudness level of our voice may also reflect our emotional state. As we become angry or exasperated, our voice usually gets louder. When we feel pity for someone, our voice tends to lower in intensity. Whether we plead, command, or pacify, the intensity level of our voice provides the listener with important clues to our intent.

Loudness levels, or volume, often are part of a culture's communicative style. Arabs, for example, enjoy loud sound. Their conversation tends to be carried out with a great deal of volume. Orientals, on the other hand, speak in a much lower volume.

In the restricted sense in which we shall use the term, *dialect* refers to the intonational pattern taken to be characteristic of the natives or residents of an area or other group. Encompassed within this pattern are many vocal elements, particularly rate of utterance, duration of vocal sounds, and inflectional peculiarities. This intonational pattern is one basis on which we label people as Southerners, Midwesterners, or Easterners, as Mexican-Americans or French-Canadian; as a resident of New York City or the bayou region of Louisiana; as a "country boy" or a "city slicker." To be sure, our labels are often inaccurate, but nonetheless we *do* label people, and dialect serves as a vocal cue.

Dialects and accents are perhaps the most relevant of all the paralanguage factors in terms of intercultural communication. We all are aware of the tendency to make fun of the strange inflectional patterns of others. We often allow dialects to determine our attitude toward other people.

While there are some exceptions, ordinarily we find dialects other than the one spoken by the listeners /evaluators receive less favorable evaluations than those considered "standard." Generally these negative responses occur because the listener associates the speaker's dialect with an ethnic or regional stereotype and then evaluates the voice in accord with the stereotype. Typical of this type of response are studies which found the following: (1) Chicano English speakers were rated lower on success, ability, and social awareness; (2) native-born Americans rated Europeans (speaking English) less positively than other native-born speakers; (3) teachers will tend to label a child as "culturally disadvantaged" especially if the speech exhibits perceived irregularities in grammer, silent pausing, and pronunciation; and (4) "standard" dialects were preferred and judged more competent than "nonstandard"—regardless who spoke— except standard dialects were more often associated with white speakers than black.[24]

Messages of Space, Time, and Silence

Up to this point we have been concerned with nonverbal messages stemming directly from the person of the communicator—his bodily messages. In this final section of the chapter we shall be concerned with how features *external* to the communicator are utilized for communication purposes. More precisely, we shall deal with space and distance, time, and silence as manipulated by people in the communication situation.

Space and Distance. The flow and shift of distance between people as they interact is part of a communication. We allow one person to stand very near to us; we keep another person at some distance. We use space and distance—proxemics—as yet one more nonverbal code in our encounters with others. Our personal space, that piece of the universe we occupy and call our own, is contained within an invisible boundary surrounding our body—and we decide who may enter and why. When our space is invaded without our permission, we react in a variety of ways. We back up and retreat, stand our ground as our hands get moist from nervousness, or sometimes react in a violent way.

The manner in which we use space often tells others something about us personally and our culture in general. For example, attitudes regarding homosexuals were studied in an experiment on social distance between "gays" and "straights." The researchers found that students sat farther away from their communication partners when they believed them to be gay.[25] In a more symbolic way, the Great Wall of

China also manifests a cultural attitude. The wall, intended to keep out "the barbarians," was a statement to the world that China wanted to be left alone.

In most instances, participants in a communication encounter are aware of the rules that govern personal space. Without ever having to articulate and discuss their feelings, they seem to know that space and territory express attitudes regarding status, dominance, affection, and attraction. The rules and procedures that govern space are learned as part of each culture, and hence spatial relationships vary from culture to culture. Many Europeans have an entirely different concept regarding public space than Americans. The European will stand very close to a stranger, while the American sees this as a violation of personal "territorial rights." Another interesting contrast may be seen in the distance between mates in various cultures. In most Western countries, a man and wife signal their relationship by walking side by side. They maintain a joint personal space. But Sudanese Arab men have their wives walk a few steps behind them. The wife may not even sit beside her husband at mealtime. The man's personal space is his alone.

In some Middle Eastern countries we can find ourselves being subjected to continual shoving and crowding on buses and in most public places, for these cultures demand very little social distance. They have learned, as part of their cultural experience, a specific orientation and outlook regarding space and privacy. The orientation can shift from culture to culture, and, as you might suspect, it can cause communication problems. In England, for example, a country where people queue up (form lines) for just about everything, Arabs are perceived as rude when they push their way to the front of lines.

A culture's use of space and distance also reflects that culture's values—it is an affirmation of what they deem important. Personal space in many Asian countries is used to communicate respect. Students do not sit close to their teachers; the distance demonstrates esteem. Distance is also used in England to reflect the cultural value of privacy. In Latin America, Greece, and Italy, where physical contact is important, people communicate in close proximity. Yet in Scotland, Sweden, and England, noncontact cultures, people do not stand very close together when they talk.

If our reaction to and use of space is learned, we can conclude that there are certain consistent patterns found among people of one particular culture. Edward T. Hall has developed a model of personal space and distance among people in the United States. His scheme is concerned with basic communication distances used in business and social relations. Table 7-1 illustrates the distance for each category and provides examples of how shifts in voice volume might occur. Because people treat social distance according to their past cultural experiences, Hall's analysis is of added interest to intercultural communicators. It

Table 7–1

**American Cultural Interpersonal Distances for
Various Categories of Interaction**

Distance	Type of Encounter	Voice Volume
Very close (3 in. to 6 in.)	Awareness of physical involvement. Love-making, comforting and protecting.	Soft whisper
Close (8 in. to 12 in.)	Details of face are easily visible. Highly personal, seldom used in public.	Audible whisper, very confidential
Near (12 in. to 20 in.)	Can hold and grasp the other person. Many dyadic social interactions occur.	Indoors, soft voice, outdoors, full voice
Neutral (20 in. to 36 in.)	Others keep at arm's length. Most common distance for social conversation.	Soft voice, low volume
Neutral (4½ ft. to 5 ft.)	Most social gatherings and business transactions.	Full voice
Public distance (5½ ft. to 8 ft.)	Business and social discourse more formal. Desks in offices are placed to hold off visitors.	Full voice with slight over-loudness
Across the room (8 ft. to 20 ft.)	Used by teachers or speakers at public gatherings.	Loud voice talking to a group
Far distances (20 ft. and more)	Public speaking by public figures.	Hailing distances, public address systems

SOURCE: Edward T. Hall, *The Silent Language* (New York: Fawcett, 1959).

provides a basis for comparison of American patterns with other cultures and their use of distances.

Subcultures also have their own unique use of space. Prostitutes, for example, are very possessive of their territory. When they mark an area as their own, even though it may be a public street, they behave as if it is their private property, and other prostitutes had better keep away. In prisons, where space is limited, controlled, and at a premium, space and territory are crucial forms of communication. Prisoner's cells, though small, are their personal islands—the one place they can call their own. Even the doling out of punishment is related to space, a reduction of space being a common reprimand. The forming of lines is yet another way space communicates to inmates.

The elements of space and distance are important when interacting in a variety of situations. Notice, for example, that Americans in group interactions tend to talk with those opposite them rather than those beside them. Seating arrangement is important in choosing a leader. In most instances, the person sitting at the head of the table is chosen to be leader. In American groups, leaders usually are accustomed to being somewhat removed physically from the rest of the group and, consequently, choose chairs at the ends of tables to sit in. In Chinese culture seating arrangements take on different meanings. The Chinese experience alienation and discomfort when they are faced directly in front of another person or on opposite sides of a desk or table. To them, this is defined as being on trial.

Furniture arrangement, as a form of communication, varies from country to country. In a courtroom in the United States the witness's chair faces outward to the people of the court—he faces his community and his peers. In Europe the witness's chair often is positioned toward the judge, the person to whom he must answer. Furniture arrangement within the home also communicates something about the culture. For example, in cultures where television viewing is important, and where conversation is not valued, the chairs in a living room will most likely be pointed at the television set rather than in a pattern that would stimulate conversation. The opposite is true, of course, in cultures such as the French and Italian where conversation is an important part of the culture. In these instances, the chairs are arranged in a manner that is conducive to communication.

Even the arrangement of office furniture can give us a clue to the character of a people. In countries that are somewhat authoritarian, such as Germany and Russia, most offices are planned so that business is conducted with the person in power sitting behind a desk. Bankers, lawyers, and government officials seldom venture from the position of power. In informal cultures (Latin America, Israel), where being comfortable is a cultural value, the desk is perceived as a hindrance to communication and visitors often sit to one side of the desk so that it does not serve as a barrier or a wall.

People's use of space is often indicative of their attitude toward the person with whom they are sharing that space. There are many white Americans who would feel comfortable in a waiting room with other whites. However, should that room be filled with black Americans, that same person might experience claustrophobia and a great deal of anxiety.

In all instances where proxemics is a factor we must keep in mind that what we infer from any given situation depends on other factors discussed earlier. The meaning of any message is related to the state of the person, the perceived relationship between the parties, the personal past history of each, and the context of the situation. These four variables help define the meaning of the space between us and the rest of the world.

Time.   The way each of us sees and treats time helps express part of our character. If we are thirty minutes late for an appointment and arrive without offering an apology, we provide certain messages about ourselves.

The North American conception of time can be divided into three basic categories: formal, informal, and technical.[26] *Formal time* involves basic relationships, like learning the number of weeks and days in a year. It also includes our outlook toward seasons of the year. *Technical time* has little meaning for the layman. It is normally used by such scientists as astronomers when they talk of tropical and sidereal years. It is in the area of *informal time* that there are the greatest implications for human interaction. With informal time we must know something about the person and/or context in which time-related words or ideas are being used. The phrase "I'll be home *in a while*," takes on many different meanings depending on the situation and who made the statement.

We also communicate with informal time without ever talking. For instance, if we are five minutes late for an appointment, no one is likely to think ill of us; but when we arrive an hour late, it is treated as a direct insult and both we and the other person are uncomfortable and disturbed.

Even the time of day or night contains potential messages. If we were to receive a phone call at four o'clock in the morning we probably would assume that it concerns an urgent matter.

Our treatment of time is also a function of status. Increased status allows us to abuse time more freely. The "boss" can arrive late for a meeting without anyone raising an eyebrow; if the secretary is late, a reprimand may be given. A rock star can keep an audience patiently waiting for a long period, but the warm up group had better start on time.

One's concepts of time are conditioned by culture. We have learned how to use and perceive time. A few instances illustrate this idea. In the United States we employ monochronic time. This is a view of time that "emphasizes schedules, segmentation, and promptness."[27] To most of us, the clock is paramount. The time-clock records our hours of work, while the bells at school alert us to potential charges of tardiness. Cultures such as the Swiss and German are even more time conscious than the Americans. This monochronic propensity toward time is not universal. Some Latin American countries have polychronic time orientations in which one is expected to be late; to them tardiness is a sign of respect. Time is not sacred; it is not one's master. Middle Eastern countries also are polychronic rather than monochronic in their use of time. In Iran, for instance, being thirty minutes late for dinner is not an uncommon occurrence. And, it matters little as to who gets served or waited on first. Native American Indians also have a rather unique conception of time. The Sioux Indians, for example, believe that they function and operate in the present—there is no past or future. They do not even have words in their language for time, late, or waiting.

Subcultures and subgroups within the United States often perceive time in a manner that is quite different from the view held by the dominant culture. Recall that in Chapter 2 we discussed how some blacks use "hang-loose time." In this is a time orientation priority that belongs to what one is doing at a particular instant. What is happening now ("Hey, man, what's happenin' ") is important. Words such as "doing time" and "serving time" help underscore the place time occupies for those people who are incarcerated. And for the hard-core poor, with very little to do and a great deal of "free time," the day is not broken up in units that center around eating, working, and sleeping. They, too, use a "clock" that keeps a time different from the one employed by middle-class America.

What these few examples demonstrate is that a culture's method of treating time tells us two things. First, it offers us specific data about an individual. And, second, it reflects the deep structure of that individual's culture; it helps us understand the relationship between attitudes, values, and behavior.

Silence.　If we reflect on the notion of silence we can see easily how it, too, sends us nonverbal cues concerning the communication situation we are in. Observe the poignant use of silence when the classical composer strategically places intervals of orchestration so that the ensuing silence marks a contrast in expression. Or someone says, "There was not even a sound, not any applause, only a deafening and profound silence."

Silence cues refer specifically to all the nonverbalized portions of an ongoing interaction in which silence affects the rate and flow of the concomitant verbal exchange. It includes all the various kinds and degrees of silence that are frequently described as cold, oppressive, defiant, disapproving or condemning, calming, approving, humble, excusing, and consenting. Silence cues have a meaning all their own that supplements the other forms of human communication.

The meaning we assign to silence is contingent on a number of factors. First, the duration of a silence can have a considerable effect on our response. If a professor asks a question of a student, and that student takes a long time to answer, the duration of the silence will influence the entire situation. The professor, the student, and the other members of the class will all infer meaning from the silence. Second, the appropriateness of the silence can be important. If, for example, the silence comes when it is not expected, we might infer a meaning quite different from silence that seems well-suited for the occasion. Third, what has just preceded the silence also has an impact. If, in mixed company and right after church, a tasteless joke is told, and silence follows the punch line, we probably would understand immediately what the silence means. Finally, the relationship existing between the participants also will exert some sway over the interpretation given to the silence. For example, some silence cues occur at the onset of an encounter and are characteristic of an individual who remains still until he decides what the other person is like.

Silence cues affect interpersonal communication by providing an interval in an ongoing interaction during which the participants have time to think, check or suppress an emotion, encode a lengthy response, or inaugurate another line of thought. Silence also functions as a feedback mechanism informing both sender and receiver as to the clarity of an idea or its significance in the overall interpersonal exchange. Silence cues may be regarded as evidence of agreement, lack of interest, injured feelings, or contempt. Like olfactory and tactile cues, silence cues transcend the verbal channel, often revealing what speech conceals.

The intercultural implications of silence are as diverse as the other nonverbal cues we have examined in this chapter. Our use of and reaction to silence is another one of those aspects of culture that has evolved within us because of our membership in a particular group. "Rapping," radio, television, and the sounds and noises that they produce, are part of our cultural experience here in the United States. In some other cultures, however, an environment that is hushed and still is the rule.

There also are cultures that hold great reverence for silence. The Buddhist wedding, for example, is basically conducted in silence. Many students of Zen believe that words often contaminate an experience, and that inner peace comes only through silence. Many American Indians hold a similar view. For them words are used with extreme care. It is silence, and not speaking, that is a sign of a great man. "One derives from silence the cornerstone of character, the virtues of self control, courage, patience and dignity."[28]

Summary

The conclusion of this chapter on nonverbal communication is an excellent place to restate a major theme because we have just finished an extensive look at cultural differences and their potential impact on intercultural communication. Diversity in culture and differences in communication styles have been shown to be potential intercultural problems. It is not only diversity, however, but also, and perhaps more important, it is our difficulty in accepting diversity which accounts for the most serious problems and challenges to intercultural communication. Awareness of cultural variations, coupled with a willingness to appreciate those variations, greatly facilitates our intercultural contacts.

Notes

1. Dean C. Barnlund, *Interpersonal Communication: Survey and Studies* (Boston: Houghton Mifflin, 1968), pp. 536–37.

2. Erving Goffman, *The Presentation of Self in Everyday Life* (New York: Doubleday, 1957), p. 2.

3. Weston LaBarre, "Paralinguistics, Kinesics, and Cultural Anthropology," in Larry A. Samovar and Richard E. Porter, eds., *Intercultural Communication: A Reader*, 2d ed. (Belmont, Calif.: Wadsworth, 1976), p. 221.

4. Judee Burgoon and Thomas Saine, *The Unspoken Dialogue: An Introduction to Nonverbal Communication* (Boston: Houghton Mifflin, 1978), p. 145.

5. Marianne LaFrance and Clara Mayo, *Moving Bodies: Nonverbal Communication in Social Relationships* (Monterey, Calif.: Brooks/Cole, 1978), p. 177.

6. Flora Davis, *Inside Intuition* (New York: Signet, 1975), p. 177.

7. Shila I. Ramsey, "Prison Codes," *Journal of Communication* 26 (1976): 40.

8. Kenneth R. Johnson, "Black Kinesics: Some Nonverbal Communication Patterns," *Florida F L Reporter*, 9 (1971): 17–20, 57.

9. Burgoon and Saine, p. 123.

10. Robert G. Harper, Arthur N. Wiens, and Joseph D. Matarazzo, *Nonverbal Communication: The State of the Art* (New York: John Wiley, 1978), p. 164.

11. Desmond Morris, et al., *Gestures: Their Origins and Distribution* (New York: Stein and Day, 1979), pp. 206–10.

12. Davis, pp. 18–19.

13. Gordon W. Hewes, "The Anthropology of Posture," *Scientific American* 196 (1957): 122–32.

14. Paul Ekman, Wallace V. Friesen, and Phoebe Ellsworth, *Emotion in the Human Face* (New York: Pergamon Books, 1971). *See also* Paul Ekman, Richard Sorenson, and Wallace V. Friesen, "Pan-Cultural Elements in Facial Displays of Emotion," *Science* 64 (1969): 86–88.

15. Davis, p. 47. *See also,* Ray L. Birdwhistell, *Kinesics and Context* (Philadelphia: University of Pennsylvania Press, 1970).

16. LaFrance and Mayo, p. 177.

17. Lawrence Rosenfeld and Jean M. Civikly, *With Words Unspoken: The Nonverbal Experience* (New York: Holt, Rinehart & Winston, 1976), p. 230.

18. J.D. Salinger, *The Catcher in the Rye* (New York: Grosset and Dunlap, 1945), p. 103.

19. Randall P. Harrison, *Beyond Words: An Introduction to Nonverbal Communication* (Englewood Cliffs, N.J.: Prentice-Hall, 1974), p. 91.

20. O.M. Watson and T.D. Graves, "Quantitative Research in Proxemic Behavior," *American Anthropologists* 68 (1966): 971–85.

21. Harper, Wiens, and Matarazzo, p. 297.

22. Ramsey, p. 40.

23. Edward T. Hall, *The Hidden Dimension* (New York: Doubleday, 1966), pp. 159–60.

24. Mark L. Knapp, *Nonverbal Communication in Human Interaction,* 2d ed. (New York: Holt, Rinehart & Winston, 1978), p. 334.

25. "Gay is Beautiful — At a Distance," *Psychology Today* (January, 1976): 101.

26. Hall, *Silent Language.*

27. Edward T. Hall, *Beyond Culture* (New York: Doubleday, 1976), p. 14.

28. Richard L. Johannesen, "The Functions of Silence: A Plea for Communication Research," *Western Speech* (1974): 27.

Additional Readings

Ashcraft, Norman and Albert E. Scheflen. *People Space: The Making and Breaking of Human Boundaries.* New York: Anchor Press/Doubleday, 1976.

Burgoon, J. K. and T. Saine. *The Unspoken Dialogue: An Introduction to Nonverbal Communication.* Boston: Houghton Mifflin, 1978, Ch. 5.

Hall, Edward T. *Beyond Culture.* New York: Anchor Press/Doubleday, 1976.

Harper, R. G., A. N. Wiens, and J. D. Matarazzo. *Nonverbal Communication: The State of the Art.* New York: John Wiley, 1978.

Little, K. B. "Cultural Variations in Social Schemata." *Journal of Personality and Social Psychology* 10 (1968): 1–7.

Morris, D., et al. *Gestures: Their Origins and Distribution.* New York: Stein and Day, 1979.

Rosenfeld, L. B. and J. M. Civikly. *With Words Unspoken: The Nonverbal Experience.* New York: Holt, Rinehart & Winston, 1976, Ch. 16.

Scheflen, A. E. *How Behavior Means.* New York: Anchor Books/Doubleday, 1974.

Concepts and Questions

1. What are some problems in studying nonverbal communication? Are there some ways to overcome some of these problems?

2. Why must we look at both intentional and unintentional nonverbal behaviors? Give a hypothetical example of each.

3. Is it easier to overcome the problems related to nonverbal actions or verbal language?

4. Explain the phrase "our nonverbal actions usually are a reflection of our culture." Give some examples.

5. How does your culture use nonverbal actions to show attitudes about another person or a situation?

6. Think of some personal experiences where you misread the nonverbal actions of someone from another culture.

7. Which one of the various types of nonverbal behaviors discussed in this chapter do you think is most important to the student of intercultural communication? Justify your answer.

Exercises

1. With the assistance of your instructor, organize an international get-together involving foreign students from several countries. Request the foreign students to bring slides of people and events of their native countries. As they show their slides, ask them to explain briefly the meanings of various nonverbal cues (e.g., dress, gestures, architecture, etc.). Did you find that the meanings assigned by you were different from the meanings explained by the foreign student? Did you feel that some explanations did not make sense? What were other problems experienced as you tried to understand the slides shown?

2. Attend a social function of members of a foreign national group and observe various nonverbal cultural elements used by the members of that particular cultural/nationality group. For instance, observe their personal appearance, dress, body movements (e.g., greetings, leaving-taking gestures), and space cues. What were the most distinctive nonverbal cues that you observed? What meanings did you assign to these cues? Check with three or four persons from that foreign country to what extent your meanings were accurate. How can you overcome the problems of misperception of nonverbal cues?

3. See a foreign film with someone from the country in which the film was produced. Observe various nonverbal elements and check with your foreign friend the meanings of nonverbal situations that do not make sense. Correlate your meanings with the meanings explained by your friend. What types of nonverbal cues were most difficult to understand? Why? To what extent do the meanings depend on the context? To what extent are nonverbal cues and culture related? How did you feel when some nonverbal messages did not make sense? Did you find subtitles helpful? Why?

IV

Improvement:
Horizons
and
Limitations

8

Becoming More Effective: A Point of View

All things are daily changing.
Plutarch

The idea that communication is an activity in which people engage and that this activity produces consequences is a thread that has been woven in and out of each preceding chapter. In this final chapter, we once again will examine the impact of those ideas. This time, however, we are concerned with effectiveness and proficiency in that activity. To this end, we will focus our attention on improving our participation in intercultural communication.

This section has four closely related goals and purposes. First, we will review some of the key concepts of our previous study and indicate how they can become potential intercultural communication problems. Second, we will explore the resolution of these problems and find some advice and counsel for improvement. Third, we will see how a change of attitude and a new set of ethical judgments toward the communication act can make us more effective intercultural communicators. And, fourth, we will explore briefly the future of intercultural communication—a future that is measured in terms of decades as well as days, a future that will be characterized by the continued development of technology, travel, and ever increasing intercultural interaction. It is inevitable that people will know more about each other, and that they also will be in closer physical contact. Both of these factors contribute to a world that is quite different from the one in which we now live. We will consider the import of this new world.

Potential Problems in Intercultural Communication

In most instances, if problems occur, it is for an assortment of reasons. If we lose our temper at a friend, does not a little introspection often reveal that it was not really our friend that prompted our anger, but rather an accumulation of events and that our friend was merely a handy target? Although we will discuss potential problems in isolation and in single categories, they most often occur in combination.

Since communication involves both a sender and a receiver, when difficulties do arise, they are usually the fault of both. During the course of our analysis, the issues we select often apply to all the participants in the interchange. In fact, trying to locate the guilty party may well be a communication problem in and of itself.

Diversity of Communication Purposes

Communication problems often occur because we all have different reasons and motivations that prompt us to interact with other people. These reasons range from the simple to the complex, covering purposes as diverse as seeking the time of day to receiving emotional catharsis. In the intercultural setting this diversity of purposes often can be a potential problem. For example, our communication purpose might be misunderstood if, while traveling in Turkey, we were to approach an elderly female and ask her to recommend a hotel or restaurant. Such an advance, by a male stranger, would be highly inappropriate in Turkey. Our innocent reason for making contact could be misconstrued.

There are countless other instances when communication purposes and goals are at such variance that they create a climate for potential problems. Visualize a situation in which a member of one culture believes that a religious ceremony is a time for joyous behavior and humorous stories, while a person from another culture sees the purpose of such ceremonies as sacred and serious. A lack of understanding regarding this diversity can create ill feelings as well as some embarrassment. An American, while traveling in Japan, stopped to take pictures of a Buddhist wedding. For him, weddings were occasions of great merriment and hence picture taking seemed a natural activity. To the Buddhists, however, weddings had a different purpose, and hence they were greatly offended by the picture taking. People use communication for a variety of purposes, and although this diversity is normal, it can be a source of misunderstanding.

Ethnocentrism

This book has stressed the notion of individual differences and the uniqueness of each person. Yet there also have been corollary themes that emphasized the role of culture in our perceptions and our attitudes. Contained in each of those discussions was the role individual differences play in our perception of ourselves and the world. This position grows out of a number of assumptions. If we accept the belief that our past influences our view of reality and the corresponding tenet that each of us may have similar but not identical personal past histories, then it should follow that another person's picture of the universe will not be exactly like ours. Yet most of us act as if our way of perceiving things is the correct and only way. We often overlook perceptual differences and conclude that if the other person doesn't see that Pablo Picasso is the greatest artist that ever lived, he simply does not know art. Actually, it may well be that he has a different past history and what is great art for him may not match our perception of art.

The problem of perceptual differences is often far deeper than the evaluation of art. In our daily activities these differences appear between different groups and subgroups. Various generations, minorities, occupations, and cultures have conflicting values and goals that will influence their orientation and interpretation of reality. We know from our own experiences that if we were to see a man with long hair hitchhiking, we most likely would stop and offer him a ride. On the other hand, people from a different generation that associated long hair with "those freaky types" might well drive right past the hitchhiker because their background causes them to view the world differently than we do. The difficulty, as we mentioned, grows out of the fact that we usually behave as if the view of the world that we hold is the right one, the correct one, and the only one.

Our culture is a major factor in perceptual discrepancies. Culture helps supply us with our perspective of reality. It therefore plays a dominant role in intercultural communication. For example, if our culture admires thin women, then we would tend to have negative reactions (at least concerning appearance) to cultures that venerate the stout female. If we perceive openness as a positive trait while another culture fosters silence, we again have perceptual differences. These differences and countless others are learned at an early age and can influence the type of communication that takes place.

When our perceptions and our subsequent communication behavior are characterized by this narrow and rigid orientation, we are guilty of ethnocentrism. Ethnocentrism, which is "the tendency to interpret or to judge all other groups, their environments, and their communication according to the categories and values of our own cul-

194

ture,"[1] is one of those communication problems that seems to cut across nearly all cultures. There are very few instances of cultures that are free of this negative characteristic. Many serious students of intercultural communication believe that ethnocentrism is not only common among most cultures, but it also is a major barrier to intercultural understanding.

Because ethnocentrism usually is learned at the unconscious level, and manifested at the conscious level, it is hard to trace its origins. Ethnocentric biases seem, in most instances, to be part of our cultural package. But regardless of who or what is the culprit, ethnocentrism is a potential communication problem that plagues most intercultural encounters.

Reflect for a moment on those situations when we have placed our cultural group above another. How do we judge Jews, Pakistanis, blacks, or the poor? Undoubtedly, we evaluate them by our group's cultural standards. Our culture tells us, in a variety of ways, how to judge others and what to use as criteria for those judgments. The danger of such evaluations is that they are often false, misleading, and arbitrary. It is truly a naive view of the world to believe and behave as if we and our culture have discovered *the* true and only set of norms. The Jew covers his head to pray, the Protestant does not—is one more correct than the other? In Saudi Arabia women cover their faces, in America they cover very little—is one more correct than the other? The Occidental speaks to God, the Oriental has God speak to him—is one more correct than the other? The American Indian values and accepts nature, the average American seeks to alter nature—is one more correct than the other? A listing of these questions is never-ending. We must remember, however, that it is not the questions that are important, but rather the dogmatic way in which we answer them. If we allow ethnocentrism to interfere with our perceptions, with our interactions and with our reactions, we will reduce the effectiveness of our efforts. To be successful we must be ever vigilant, for "we do know that ethnocentrism is strongest in moral and religious contexts, where emotionalism may overshadow rationality and cause so much hostility that communication ceases."[2]

Lack of Trust

When we trust other persons they usually are sending both verbal and nonverbal messages that inform us that they are the type of persons we wish to take into our confidence—the type of persons who, because we can trust them, make us feel comfortable and at ease. As we reflect upon the people we have met, a long list of traits that encourage and discourage trust becomes apparent. For example, how often do we trust someone who is critical of whatever we do or say? Do we confide in the individuals who, by words or deeds, create a partition between themselves and us? And what about the person who seldom smiles? In all three of these instances we are faced with someone who makes trusting rather difficult. On the other hand, notice how we tend to trust the person who makes us feel comfortable and manifests concern for us and our ideas. In short, we reveal more and are freer when our partner allows us the opportunity to be honest and open instead of inhibited and restrained.

The intercultural setting, because of its unique characteristics, is often a communication exchange that is marked by a lack of trust. Most of us are reluctant to take personal risks with strangers. We tend to perceive differences in color and culture to be far greater than they really are. Individual differences often are more profound than are cultural variations. Yet even knowing this fact, in most intercultural situations we let the differences inhibit communication. Instead of finding enjoyment and stimulation from cultural contact, we develop feelings that make trusting extremely complicated. In the United States this lack of trust is perhaps most evident in those situations involving a black person or a Hispanic who is interacting with a white person. Most of this mistrust centers on intent and background. When this happens there is very little opportunity for meaningful communication. ". . . It is so easy for people who bear suspicion or hostility toward each other to miss the basic assumptions upon which a message rests. . . . If this occurs, then the communicators are talking at different levels."[3]

Withdrawal

It is nearly impossible for communication to take place when one of the participants has, for whatever reason, psychologically withdrawn from the encounter. Although it is a somber observation of modern man, feelings of withdrawal, apathy, and alienation seem to be more prevalent now than ever before. We can only speculate as to the causes behind our feelings of estrangement. Perhaps it is the vastness and unresponsiveness of our institutions, or the fear and distrust of other people that seem to have accompanied urban expansion. Whatever the reason, many of us have lost faith in communication as a means of resolving our problems, and have withdrawn from personal interaction with others.

The problems of withdrawal are so overt that we need only touch on them. When individuals retreat from communication we can no longer learn from them, or offer them support. And, if communication truly is reciprocal, they in turn cannot profit from their contact with us.

There are many instances, on both the international and domestic level, where withdrawal marks the intercultural exchange. History is replete with examples of how one nation refused to attend (withdrew from) an important peace conference. For decades the peoples and governments of the United States and China refused to talk to each other. It was only after both parties agreed to interact that any kind of accord was reached. The vivid example of Israel and Egypt also underscores the folly of withdrawal. We need to reflect on our own behavior and ask ourselves how many times we have retreated from communication. In many of these instances the other person might well have been someone of a different color or cultural background. When this happens communication ceases and all attempts at mutual understanding are lost.

Lack of Empathy

As producers and consumers of messages it behooves us to understand how to send our messages and also what to make of the messages we receive from others. One important factor in making decisions about what to say, and in comprehending what other people intended to say, centers on the issue of empathy, which is the "ability to feel like another or to place oneself in another's shoes."[4] To communicate effectively with other people, we must be able to create inner images that give us some insight into their feelings and characteristics. This sharing of experiences is a difficult task, for empathy hinges on the assumption that we are able to understand and in some way share the internal states of those whom we resemble. Yet the fact remains, that however similar we may appear to be, there is something distinctive and unique about each of us. Our internal states are elusive, fleeting, and only known to us in forms and shapes resembling distorted shadows. Hence, knowing the other person, predicting their reactions, and anticipating their needs, is a troublesome assignment.

Our inability to understand completely, to appreciate, accept, and even take pleasure in these individual and cultural differences is but one problem we face in trying to develop empathy. In addition, there appears to be a number of behaviors we often employ that keep us from understanding the feelings, thoughts, and motives of another person. Perhaps the most common of all barriers to empathy is *a constant self-focus*. It is difficult to concentrate on another person if we are consumed by thoughts of ourselves. If the main focus of our attention is directed toward thoughts of how much the other person likes our boots or hair style, we certainly are not in a position to expend much energy in the direction of developing empathy.

The tendency to note only some features at the exclusion of others often

197

causes us to misuse the data we gather about another person. If, for example, we notice only a person's skin color or surname, and from this limited information assume we know all there is to know about that person, we are apt to do a poor job of empathizing with that person. Admittedly color and names offer us some information about the person in front of us, but this type of data must be considered along with a whole host of other behaviors being generated by the person. Although it is an obvious analogy, we should remember that most outward features only represent the tip of the iceberg.

The stereotyped notions concerning race and culture that we carry around in our heads also serve as potential inhibiters to empathy. If we have the idea that "all English people dislike the Irish," we might allow this stereotype to influence our view of an English person who happens to hold no ill feelings toward the Irish. Stereotyped notions are part of our personalities, so we must be careful not to allow these generalizations to serve as our models of other people.

Lack of previous knowledge about a certain group, class, or person also impedes the development of empathy. If we have never been around Mexicans nor had an opportunity to share in their culture, it might be quite easy for us to misread some of their behavior associated with their concept of time (a somewhat laissez faire attitude toward the clock). This lack of knowledge could cause us to draw a conclusion from some specific action that is not at all related to the real motivation behind the behavior.

We often *engage in behavior that keeps other people from wanting to reveal information about themselves.* This is called defensive communication. If people are "put off" by our actions, they are not likely to disclose very much to us. It is nearly impossible to make accurate predictions concerning how others will act if, by our behavior, we have created a situation that makes it difficult for them to be natural and open. During the course of defensive communication we are apt to receive very little information that will contribute to our knowing the other person. Because they are so common, it might be helpful for us to examine how some defensive actions stifle empathy.

When we appear to be *evaluating* other people, whether by what we say or what we do, we are likely to make them feel defensive toward us. Most of us, if we feel we are being evaluated, will be hesitant to offer communication that will foster empathy. Do we not experience a potential communication problem when, after sharing some personal information, the other person quickly lectures us on the rashness of our act? After a few minutes of criticism and ridicule we will probably decide not to disclose any other private information to that particular person.

When we appear to be *controlling* another individual we are employing communication behavior that will make him defensive and guarded. Notice the next time a salesman is overly aggressive toward you and tries to control your actions and attitudes. You will most likely respond to his efforts by being defensive toward him.

Most of us also have an aversion to revealing very much to the person who we deem to be *neutral* toward us and our ideas. Empathy, which is most effective when it is reciprocal, cannot take place when one of the individuals becomes defensive over the neutrality and disinterest being manifested by the other person. Again, we must answer this question: "How much do I disclose to a person who is neutral toward me and to what I am saying?"

A communication attitude of *superiority*, which produces defensive behavior, seldom offers us the kind of information we need to empathize. Instead, superiority puts another person in an uncomfortable position and keeps him from wanting to discuss anything personal or important. Imagine how defensive we would become if someone from France spent the bulk of his time telling us how French was the only pure language. Both parties would have some difficulty gaining insight into the other.

A potential communication problem is also common when we interact with a person who manifests *certainty*. If someone is dogmatic, and communicates as if he has answers to questions we have not even asked, we are likely to become defensive around that person. In the case of the dogmatic person our defensiveness may take the form of silence, and it is probable that this lack of communication will not be conducive to empathy. Very little is revealed when people are not interacting at all levels.

Two final notes regarding empathy. First, under normal conditions it is extremely difficult to transpose yourself into the personality of another person. When we add the ingredient of culture, the process becomes even more complicated. This section on the problems of developing empathy concludes, therefore, with an appeal that we be watchful of those occasions when we find ourselves only making mild attempts at empathizing, for it will be at those instances when communication is least effective. Second, because of the importance of empathy to intercultural communication, we shall return to this topic later when advice for improving interaction among people of different backgrounds is offered.

Stereotyping

Our propensity for stereotyping is perhaps one of the most serious problems in intercultural communication. Although we examined stereotyping in some detail in Chapter 5, it is an issue of such importance that it warrants further consideration. Recall that, in general terms, stereotyping involves our beliefs about groups of individuals based on previously formed opinions, perceptions, and attitudes. Stereotyping is very common in intercultural settings. The widespread nature of stereotyping can best be pointed out by asking ourselves this question: "How often am I guilty of jumping to conclusions and treating a specific individual as if he or she were just like the preconceived model I carry around in my head?" Most of us would have to conclude that our behavior toward others is often characterized by some degree of stereotyping.

As just noted, the pervasive nature of stereotyping is most evident in the intercultural setting. It is in this context that we tend to stereotype people and groups based on very little knowledge or contact. It is both effortless and comfortable to be able to quickly say "All Jews are . . . " or "He is a Mexican, therefore he must . . . " Such conclusions take little energy, and also exonerate the individual from any other reflection or observation. He is able, often without ever knowing a Jew or a Mexican, to act as if he knows all about the person who stands before him. It is, in short, a lazy method of interaction.

Not only is stereotyping an indolent way of perceiving and communicating with other people, but for many it is a defense mechanism and a device for reducing anxiety. To depend on preconceptions and stereotypes is a common defense technique for reducing culture shock.[5] And as we all realize, culture shock is that overwhelming and disturbing feeling we experience when we are thrust into a situation or environment that contains very few familiar symbols or behaviors. What happens is that we become frustrated and simply do not know how to act. In these instances, stereotyping often takes over. Stereotyping is not necessary, but it is often easier than suspending conclusions and coping with ambiguity. Because many of us are lazy, and reluctant to expend the energy necessary to know others in alien situations, we are willing to reduce our confusion by accepting misleading information. The problem, however, is that stereotypes, as pictures in our head, are usually rigid, resistant to change, used as defense mechanisms, incorrect, and often highly unfavorable. This type of list, as we surely must realize, is not conducive to successful intercultural communication. In fact, this sort of fixation on negative traits keeps both parties from ever experiencing the joy of knowing about another person and his culture. In summary, to be negative and to overgeneralize (stereotyping) can only serve to hinder communication.

Power

Our concern with power begins with these two assertions: (1) In every communication relationship there is some degree of power. (2) It is not power that represents the potential communication problem, but the misuse of power. Let us now examine these two statements and relate them to intercultural communication.

In most instances power so permeates the encounter that most of us just assume its presence. From parent-child relationships to world power politics, we learn about power. The methods of power are as diverse as they are widespread. People and cultures have employed guns, bombs, language, space, money, and even history as devices for controlling others. Cries of black, brown, gray, red, and gay power only serve to attest to the importance of power in the intercultural context. Understanding power and its effect on communication, therefore, is an important part of understanding intercultural communication.

Our degree of power is contingent upon the person(s) we are interacting with and the resources that we control. In intercultural communication these two factors take on added significance, for the sources of power are culturally based, and what one culture deems as a source of power another culture may not even consider a power variable. For example, in England one's language is often a sign of potential power. It signals one's class and station in that culture. There are countless cultures, however, where language is not a consideration. There also are instances when one culture believes that power is derived from simply being a member of that particular culture. The whites' relationship with the blacks in the United States is often an example of this assumed power, and, for over a century whites in the United States have been hesitant to relinquish this power. It is easy to see how this use, or misuse, of power, when employed to control and to determine another's behavior, can restrict openness and communication. "To allow customary subservience or power a place in human interaction is to introduce an inevitable obstruction."[6] Adherence to the following philosophy could help us avoid that obstruction.

> The ideal power relationship . . . is not concerned with the idea of control . . . . Rather, the desire is to attribute to all . . . groups the credibility that allows them positive influence in communication situations.[7]

Perhaps the most appropriate way to end this section on potential problems is to try to place all seven propositions under one heading. Looking for just such a phrase or summary we recall the words of a famous modern philosopher who was searching for a cause behind much of man's failure. His plight is analogous to ours. For where do we look for dragons to slay or metaphors to explain? We believe that Pogo, our modern sage, gave us the answer when he said, "We have met the enemy, and he is us." So be it with communication problems.

201

If problems occur, we must not look to someone else as a means of locating and placing blame—we must look to ourselves. We are the enemy.

Improving Intercultural Communication

Sincere and conscientious attempts to improve intercultural communication are neither new nor original with this book. Since World War II we have had to learn to deal with an entire new series of relationships. During the fifties and sixties, as we saw in Chapter 1, travel and new and advanced technology brought about more and closer intercultural contact. During the 1970s these earlier trends accelerated and were added to by problems of shortages of natural resources, forced integration, nuclear proliferation, and an ever-increasing distance between the world's have's and have-not's. As the issues become more acute, so does the need for improved intercultural communication. What those who offer suggestions rely on are the observations of people who have had experience dealing with intercultural communication. We have tried, thus far, to share with you some of the benefits of their experience.

The theme throughout this book has been that successful intercultural interaction is based on effective communication. The same attitudes and skills that we need to develop to communicate in general apply to intercultural communication, only more so. To be communicative is to be open, responsive, and nonjudgmental. It may be difficult to achieve these attitudes, especially in intercultural interactions, but it is not impossible. Let us now turn our attention to those techniques, devices, and philosophies that can help us develop those skills and attitudes.

Know Yourself

Perhaps the first thing we can do to improve our intercultural communication and resolve many of our problems is to know ourselves. By knowing ourself we are not referring to any mystical notions or deep psychological soul searching, but rather to the simple act of identifying those attitudes, opinions, and biases that we all carry around. These attributes help determine not only what we say but what we hear others say. If we hold a certain attitude toward homosexuals, and a man who is a homosexual talks to us, our response to what he says will be colored by our precommunication attitude. Knowing our likes, dislikes, and degrees of personal ethnocentrism enables us to place them out in the open so that we can identify them and deal with them.

This is essential for successful intercultural communication. Hidden personal premises, be they directed at ideas, people, or entire cultures, are often a cause of many of our problems.

The second step in knowing ourself is somewhat more difficult than simply identifying our prejudices and predispositions. It involves discovering the kind of image we portray to the rest of the world. That is to say, how do we communicate? The importance of this type of introspection cannot be stressed enough. We all have heard stories regarding how foreigners view Americans who travel abroad. The "Ugly American" example might be trite, but often it is true. Therefore, if we are to improve our communication and understand the reaction of others toward us, we must have some ideas of how other people perceive us. If, for instance, we see ourself as serious and austere, while in reality we present a different image to people, we will have a hard time trying to determine why people react to us as they do. We must, therefore, take stock of our actions, both verbal and nonverbal, if we are to understand why people behave around us as they do.

What is suggested here is that we identify what is called our "communicative style." Our individual and cultural styles include "the topics people prefer to discuss, their favorite forms of interaction—ritual, repartee, argument, self-disclosure—and the depth of involvement they demand of each other. It includes the extent to which communicants rely upon the same channels—vocal, verbal, physical—for conveying information, and the extent to which they are tuned to the same level of meaning, that is, to the factual and emotional content of messages. The use of a common vocabulary and even preference for similar metaphors. . . . "[8] Our styles even include the way we employ time and space.

If we have a fairly accurate picture of how we present ourself, our individual and cultural communicative styles, we will have taken the first step toward improving our communication, for we would now be able to understand better the reactions of others, and also be in a position to make the necessary adaptations in our style as we move from one communication context to another.

Discovering how other people perceive us is not an easy task. It is somewhat awkward and highly irregular for us to walk around asking people what they think of us. We must, therefore, be sensitive to the feedback we receive, and perceptive in the reading of that feedback. If we look menacing when we are not, and fail to be aware of that image, we will not be able to accurately formulate our messages or even understand the messages we receive from others.

We must learn to ask ourselves questions such as the following: Do I give people my undivided attention? Do I seem at ease or tense? Do I often change the subject after people finish a sentence? Do I deprecate the statements of others? Do I smile often? Do I interrupt repeatedly?

And do I show sympathy when someone has a problem? In addition to these questions, we can gain insight into ourselves by observing the topics we select to talk about when the choice is ours. We also can gain some personal knowledge by noting the type of people toward whom we gravitate. Our tone of voice, our expressions, our apparent receptiveness to the responses of others, and literally hundreds of other factors all have an impact on those we wish to reach. Frequently overlooked, these subtleties of communication often affect a person's reaction to us and our message.

Use a Shared Code

In Chapter 6 we discussed the idea that meanings are in people not in words. This basic precept of language serves as a tool for improvement. Stated as a positive axiom for successful communication, both parties should share a common code. There are countless subcodes contained within the English language, and to improve our communication we must know the specific code being used by the other person. If he uses a jargon that is indigenous to a certain group, we must know that jargon as part of the code. If he uses a black argot and says "Am I right Leroy, you was cribbin' over there then," we also must attempt to share that symbol system if communication is going to take place.

As the last example indicates, the ambiguity of our language is compounded when we attempt to share our ideas with someone considerably removed from our specific background and frame of reference. Although it is a stereotyped illustration, try to imagine the difficulty of sharing a code if one person uses street argot from the "hip" culture ("Man, that's cool") and the other person is from a small rural community that has developed yet another form of slang. Admitting the exaggerated nature of our example, it nevertheless underscores the necessity for sharing a common code.

The importance of a shared code is greatly compounded when a foreign language is being spoken. The issue of translation has already been discussed elsewhere in the book, so our purpose here is to remember that vocabulary, syntax, and dialects represent only a small portion of the variables of the spoken code. We must always work toward trying to break the code—to understand the picture in the head of the other person. That picture will tell us more about what is being discussed than will the sound of the word. Nonverbal behavior also shifts from culture to culture. For example, in Japan a female may cover her mouth as a sign of shyness, while in America that same activity is apt to be stimulated by fear.

Because nonverbal differences are often subtle they tend to be over-looked. Yet nonverbal actions usually offer insight into what is being communicated and at the same time they also are offering a glimpse into the deep structure of the culture. Hence, we must be aware of these nonverbal elements as we begin our intercultural training.

Take Time

The notion of taking time when communicating actually includes two separate observations. The first relates to our common tendency to jump to conclusions. We all know how hard it is to suspend judgment and hold off on our evaluations. Think of those occasions when we decided we did not like a particular class even before we gave it an opportunity to get started and yet ultimately enjoyed the experience. In communication we often end up doing much the same thing. We finish the thought or idea for the other person before he has finished talking, and in many instances it is only our conception of what he would have said. There is no positive compensation for a quick deci-sion, particularly if that decision was made without sufficient evidence. In fact, we most likely will discover that by suspending our conclu-sions, and taking time to communicate, we might be learning things we did not know. In this way we reap the rewards that accompany increased understanding.

When the parties are from different cultures the need to defer conclusions becomes even more manifest. If we do not know the world view, value structure, family orientation, nonverbal codes, and the like, of the other culture we might rush to a false conclusion regarding their communicative behavior. For example, if in our head we do not allow a Jewish person to finish a story, we may well miss the point of the entire transaction, for story telling, and the embellishing of a sim-ple tale, is an important aspect of the Jewish culture. By taking time, therefore, we not only discover the person's main idea, but we also might enjoy the story.

The second way we must learn to take time involves not ourselves but the other person. We must allow the other person the time neces-sary to accomplish his purpose. We have repeatedly seen that each person and culture has a communication style that is unique. Some cultural nonverbal styles call for periods of silence and long pauses. We must learn to respect these phases in the encounter and allow the other person enough time to utilize those periods. We should try to cultivate the necessary patience that will offer us and the other person the time needed to think through and explore ideas and feelings.

Consider the Physical and Human Setting

It has been stressed that meaning and intent are conveyed by more than words. Our total personality and all of our actions come into play each time we are part of a communication experience. In addition, many other factors influence the overall impact of the communication act. As participants in that act we must be aware of the entire setting in which we find ourselves. Consider, for example, the impact of timing, physical setting, and custom on human interaction.

Being aware of *timing* often can make the difference between a successful engagement and one that is characterized by ill feelings and antagonism. What are the circumstances under which someone should tell his or her parents that they plan to drop out of college? Have they rendered their decision at the same time their father has lost his job? Or try to picture attempting to talk over some important business transaction during a period that our communication partner believed to be a solemn occasion. In short, the time we select to communicate might well be as important as the message itself. Few professors will sympathize with the student who waits until the last week of the semester to announce "I would like to come to your office and talk about the midterm examination I missed a few months ago." This is poor timing.

Physical setting must also be taken into consideration. We must learn to be aware of some of the meanings various cultures associate with certain places, settings, and locations. The Hindus view their temples in a somewhat different light from the non-Hindu. Knowing that difference might well be important if we were to meet and communicate with a Hindu. For example, it would be very embarrassing to offer a humorous anecdote in an environment that the other person deems sacred.

Custom and past practice is a concept that is very important in intercultural communication. It refers to our being cognizant of the total situation. Our encounters will be influenced by the degree to which our communication conforms to, or departs from, the expectations of the other person. We will be unsuccessful if custom calls for us to remain standing when we enter a room but instead we take a seat. When, if at all, do we bow? When, if at all, do we offer our hand? These and other questions of custom must be dealt with.

Improve Your Communication Skills

Although our primary focus has been to understand intercultural communication, we also have noted that one needs that knowledge if communicative behavior is to improve. In addition to the improvement that grows out of increased understanding, however, we also can expect to improve our communication if we develop greater proficiency in some basic and practical interactive communication skills. The four most common skills that can aid communication are: (1) interest, (2) organization, (3) delivery, and (4) message reception. The essential nature of these four skills is so evident that we need only remind you of how each operates during the interchange.

In most instances we decide what messages we send to other people. No one tells us to select the words we pick. It is our choice. Because of this, we have no assurance that what *interests* us will interest another person. In most cases, since the selection was highly personal, there is a good chance that it will not interest the receiver. We must, therefore, make sure our messages not only represent our ideas and feelings, but also contain the necessary ingredients to hold attention.

The message we send should not only be interesting but should also be well *organized* and easy to follow. Reflect for a moment on how much of our communication is characterized by messages that are unclear, poorly organized, and generally difficult to follow. We all are guilty of allowing our thoughts and our words to ramble. How presumptuous of us to assume that people will attend to our disorganized verbal wanderings.

We discussed the concept of *delivering* the messages when we talked about potential communication problems. At this point we simply reverse our analysis and speak of improvement of problems. We need only point out that the way we use our voice and body can have a significant influence on the entire meeting. If, by our sounds and actions, we manifest boredom and disinterest, we will not have a very rewarding experience. On the other hand, if our voice and actions show enthusiasm and hold interest, we are likely to be compensated for our efforts.

Finally, we come to *message reception* as a basic communication skill. Too often we assume that when we start talking we can stop listening and watching. We falsely believe that communication is a one-way process, and we merely have to wait our turn to talk and take part. This, of course, is not true. Communication is a dynamic, on-going, interactive process that sees us as both sender and receiver at the same time. Hence, we must develop the skill of being alert to all cues in the environment, and at all times. Even more serious is the error of inattentiveness. This error is compounded by the fact that message reception is one of the most important, most difficult, and most neglected skills in communication. It demands that we concentrate not only on the explicit messages another person is sending, but on the implicit meanings communicated verbally and nonverbally.

Encourage Feedback

The importance of feedback to human communication has already been stressed. So, in this final section we will examine feedback from still another perspective. This time our orientation will focus on how to use and encourage feedback effectively.

Recall that we have seen that feedback enables us to adapt future messages because we are aware of the response produced by earlier messages. Feedback "enables communicators to correct and adjust messages so that they say what the communicators want them to say, and so that requests for responses are understood accurately by the receiver. Without feedback there is no way to monitor the communication process, no way to seek integration and agreement."[9]

Granting that feedback is important, we must learn to create an atmosphere whereby other people are encouraged to offer us feedback. Therefore, let us examine a number of ways we can create situations that encourage others to give us information about ourselves and our messages.

Perhaps there will be occasions when silence instead of words will inspire feedback. If we want the other person to speak up or respond in some nonverbal way, we may want to remain silent and wait. We all probably remember a professor who had the habit of ending each sentence or idea with the phrase "Are there any questions?" The only problem with this technique was that he never paused long enough to allow anyone to respond but would immediately move on to a new idea. His lack of pause and silence did not encourage feedback, and instead forfeited an important method of checking on the success of his communication.

Nonverbal feedback often is as useful as verbal. When we examined nonverbal communication we saw that our nonverbal responses often were harder to control and censor than our verbal. To improve our use of feedback we must, therefore, be tuned in to all aspects of the situation. We must not only recognize the obvious nonverbal signs, like an entire group of people standing up and walking out of the hall during our presentation, but also the more subtle and elusive responses we make with our eyes, fingers, and the like.

We also can encourage feedback by using ourselves as a model of an efficient feedback system. If we offer feedback to others it is likely that this example will become contagious, and people around us will do the same.

Asking questions is also an excellent method of gathering information. We can ask specific questions such as "What do you mean when you say John is lazy?" Or we can ask questions with simple words and phrases such as "What?" or "How come?" In either instance we gather additional data.

Finally, the quality and quantity of available feedback cues shifts from culture to culture. In cultures that are very amicable and animated, such as the Italian and Jewish cultures, there is usually an abundance of data to be evaluated. In most oriental cultures, however, outward displays of emotions and feelings, either by words or actions, often are lacking. Hence, in these instances the communicator must take great care when reading the responses produced by his messages.

Develop Empathy

A lack of empathy nearly always represents a potential communication problem. Our inability to understand and appreciate the point of view and life orientation of others often keeps us from effectively communicating with them. The greater the difference between ourselves and others, the harder it is to empathize. For not only do we lack a common background, but most of us have very little tolerance for people who do not share our particular world view and value system. Our ability to empathize can be greatly enhanced by avoiding some of the pitfalls mentioned earlier in this chapter (see pp. 197–199).

In addition, there are six steps we can follow to improve our skill in developing empathy. We will look briefly at these steps and see how each of them, working in conjunction with the others, can help us understand and respect another person's experiences.

The first step in developing empathy is to *assume there are differences* among individuals and cultures. The philosophical assumption necessary for empathy is a multiple-reality theory, which holds that not all people see the same view of the world. The second step is to *know ourselves*. This has already been discussed but we mention it here because it is necessary for the steps that follow. In the third step, the self-identity that was part of stage two is temporarily set aside for what is called *suspended-self*. "One way of thinking about this procedure is to imagine that the self, or identity, is an arbitrary boundary that we draw between ourselves and the rest of the world, including other people. The suspension of self is the temporary expansion of this boundary— the elimination of separation between self and environment."[10] In the fourth step we *imaginatively put ourselves in the other person's place*. Once we let our imagination inside the other person we are ready for the fifth step—*the empathic experience*. While this experience is still imaginative, it nevertheless comes close to our experience and feelings. Finally, we must *reestablish self*. Granting the excitement and exhilaration of sharing another's experience, we must, however, be able to return to ourselves. To be able to see ourselves and our culture once again.[11]

By learning how to use these six steps we all might be able to

209

overcome our ethnocentric tendencies while becoming more sensitive to the needs, values, and goals of other people.

Seek the Commonalities among Diverse Cultures

Although there has been an attempt to avoid it, this type of book tends to overemphasize the differences existing between people and cultures. Admittedly some of these differences are important; however, in many ways it is our likenesses that enable us to find common ground and establish rapport. It might be interesting to know that "an American child sticks out his tongue to show defiance, a Tibetan to show courtesy to a stranger, and a Chinese to express wonderment,"[12] but it is more important to know that they also share a series of more crucial characteristics that link them together. These likenesses are as obvious as the fact that we all share the same planet, and as subtle as our desire to be free from external restraint. The effective intercultural communicator is aware of these likenesses and seeks to develop them as a means of establishing a bond between himself and the rest of humanity. To know of our commonalities, and to be able to deal with them, is not a philosophical issue, but rather a practical matter. For example, there is nothing religious or metaphysical in appreciating and utilizing the notion that all people seek to avoid stress and try to locate some degree of happiness. It is knowing this kind of general information, combined with the important specifics of a particular culture, that marks the person who is successful in traveling in and out of various intercultural settings.

Our Ethical Responsibilities

There is not a single chapter of this book that has not stressed the theme that culture and communication are inseparable. They are interrelated, like the object and the shadow. There are also corresponding topics, perhaps not as obvious, but just as important, that have traveled with us in and out of every page. They are, simply stated, that (1) communication focuses on people and (2) our actions (or lack of them) have an effect on those people. It is these two precepts that serve as the nucleus of this section.

There is no need here in the final chapter of this book, to stop and review these two ideas in more detail. As we have seen repeatedly, we cannot have communication without it having an influence on other people. Like the sea and sand, if we have one we have the other. We, therefore, will forego review and highlight the consequences of this interrelationship.

In the boldest of terms, if we believe that our communicative behavior has an effect on people, then it follows that we must accept a great personal responsibility for that behavior. Quite simply, communication is an instrumental act and whether it is employed to sell used cars, get elected, ingratiate yourself to an employer, punish children, or deceive teachers, it will have an impact that is either good or bad, desirable or undesirable. Obviously, most cultures recognize the ethical dimensions of communication as we do in our libel, slander, truth in advertising, and campaign practices laws. But just because the majority of our own communication does not involve mass media does not relieve us of considering the effects of our behavior in interpersonal settings.

When we transpose the consequences of our communicative behavior to the intercultural context, the problems and issues are even more complex. In the intercultural encounter, because of the diversity of backgrounds, it is much more difficult to assess and predict the type of response our messages and actions will produce. For example, we have learned, as part of our cultural package, how to thank someone. That is to say, we can predict, with some degree of accuracy, what others expect from us and how they will respond to our signs of appreciation. As we move to other cultures, however, these predictions are not as easy to make. In Latin America one must be profuse in offering thanks, while in England one is to offer very little thanks since too much esteem is considered offensive. Yet in all three instances (United States, Latin America, and England) what we do will affect the other person. There even are more profound cases. In many Eastern cultures (Japan and Indonesia) the desire for interpersonal harmony is an overriding communication value. Members of these cultures will do most anything to keep from disrupting this harmony. They simply smile and say yes to most comments. As we can infer, this cultural trait makes knowing the other person quite involved. But again we must hark back to the main point of this section—our behavior affects other people so we must be aware of the consequences. We must continuously ask ourselves if we are behaving in a way that reaffirms a belief in the intrinsic worth of the human personality, a philosophy that maintains that all people have the same rights. Is our communication contributing to the fulfillment of those rights? It seems to us that anything less would only diminish us and our communication partner. One of the clearest statements and summaries of this entire issue was found not in a book on ethics, but a textbook on business:

> Without indulging in too great refinements, let us remind ourselves that communication also has at bottom a moral aspect. It does, when all is said, *anticipate a change in the conduct of the recipient*. If the change has any large significance it means an interposing or interference with

the autonomy of the other person or persons. And *the tampering with personal drives and desires is a moral act* even if its upshot is not a far-reaching one, or is a beneficial result. To seek to persuade behavior into a new direction may be wholly justifiable and the result in terms of behavior consequences may be salutary. But the judgment of benefit or detriment is *not* for the communicator safely to reach *by himself. He is assuming a moral responsibility*. And he had better be aware of the area with which he concerns himself and the responsibility he assumes. He should be willing to assert as to any given new policy, "I stand behind this as having *good personal consequences for the individuals whom it will affect*." That judgment speaks a moral concern and desired moral outcome. [13]

Futurism—What's Next, and Next, and Next

This book concludes in the same way it started—with a declaration regarding the future of intercultural communication. If we have remained throughout this experience, we are different people from the ones we were when we began. For we have now read about intercultural communication. And, therefore, for better or for worse, with or without consent, we have changed. This change, and the countless others that have taken place since we started this volume, have been inevitable. As the quotation that began this chapter pointed out, "All things are daily changing." And as Bob Dylan repeated nearly two thousand years after Plutarch's observation, "The times they are a-changin'."

The inescapable nature of change is constantly creating a different world. None of us—our institutions, our values, or even our faces—is spared being touched by time. The study of intercultural communication, if it is to be a viable discipline, must be aware of, and able to adapt to, these changes. Trying to predict the future, however, is a very difficult assignment. For who among us can say, with any degree of accuracy, what tommorow will be like? And when we talk about thousands upon thousands of tomorrows, the problem seems almost impossible. Yet we must be ready for the tomorrows if we and culture are to prevail. One way to be ready is to use what we have learned from the past—for it tells us something of the future. We have learned, for example, that science seems to have no bounds. They can make beer cans we open with one hand, television sets we operate without moving from our chair, and even a baby. The next hundred years will most likely bring, at least to the industrialized nations, a technology that may have us living in outer space, using computers to do most of our work, and spending the bulk of our time with mediated experiences. We even may be visiting with people from other planets. (If not in space, at least at Disneyland.)

What about intercultural communication's past? What does it tell us about the future? Allowing us the freedom to generalize, we need only to be reminded of the history of intercultural communication mentioned in Chapter 1 and again this chapter—a history dotted with change, problems, conflicts, and people endeavoring to respond to these forces. The next few decades will see the continuation of those activities, activities that will increase both the amount of intercultural contact and the perplexities associated with that contact. Travel will become more commonplace, communication satellites more abundant, and demands for mobility more vehement. There also will be changes in intercultural contact that will be much more profound than the three just mentioned. Those three will bring us together, but the quality of that contact will be greatly influenced by three additional changes that will compel us to re-evaluate our relationships with other people and other cultures. They are the issues of world population, shortages in food and natural resources, and the ever-increasing gulf growing between the have's and have-not's of the world.

These three problems are so interrelated that if we touch one area we must touch the others. Let us look briefly at these topics and see if we can find out their relationship to each other and to intercultural communication.

The seriousness of overpopulation is best explained by citing statistics from the United Nations Statistical Office.

> The world's population reached a total of 3.56 billion in mid-1970, or a 272 million increase over 1969. Latest statistical data also indicate that if the present rate of population growth remains at 2.0 percent, the world's population will double by the year 2006.[14]

If these statistics were not alarming enough, the world's population is increasing daily by an average of 180,000 persons. It is not the statistics in and of themselves that impact intercultural communication, but the way these population figures affect the other two ideas we mentioned.

As the population of the world increases we are discovering that there is not a consistent or equitable distribution of people, resources, and wealth. For example, in India the population density per square mile is 654.7, while in Australia it is 7.0. The unevenness of the earth's natural resources is even more obvious. The Arabs have the oil, the Japanese do not. The garbage disposals in the United States seem to consume more food than do the people of Bangladesh. The list could fill page after page, each item demonstrating a lack of equality regarding space and resources. This disparity is growing at a rapid rate. And with it the distance between those who have an opportunity for "the good life" and those who can only look forward to a life of hardship and possible starvation is also growing.

Perhaps it is time to pause and be more specific regarding how these doomsday prophecies relate to intercultural communication. The first intercultural connection is somewhat philosophical. "Never before have we had the opportunity to know so much about the world we inhabit—its peoples, its natural resources, its technological potential. But it is also true that the quality of life, and respect for the individual worth of each person may be lessening."[15] If this is true, and we are indeed isolating ourselves in every respect but as "world tourists and traders," then the challenges for intercultural communication are quite clear. We cannot continue to ignore the major differences existing between the peoples of the world. If these gulfs are allowed to grow, we might well have a chasm that could confront the world with a major war—a war between the underdeveloped cultures with their large populations and the highly technical cultures with their smaller populations.

We can afford to overlook these major differences for only so long. When there are billions of people who are desperate, and they can see millions of other people who appear free from despair, they will care very little about the consequences of their actions. In the 1960s the United States witnessed a microcosm of this same phenomenon when the people who were living in the major ghettos sensed the hopelessness of their situation and attempted to destroy many of the cities in the United States. There was very little communication taking place between the affected cultures. We would, however, suggest that there were alternatives then as there are actions we can take now. It is not too late. We can begin to accept cultural pluralism while still seeing the oneness among all cultures. We must accept the notion that the web of life, nature's interdependence, applies to all creatures and living things—including man. What we are suggesting is that all people, and all cultures, are inexplicably connected to each other. It matters very little if one wears gold chains around one's neck or gold rings in one's ear, long dresses or no dresses, sees God or hears God—we share the same planet. We all seek pleasures and joys and try to avoid pain. This alone should be enough of a bond to keep us ever mindful of our intercultural behavior and our intercultural obligations. What we must try to do is become multicultural persons. "What is universal about the multicultural person is his abiding commitment to essential similarities between people everywhere, while paradoxically maintaining an equally strong commitment to their differences."[16] The same idea was expressed over two hundred years ago by Comenius:

To hate a man because he was born in another country, because he speaks a different language, or because he takes a different view of

214

this subject or that, is a great folly. Desist, I implore you, for we are all equally human. . . . Let us have but one end in view, the welfare of humanity.

For those of us who would say that such an orientation is simplistic and sophomoric, the only answer is that you are correct, but we would also ask *you* for alternatives. Until that time we must learn to understand one another and be able to communicate our wants, desires, and frustrations. This search for understanding has been the central aim of this book. If we have been at all successful, we will not only be better prepared for our next intercultural encounter, but also for our next, and next, and next.

Peace!

Notes

1. Sharon Ruhly, *Orientations to Intercultural Communication* (Chicago: Science Research Associates, 1976), p. 22.

2. Richard E. Porter and Larry A. Samovar, "Communicating Interculturally" in Larry A. Samovar and Richard E. Porter, eds., *Intercultural Communication: A Reader*, 2d ed. (Belmont, Calif.: Wadsworth, 1976), p. 11.

3. Arthur L. Smith, *Transracial Communication* (Englewood Cliffs, N.J.: Prentice-Hall, 1973), p. 71.

4. Arthur Combs and Donald Snygg, *Individual Behavior: A Perceptual Approach to Behavior* (New York: Harper & Row, 1959), pp. 234–36.

5. La Ray M. Barna, "How Culture Shock Affects Communication" (Paper presented in the Distinguished Scholars Program at the 1976 Communication Association of the Pacific Annual Convention, Koke, Japan, June, 1976), p. 14.

6. Smith, p. 119.

7. Jon A. Blubaugh and Dorthy L. Pennington, *Crossing Differences: Interracial Communication* (Columbus, Ohio: Charles E. Merrill, 1976), p. 39.

8. Dean C. Barnlund, *Public and Private Self in Japan and the United States: Communication Styles of Two Cultures* (Tokyo: Simul Press, 1975), p. 15.

9. William D. Brooks and Phillip Emmert, *Interpersonal Communication* (Dubuque, Iowa: Wm. C. Brown, 1976), pp. 147–48.

10. Milton J. Bennett, "Overcoming the Golden Rule: Sympathy and Empathy" (Paper delivered at the 29th Annual Conference of the International Communication Association, Philadelphia, May, 1979), p. 31.

11. Bennett, pp. 29–34.

12. Yu-Kuang Chu, "Six Suggestions for Learning about Peoples and Cultures" in Seymour Fersh, ed., *Learning About People and Cultures* (Evanston, Ill.: McDougal & Littell, 1974), p. 52.

13. Ordway Tead, *Administration: Its Purpose and Performance* (New York: Harper & Row, 1959), p. 46.

14. Morris Harth, ed., *Family '72 Almanac, New York Times Edition* (New York: *New York Times*, 1972), p. 256.

15. Seymour Fersh, ed., *Learning about People and Cultures* (Evanston, Ill.: McDougal & Littell, 1974), p. 119.

16. Peter S. Adler, "Beyond Cultural Identity: Reflections on Cultural and Multicultural Man" in Richard W. Brislin, ed., *Topics in Culture Learning*, Vol. 2 (Honolulu: East-West Center, 1974), p. 25. Also in Larry A. Samovar and Richard E. Porter, eds., *Intercultural Communication: A Reader*, 2d ed. (Belmont, Calif.: Wadsworth, 1976), p. 364.

Additional Readings

Barnlund, Dean C. *Public and Private Self in Japan and the United States: Communication Styles of Two Cultures.* Tokyo: Simul Press, 1975.

Fersh, Seymour, ed., *Learning about Peoples and Cultures.* Evanston, Ill.: McDougal & Littell, 1974.

Jacobson, Wally D. *Power and Interpersonal Relations.* Belmont, Calif.: Wadsworth, 1972.

Ruben, Brent D., L.R. Alsking, and D.J. Kealey, "Cross-Cultural Effectiveness" in David S. Hoopes, Paul B. Pedersen, and George W. Renwick, eds., *Overview of Intercultural Education, Training, and Research, Volume I: Theory.* Society for Intercultural Education, Training and Research, 1977.

Samovar, Larry A. and Richard E. Porter, eds., *Intercultural Communication: A Reader*, 2d ed. Belmont, Calif.: Wadsworth, 1976, Chs. 6 and 7.

Seelye, H.N. *Teaching Culture: Strategies for Foreign Language Educators.* Skokie, Ill.: National Textbook Company, 1976.

Concepts and Questions

1. List some examples of ethnocentrism that seem to be part of the American character.

2. List some intercultural communication problems that were not mentioned in this chapter.

3. Granting the notion of individual and cultural differences, can we ever truly empathize with another person? How do cultural differences compound the problem?

4. What is the relationship between stereotyping and ethnocentrism?

5. Think of some ways of improving intercultural communication that were not discussed in this chapter.

6. Do you see a future where people of different cultures become closer together or one where they become increasingly isolated from each other?

Exercises

1. Interview the foreign student adviser on your campus to find out the ten most important communication problems experienced by her or him in interacting with foreign students. Discuss the possibility of organizing a short orientation session for foreign students and for the staff of the foreign student adviser's office. What concepts or principles of intercultural communication would you include in the orientation session? Why? How does the list of problems obtained from the foreign student adviser compare with the problems discussed in this chapter? What concepts from this chapter would you include in your orientation session? Why?

2. With other members of your intercultural communication class, make a rank-ordered list of the five most common communication problems encountered by American students in their interactions with foreign students. Discuss these problems to find the most useful and practical solutions.

3. In consultation with your instructor select five books or articles dealing with intercultural communication training. Analyze these books or articles to identify the principles or guidelines that are most often suggested in the training programs. Compare these principles with the concepts or principles discussed in this chapter with a view to suggest areas of improvement for the authors of your present text.

Index